Voices of an American Utopia:
The Oneida Community in Their Own Words

Edited by
Anthony Wonderley,
Susan Belasco,
Thomas A. Guiler, and
Laura Wayland-Smith Hatch

Oneida Community Mansion House
2024

Voices of an American Utopia: The Oneida Community in Their Own Words
Edited by Anthony Wonderley, Susan Belasco, Thomas A. Guiler, and
Laura Wayland-Smith Hatch

First Edition

All figures are from the collections of the Oneida Community Mansion House.

Copyright © 2024 by Oneida Community Mansion House. All rights reserved.
No part of this book may be reproduced by any means without the written consent
of the Oneida Community Mansion House.

Published by:
Oneida Community Mansion House
170 Kenwood Ave.
Oneida, NY 13421

ISBN: 978-1-7372782-3-8

Table of Contents

Captions to Illustrations VII

Foreword by Thomas A. Guiler XI

Preface XIII

Chapter 1. The Oneida Community 1

Chapter 2. Histories 21

    Part One: "One of the Four" by Harriet Skinner 21

        Text 1: [The Noyes Family in Putney] "One of the Four: A Memoir of Charlotte A. Miller, I," *Oneida Circular*, March 8, 1875, p. 75 25

        Text 2: [Childhood in Putney] "One of the Four: A Memoir of Charlotte A. Miller, II," *Oneida Circular*, March 15, 1875, p. 83-84 28

        Text 3: [Education] "One of the Four: A Memoir of Charlotte A. Miller, III," *Oneida Circular*, March 22, 1875, p. 90-91 32

        Text 4: [Importance of Religion] "One of the Four: A Memoir of Charlotte A. Miller, IV," *Oneida Circular*, March 29, 1875, p. 98 34

        Text 5: [Religious Revivals and Perfectionism] "One of the Four: A Memoir of Charlotte A. Miller, V," *Oneida Circular*, April 5, 1875, p. 106-107 36

        Text 6: [Early Preaching Career of John Humphrey Noyes] "One of the Four: A Memoir of Charlotte A. Miller, VI," *Oneida Circular*, April 12, 1875, p. 113-114 39

        Text 7: [School in Putney, 1836] Excerpts from "One of the Four: A Memoir of Charlotte A. Miller, VII," *Oneida Circular*, April 19, 1875, p. 122 43

Text 8: [Early Publishing Career of John Humphrey Noyes] Excerpts from "One of the Four: A Memoir of Charlotte A. Miller, IX," *Oneida Circular*, May 3, 1875, p. 137-38....................44

Text 9: [Noyes and Partnership with John R. Miller] Excerpts from "One of the Four: A Memoir of Charlotte A. Miller, X," *Oneida Circular*, May 10, 1875, p. 145-146 45

Text 10: [Departure from Putney to Central New York] Excerpts from "One of the Four: A Memoir of Charlotte A. Miller, XI," *Oneida Circular*, May 17, 1875, p. 153-154 48

Text 11: [Life in the Community: Children and Women's Rights] "One of the Four: A Memoir of Charlotte A. Miller, XII," *Oneida Circular*, May 24, 1875, p. 165-66....................49

Text 12: [Death of Mary Cragin] Excerpts from "One of the Four: "A Memoir of Charlotte A. Miller, XIII," *Oneida Circular* 12, No. 22, May 31, 1875, p. 170-171 52

Text 13: [Women and Childbearing] Excerpts from "One of the Four: A Memoir of Charlotte A. Miller, XIV," *Oneida Circular*, June 7, 1875, p. 178....................53

Part Two: "A Community Transplanted" by [H.H.S. (Harriet Noyes Skinner)]....................54

Text 14: [Early Life of the Community in Putney] Excerpt from A Community Transplanted. From Putney to Oneida, I," *American Socialist*, August 14, 1879, pp. 261-262. 55

Text 15: [Perfectionism in the Early Community] Excerpt from "A Community Transplanted. From Putney to Oneida, II," *American Socialist*, August 21, 1879, p. 269-270....................59

Text 16: [Community Organization in Putney] "A Community Transplanted. From Putney to Oneida, III," *American Socialist*, August 28, 1879, p. 277 60

Text 17: [Beauty of Central New York Location] Excerpt from "A Community Transplanted. From Putney to Oneida, IV," *American Socialist*, September 4, 1879, p. 285....................63

Text 18: [Work in the Early Days at Oneida] "A Community Transplanted. From Putney to Oneida, V," *American Socialist*, September 11, 1879, p. 293-294..64

Text 19: [Water Power and the Community] "A Community Transplanted--From Putney to Oneida, VII," *American Socialist*, September 25, 1879, p. 309..67

Text 20: [The Community and the Oneida Nation] Excerpt from "A Community Transplanted--From Putney to Oneida, VIII," *American Socialist*, October 2, 1879, p. 317..69

Text 21: [The Community and Other Religious Movements] Excerpt from "A Community Transplanted--From Putney to Oneida, IX," *American Socialist*, October 9, 1879, p. 325.................71

Part Three: "[Childhood Friends]" by Charlotte Miller........................73

Text 22: "[Childhood Friends]" by Charlotte Miller, "One of the Four: A Memoir of Charlotte A. Miller, XVIII," *Oneida Circular*, July 12, 1875, p. 222-23...75

Chapter 3. Doctrines..81

Part One: The Bible Argument 81

Text 23: Excerpts from "Bible Argument" by John Humphrey Noyes 85

Part Two: Complex Marriage 89

Text 24: "Decadence of Marriage I," *Oneida Circular* 13, No. 4, January 27, 1876, p. 28. Signed J.W.T. (James W. Towner)....................91

Text 25: "Decadence of Marriage II," *Oneida Circular* 13, No. 5, February 3, 1876, p. 36. Signed J.W.T. (James W. Towner)....................93

Part Three: Education 95

Text 26: "Home-Talk—No. 131, Reported July 28, 1850. "Education," [John Humphrey Noyes], *Circular*, October 10, 1852, p. 195..95

Part Four: Mutual Criticism 97

 Text 27: From "Criticism," H., *Circular*, March 21, 1852, p. 74 98

 Text 28: From "A Community Journal: Criticism," *Circular*, March 26, 1863, p. 14 99

Part Five: Community Property and Legal Obligations 101

 Text 29: The Oneida Community's Agreement Not to Sue by [James W. Towner] 103

Chapter 4. Business 109

Part One: Trap Manufacturing 109

 Text 30: [Sewall Newhouse and the Trap Business] "A Community Transplanted. From Putney to Oneida, VI," *American Socialist*, September 18, 1879, p. 301 109

Part Two: Farming, Fruit, and Canning 112

 Text 31: "Corn Packing: Patent Litigation [1]," J.W.T. [James W. Towner], *Oneida Circular*, November 23, 1874, p. 380 113

 Text 32: "Corn Packing: Patent Litigation [2]," J.W.T. [James W. Towner], December 27, 1876, p. 412 115

Part Three: The Silk Thread Business 117

 Text 33: "Silk-Manufacturing in the O.C.: Its Conception," by C.A.C. [Charles A. Cragin], *Circular*, December 3, 1866, p. 299 117

 Text 34: From "Community Gossip: The Silk Maker's Bulletin" by H [Harriet Worden], *Circular*, August 6, 1866, p. 164 120

Part Four: Silverware 121

 Text 35: "1877—The Iron Spoon" by [George E. Cragin], *Quadrangle*, September 1913, p. 15-17. 121

Chapter 5. Practices 127

    Part One: Governance 127

        Text 36: "Internal Governance" from William Alfred Hinds, *American Communities and Co-operative Colonies*, 2nd rev., 3rd ed. (Chicago: Charles H. Kerr, 1908, originally published 1878), p. 197-202 128

    Part Two: Dress Reform 132

        Text 37: "Origin of the Short Dress Costume" by [Harriet Skinner], *Circular*, August 28, 1856, p. 126 137

        Text 38: [On the Short Dress and Short Hair], Harriet M. Worden, *Oneida Circular*, February 6, 1871, p. 46 139

        Text 39: On the Short Dress (1895), Tirzah Herrick (née Miller), *The Quadrangle*, September-November 1912, p. 13-14 141

    Part Three: Childcare 141

        Text 40: "Our Youngest" by [Harriet Skinner] *Oneida Circular*, June 23, 1873, p. 205-6 144

        Text 41: "The Crushing System" by R, [Harriet Worden], *Oneida Circular*, February 23, 1874, p. 68 151

    Part Four: Outdoor Mingling...153

        Text 42: "The Corn-cutting Bee," Charlotte Miller, *Circular*, November 10, 1852, p. 196 154

    Part Five: Women Speaking Up...155

        Text 43: "Woman's Rights" (1853) by Charlotte A. Miller, *Circular*, April 27, 1853, p. 196 156

    Part Six: Diet 157

        Text 44: "Community Eating" by Harriet Skinner. *Circular*, July 5, 1869, p. 127-128 158

Part Seven: Influence of Women 159

    Text 45: "Subjugating the Tobacco Principality" by Harriet
    Worden, Oneida Circular, June 12, 1871, p. 188-189. 159

Part Eight: Visitors to the Mansion House 164

    Text 46: "Stranger's Guide to the O.C.," *Circular*,
    March 21, 1870, p. 1 164

Chapter 6. Conclusion 175

Bibliography 183

Index 189

Illustrations & Captions

Figure 1. John Noyes (1811-1886), about 1840 2

Figure 2. Vue générale d'un phalanstère, an imaginary scene of Fourierist life in a lithograph by Jules Arnout, early 1840s. In late 1844, Albert Brisbane "returned from France with a huge engravedaerial view of an ideal phalanx, which helped to spread the doctrine to impressionistic American audiences" (Guarneri, Utopian Alternative, 28). This copy of the same print, still on view in the Mansion House, was presented to the Oneida Community by French Fourierist Victor Considerant in 1875 5

Figure 3. Charles Fourier 5

Figure 4. The earliest Perfectionist settlement on Oneida Creek, painted from the boyhood memory of George F. Cragin, about 1915. Prominent in the left foreground is Jonathan Burt's sawmill, then (to the right), the Burt house, an Oneida Indian log cabin, and–partially visible on the right edge—a blacksmith shop. 6

Figure 5. Early Mansion House complex, about 1851. A drawing by Charlotte Miller depicts the original Mansion House of 1848, a three-story structure (center) that grew quickly with the addition of two wings and a woodshed. The Children's House of 1849 is visible behind the Mansion House. An earlier farmhouse can be seen to the right. 8

Figure 6. Young women show off their characteristic apparel (short dress and pantalet), 1865. 9

Figure 7. The Oneida Community gather for a bee to hoe and rake, 1867. 10

Figure 8. Sewell O. Newhouse (1806-1888) Blacksmith and inventor of the Newhouse Trap. 13

Figure 9. Photograph of the main Community buildings in 1865. Visible (left to right) are the first Mansion House (1848), the Children's House (1849), the permanent Mansion House (1862), and the "Tontine" (1863). 15

Figure 10.	Print of the main Community buildings, about 1865. This view illustrates how the Perfectionists wanted their home to be perceived by the outside world. It probably was rendered from a photograph, very possibly the one given as Figure 9	15
Figure 11.	John Noyes (1811-1886), about 1863.	17
Figure 12.	Harriet Skinner (1817-1893)	21
Figure 13.	John L. Skinner (1803-1889)	22
Figure 14.	The *Oneida Circular* – Photo by Jim Demarest	23
Figure 15.	Polly Hayes Noyes (1780-1866) in her later years.	27
Figure 16.	George Washington Noyes (1822-1870)	44
Figure 17.	*American Socialist* – Photo by Jim Demarest	54
Figure 18.	John R. Miller (1813-1854)	73
Figure 19.	Charlotte Miller (1819-1874)	74
Figure 20.	Jonathan Burt (1806-1886)	81
Figure 21.	*Bible Argument* - Photo by Jim Demarest	82
Figure 22.	James Towner (1823-1913)	90
Figure 23.	*Circular* – Photo by Jim Demarest	98
Figure 24.	Jessie Kinsley	102
Figure 25.	The Oneida Community's Agreement Not to Sue Handwritten Scroll – Photo by Jim Demarest	103
Figure 26.	Newhouse's "Great Bear Tamer Trap"	110
Figure 27.	Strawberries Label	112
Figure 28.	Silk Twist Label	117

Figure 29.	George E. Cragin (1840-1915)	120
Figure 30.	*Quadrangle* – Photo by Jim Demarest	121
Figure 31.	Oneida Community silverware advertisement	123
Figure 32.	William Hinds (1833-1910)	127
Figure 33.	*American Communities* – Photo by Jim Demarest	128
Figure 34.	Harriet M. Worden (1840-1891)	131
Figure 35.	Theodore R. Noyes	132
Figure 36.	Tirzah Miller (1843-1902)	135
Figure 37.	Pierrepont B. Noyes (1870-1959)	132
Figure 38.	Corinna Ackley (1872-1968)	143
Figure 39.	Alice Ackley (1847-1922)	143
Figure 40.	William H. Woolworth (1824-1904)	162
Figure 41.	Oneida Community members greet visitors in the Reception Room.	166
Figure 42.	Oneida Community men and women reading, studying, and learning in the Mansion House library.	175
Figure 43.	Ellen Nash Wright, Portia Underhill Allen, and Constance Bradley Reed in the flower garden, once on the northwest end of the North Lawn. Bouquets were sold to the many visitors.	177

Illustrations & Captions IX

Foreword

People have been writing about the Oneida Community ever since the first Perfectionists settled in Central New York in 1848. Admirers praised their handsome home, the Mansion House, their fine animal traps, their gracious hospitality, and their devout faith. Others, taking a less charitable view, launched polemics against their unconventional sexual practices, mocked the way Community women dressed and cropped their hair, and accused the Community of blasphemy, adultery, and more. Reporters, self-righteous preachers, and admirers penned pieced in periodicals from Frank Leslie's *Illustrated Newspaper* to bawdy mid-twentieth century men's magazines have all spoken on behalf of or about the Community and its legacy for over 175 years.

But what did the Community write about itself?

Indeed, the Community did speak for itself—extensively. Many of its members penned religious manifestos, memoirs, and autobiographies both during the Communal era as well as afterwards. Its founder, John Humphrey Noyes, as one docent at the Oneida Community Mansion House often says, "did not have an unpublished thought." His son, Pierrepont B. Noyes, wrote a memoir about growing up in the Community as well as a chronicle of its transition to a joint-stock corporation that led the world in silverware. Other members such as Harriet Worden, Corinna Ackley Noyes, Harriet Skinner, and others wrote of their time in the Community—giving us tremendous insight into daily life of the Community for over thirty years.

As a collective, the Community was a prolific publisher and produced a number of periodicals including *The Circular* and the *O.C. Daily Journal* that contained news from the Community, explanations of their practices and beliefs, religious treatises, updates on their business dealings, and much more. They also published their "Mutual Criticism" sessions where in Community members were constructively critiqued for their shortcomings in a quest for Perfection. They also published Noyes's nightly "Home Talks" in which he addressed the Community on any number of topics. This is only the published record. Members of the Oneida Community were prodigious letter writers and diarists leaving behind a massive archive that now resides at the Special Collections Research Center at Syracuse University. Another way in which the Community spoke for itself was that it kept a massive photographic record, not only of their buildings, business activities, and lifestyle, but also portraiture—something rare among even the wealthiest families in America.

Indeed, the Oneida Community is one of the best documented intentional communities in American History.

Over the course of his career, Tony Wonderley has been a leading scholar of the Oneida Community with a long publication record that includes compilations of Community writings, articles on their businesses, many museum exhibits and presentations, and one of the best and most comprehensive histories of the Community from its founding through the collapse of Oneida Limited in the early 2000s.

Voices of an American Utopia is his latest contribution to works on the Community. In many ways, this is a companion or supplement to the very first compilation of Community writings to be published in 1970, Constance Noyes Robertson's *Oneida Community: An Autobiography, 1851-1876*, which drew on articles from Community periodicals to shed light on the Community's practices, architecture, businesses, child rearing, and the important role of women in the Community. What further sets this volume apart is that it also lets their photographic record speak as this book is lavishly documented with not only the words of the Community but also their faces—allowing the reader to put words to the likenesses of the Community members who wrote them.

With this new volume, Wonderley dives deeper into many of the issues Robertson did, but also uncovers never-before-reproduced writings that reveal important new details about the Community. Indeed, through Wonderley's deft editing, the voices of the people who lived, worked, and played in the Oneida Community ring loud and clear and give insight to the past for a new generation of people who look to the Oneida Community for inspiration to imagine a different way of living.

In the process of preparing Tony's manuscript for publication, we expanded the scope and reorganized his original project with additional readings and illustrations. Susan Belasco found, transcribed, and edited new materials; Laura Wayland-Smith Hatch contributed illustrations and captions; Jim Demarest photographed the publications and scroll; and Lauren Pawlika assisted with proofreading. All of us are grateful to Tony for providing us with this rare opportunity to create a collection of original materials written by Oneida Community members.

Thomas A. Guiler
Director of Museum Affairs
Oneida Community Mansion House
Summer 2024

Preface

The Oneida Community (1848-1880) was the most radically successful social experiment in American history. It comprised about two hundred-fifty people dedicated to living together as one family sharing all property, work, and love in Oneida, New York. This group built the country's first truly collective residence, a house in which men and women freely mingled under one roof. Within, they instituted cooperative household arrangements with men and women working in positions of comparative equality. They pioneered a new style of female clothing which permitted women to work indoors and out in comfort. They invented a unique system of raising children with collectivized childcare. They innovated household arrangements while working out effective means of governance. They crafted a labor system in which committees assigned tasks and work brought satisfaction. They created a subsistence regime fostering spirituality and resulting in practical gender equality. Later on, the Oneida Community became one of the most economically successful communes of all time, its prosperity based not on agriculture but on factory production.

Bucking the prevailing Victorian sentiment set against them, the Community developed a system of group marriage in which, they asserted, women were freed from "matrimonial bondage." The Oneidans, furthermore, claimed to have corrected one of the greatest sources of human misery: unwanted, unchosen pregnancies. This was accomplished by practicing a form of birth control prohibiting male ejaculation during sexual intercourse. And that, they said, freed the women from "propagative drudgery." In its later years, Oneida started up a eugenics program—even possibly humankind's first—to produce a spiritually elevated group of people who would benefit humankind.

It is a remarkable story, one that has been told before. Members of the Oneida Community narrated much of it themselves in the pages of the newspaper-like publications they sent out into the world.[1] A number of historians have recounted it in our own day.[2] I have also told their tale.[3] But while my conceit has been to speak for them as a chronicler, I am aware of the arrogance of the living. I believe people of the past who spoke for themselves should be encouraged to do so today. And, indeed, the closest we can come to experiencing the past is to imbibe its voices on the printed page.

Early efforts to anthologize these voices include Oneida Community-descendant Constance Robertson who collected what she regarded as the most informative and characteristic of their writings in *The Oneida Community: An Autobiography* (1970). Since then, I have published three books of primary sources that examine specific aspects of the Community: *The Days of My Youth: A Childhood Memoir of Life in the Oneida Community*, by Corinna Ackley Noyes (2011); *John Humphrey Noyes on Sexual Relations in the Oneida Community: Four Essential*

Texts (2012); and *Writings from Wallingford: The Connecticut Outpost of the Oneida Community* (2020).

This new collection of forty-six, little-known writings evokes the Perfectionists' commitment, intelligence, happiness, and common sense within the main Oneida Community context. Together they comprise a sourcebook that introduces us to the primary tenets of Perfectionism. Published here for the first time since their initial appearance in the 19th century, these writings enlarge our understanding of the Oneida Community, of communitarianism, and of utopianism.

Note on the Texts: All of the texts in this collection are taken from original sources in the collection of the Oneida Community Mansion House. Each text has been checked against the original for accuracy. In most cases, the original spellings, punctuation, and wordings have been maintained and typographical errors in the original have been corrected; only in the interest of clarity or ease of reading for the contemporary reader have any minor alterations been made to the texts. In the cases where the original texts have been excerpted and some extraneous content has been omitted, the deletions are indicated by ellipses marks.

Anthony Wonderley

Notes

1. The Oneida Community's periodical, a newspaper-like magazine usually published weekly, went through several changes of name: *Spiritual Magazine* (begun in Putney and published 1848-50 in Oneida), *Free Church Circular* (1850-51), *Circular* (1851-70), *Oneida Circular* (1871-76) and *American Socialist* (1876-79). A newsletter printed for internal consumption (*Daily Journal*, 1866-68) was preceded by the "*Community Journal*" (1863-64) which exists in typescript at the Mansion House. Another source of information is the *Quadrangle*, a journal published irregularly out of the Mansion House by Oneida Community descendants between 1908 and 1938. The *Oneida Community Journal* (1987-present) is the biannual periodical of the not-for-profit museum, the Oneida Community Mansion House.
2. Maren Lockwood Carden, *Oneida: Utopian Community to Modern Corporation* (Syracuse, NY: Syracuse University Press, 1998, originally published 1969); Spencer Klaw, *Without Sin: The Life and Death of the Oneida Community* (New York: Allen Lane, Penguin, 1993); Constance Noyes Robertson, *Oneida Community: An Autobiography, 1851-1876* (Syracuse, NY: Syracuse University Press, 1970) and

Oneida Community: The Breakup, 1876-1881 (Syracuse, NY: Syracuse University Press, 1972); Ellen Wayland-Smith, *Oneida: From Free Love Utopia to the Well-Set Table—An American Story* (New York: Picador, 2016); and Carol Stone White, *A Taste of Heaven on Earth: Harnessing the Energies of Love* (Eugene, Oregon: Resource Publications, 2020). The literature of the Oneida Community also includes two Oneida Community diaries edited and commentated by Robert S. Fogarty: *Special Love/Special Sex: An Oneida Community Diary* (Syracuse, NY: Syracuse University Press, 1994), and *Desire and Duty at Oneida: Tirzah Miller's Intimate Memoir* (Bloomington: University of Indiana Press, 2000). Three works by Lawrence Foster are also basic to this literature: *Religion and Sexuality: The Shakers, the Mormons, and the Oneida Community* (Urbana: University of Illinois Press, 1984, originally published 1981); *Women, Family, and Utopia: Communal Experiments of the Shakers, the Oneida Community, and the Mormons* (Syracuse, NY: Syracuse University Press, 1991), and (edited and commentated by Foster) *Free Love in Utopia: John Humphrey Noyes and the Origin of the Oneida Community*, Compiled by George Wallingford Noyes (Urbana: University of Illinois Press, 2001).
3. Anthony Wonderley, *Oneida Utopia: A Community Searching for Human Happiness and Prosperity* (Ithaca, NY: Cornell University Press, 2017).

Chapter 1. The Oneida Community

Communitarian Dreams and Putney Precedents

The Oneida Community was germinated in the Second Great Awakening—a wave of Protestant revival excitement that swept over the Northeast about 1830. The epicenter of the religious excitement was upstate New York along the Erie Canal corridor, the so-called Burned Over District (the "Burnt District," they called it), which experienced more than 1,300 revivals. There it was that the popular exhorter, Charles Finney, advanced a brand of the Wesleyan belief that perfect holiness and salvation from sin might be achieved in the here and now. Reasoning from the Christian premise of redemption, a person able to become one with Christ would thereby be freed from sin. To be free of sin in a religious sense is to be perfect.

Those who reasoned in this fashion—Perfectionists—felt themselves to be exempt from external earthly authority. That outlook encouraged the further presumption that they were not subject to legalistic strictures. The bonds they most frequently insisted they were free of were marriage relations. That thought led them, in turn, to devalue, to de-emphasize the purely physical contact between husband and wife. Perfectionists near Syracuse in 1834 took up the notion of spiritual affinity, a mystical bond of true love between a man and a woman forged in heaven. Accordingly, some of the leading evangelists paired themselves up, platonically, to demonstrate mastery over the flesh. Such relationships tended to become sexual and brought to Perfectionism a reputation for lurid scandal long preceding that of the Oneida Community.

One convert to the new faith was John Humphrey Noyes (**Figure 1**) a young Vermonter who came to believe that faith-based Perfectionism needed one more precept to work—in effect, an "on" switch. The individual, Noyes proposed, activated his or her state of inner redemption by publicly announcing allegiance to Perfectionism. For Noyes himself, the confession of Christ was equally an acknowledgment of being divinely appointed to advance God's work. That, one would suppose, brought a great inner strength of certainty. Thereafter, Noyes became an important figure in the Perfectionist movement. He wielded influence mainly by publishing a periodical that enjoyed wide currency.

As the Perfectionist movement became increasingly identified with sex, Noyes formulated a bold theory of sexual communism. If all things in heaven are held in common, he reasoned, and if people there truly love one another, then the way of heaven is that all men and women love each other in all ways—unselfishly and physically. This implied sexual communism. And, although Noyes did not practice what he preached, this view of intimate relations would become the keystone of life in the future Oneida Community. Further, and as the Oneida Community was to discover, this interpretation of heterosexual relations implicitly accorded men and women the same right to engage in sex. Eventually called "complex marriage," the practice was charged with the potential to further a sense of sexual equality. Complex

Figure 1: John Humphrey Noyes (1811-1886), about 1840

marriage would become the keystone of life in the future Oneida Community.

Embarrassed by the sexual infamy of the early Perfectionist movement, Noyes retreated to his hometown of Putney, Vermont, to recruit his own cadres untainted by the excesses of others. Beginning in 1836, his first followers included younger siblings Harriet, Charlotte, and George, their future spouses, and a couple named Cragin. His converts included Harriet Holton, the woman he married early on in his Putney sojourn. All these disciples acknowledged their fealty to Noyes as emissary of God. In future years, several of them would comprise the core of the

Oneida Community's "central committee," an informal group of advisors close to Noyes.

Noyes had long been drawn to the printed word with the idea that the penny press of his day represented a technological revolution in communication. Harnessed to the gospel cause, the press would spread the good word and constitute the central, regulating office of Noyes's church. His experience with the short-lived Perfectionist magazine had strengthened this view. Now, in Putney, he was able to acquire his own printing press. Noyes and his adherents would continue to publish a periodical, more or less biweekly, for upwards of forty years. The group eventually numbered about two dozen adults who, when not printing, devoted themselves to studying religious topics. Out of this practice came a taste for forging group consensus in collective discussion. Later, these would flower into the daily communal meetings characteristic of Oneida. However, there was not any impulse toward gender equality. In Putney, the superiority of men over women was never questioned.

As time passed, the group became increasingly committed to communism by assuming collective ownership of everything originally owned by individual members. As the Putney Perfectionists were becoming a community of pooled property, they took an interest in similarly inclined groups around them. During the nineteenth century, dozens of Utopian movements were organized, such as the Moravians, the Mormons, the New Harmonists, and the Amana Community. But the brand of sectarian communitarianism best known to them was the Shakers, a religious sect founded about 1779 near Albany. Shakers called themselves the United Society of Believers in Christ's Second Coming in the conviction that their founder, Englishwoman Ann Lee, was an incarnation of Christ. In following her teachings, they initiated, as they thought, the kingdom of Christ on earth. Based on the belief that lust was the cause of evil, Shakers were celibate and practiced a nearly complete segregation of men and women.[1]

By 1830, Shakers may have numbered about five thousand members residing in some nineteen societies located in several states. Each society was an essentially autonomous, self-sufficient farming settlement which also produced such saleable products as garden seeds, medicinal herbs, preserved fruits and vegetables, and finely wrought furniture. Typically, a society was divided into four families, each comprising a cluster of buildings with about a hundred people. In each family, men and women worked separately at tasks which they, in common with the world around them, regarded as gender appropriate. Each of the families had parallel organizations for men and women, each with its own leaders. Children, brought into the family with their parents or adopted by the order from orphanages, were kept physically apart from the adult world.[2]

John Noyes was a student of Shaker doctrines which clearly influenced his thinking about Christian communism. Of course, he profoundly disagreed with the

Shaker idea that sex was bad and that such a view could be justified from scripture. As he wrote in *The Berean: A Manual for the Help of Those Who Seek the Faith of the Primitive Church* (1847): "An unauthorized and evil use is made of the text, 'In the resurrection they neither marry, nor are given in marriage.'" He insisted, "when it is taken for proof that the distinction between the sexes—the very image of God—is to be obliterated in heaven, and all the glorious offices and affections growing out of that distinction are to have an end."[3] Noyes based his belief on his own interpretation of Matthew 22:30: "For in the resurrection they neither marry nor are given in marriage, but are like angels of God in heaven" (King James Version). To Noyes, this was evidence for his belief in "complex marriage," that all adults were spouses to one another. He did, however, regard Shaker abstinence as an ethically justifiable form of birth control. At this time, Shakers were increasingly recognized for successful communal living. Noyes himself—much later—credited that sect with having demonstrated the practicality of communal life.[4] And, because the Shakers recognized no personal ownership, they also demonstrated the possibilities of communism.

There were also non-religious communards who looked hopefully on the world around them with a view to changing it for the better. Idealists of this stripe imagined they could fashion a utopian state of harmony in which social life could be satisfying for all. They offered a model for better living they assumed others would admire and want to imitate. Noyes was particularly influenced by Brook Farm, the Transcendentalist community established in 1841 and inspired by the works of Ralph Waldo Emerson, whom he much admired. Noyes also admired Fruitlands, another secular society inspired by Transcendentalism. For these groups and in Noyes's mind, utopian communities would voluntarily and peacefully improve society. Nonreligious communitarianism or utopianism was thus a reform movement similar to abolitionism and women's rights in its intent to improve the world.

The brand of nonreligious communitarianism which the Putneyites studied most closely was Fourierism—a popular movement that engulfed America in the early 1840s. (**Figure 2**) Its originator, Frenchman Charles Fourier (1772-1837) (**Figure 3**), believed humans acted according to instincts and talents he called "passions." There were supposed to be 12 passions distributed among 810 personality types. If the precise mix of personality types were assembled in the correct number of people living together in a common residence (a phalanstery or phalanx), the result would be social harmony—utopia. Work would become enjoyable—"attractive"—because people were following out their innate self-interests and doing what they were meant to do. The key assertion of Fourierism was that "passional attraction"—meaning personal inclination and occupational leaning—rendered labor attractive. Further, phalanstery life would improve the lot of women. Working closely together with men, women would be liberated from the isolated households which had doomed them to the economic servitude of domestic work.[5]

The American Fourierist movement, called Associationism, may have

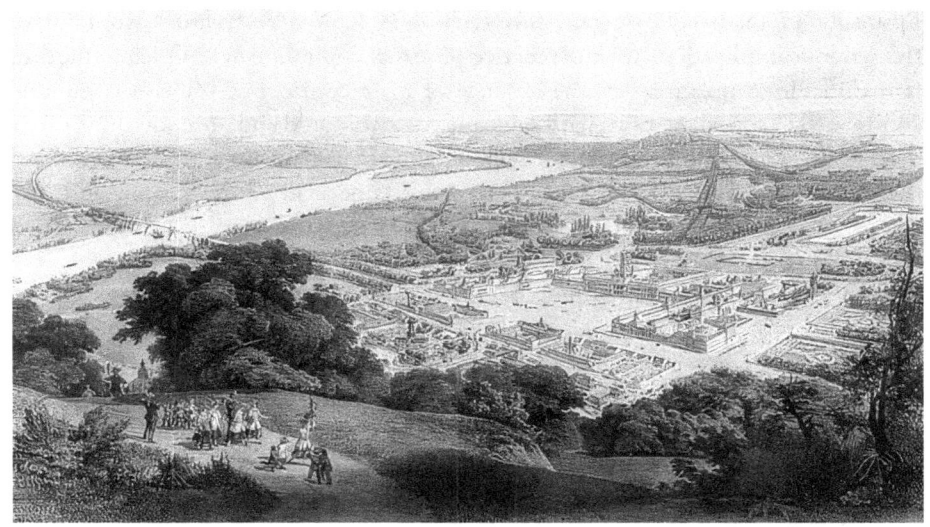

Figure 2: "Vue générale d'un phalanstère," an imaginary scene of Fourierist life in a lithograph by Jules Arnout, early 1840s. In late 1844, Albert Brisbane "returned from France with a huge engraved aerial view of an ideal phalanx, which helped to spread the doctrine to impressionistic American audiences" (Guarneri, *Utopian Alternative*, 28). This copy of the same print, still on view in the Mansion House, was presented to the Oneida Community by French Fourierist Victor Considerant in 1875.

numbered as many as 100,000 adherents. The dissemination of the movement resulted, in large measure, from the printed word, especially in the form of Albert Brisbane's columns on the subject which ran in the *New York Tribune* in 1842-1843.[6] This body of writing impacted the thinking of Noyes and the Putneyites. It taught them that work could become fun if men and women engaged in it together. Fourieristic writing equipped them with the vocabulary to express the benefits of communal labor and of communal residence in a unitary home. More generally, Brisbane and Fourier probably reenforced the love Putneyite Perfectionists were developing for fruit trees. Brisbane and Fourier also may have ignited the interest in gender equality soon to flower at Oneida.[7]

In the meantime, Noyes set out to improve conjugal relations by developing a form of birth control that would prove crucial to practicing sexual communism at Oneida.

"Male continence," as he called it, meant coitus in which the man did not ejaculate.

Figure 3: Charles Fourier

The Oneida Community   5

Resulting in relatively safe sex, this technique (coitus reservatus) would have tremendous implications for the practice of sexual communism at Oneida. Indeed, it is difficult to imagine—in the absence of male continence—how a commune committed to sexual relations with multiple partners could end up as anything other than a support group for pregnant women and their offspring. At the same time, the recognition that women were freed from the necessity of pregnancy and that their experience of sex could be, as Noyes put it, "very satisfactory."[8] These ideas had radical potential for developing gender relations of greater equality.

Further, Noyes developed the doctrine of salvation from sin to the radical position that salvation, once attained, was absolute and forever. Having gone so far with the purely faith-based religion, he began adding qualifications to make it governable and functional. When he considered the essentially individualistic and egalitarian nature of Perfectionism, Noyes decided that a hierarchical organization would be acceptable providing a divinely appointed leader could impart beneficial instruction. To that, he added the caveat that becoming perfect was likely to be a gradual process. Perfectionism, he implied, was not only progressive, but it was also something that might reasonably be mistaken for or combined with social improvement.

Many Americans of the time expected the return of Christ and the end of the world momentarily. The biggest end-time excitement originated with Baptist minister William Miller who predicted the return of Christ to render judgment on humankind in 1843 or 1844. Conveyed in millions of books, pamphlets, periodicals and tracts, these ideas resulted in a substantial movement of many thousands of adherents. In contrast to the Millerites, Noyes offered a complicated interpretation of history involving two world ages and three advent occurrences. More importantly, he rejected the idea of an apocalypse signaling Christ's return and instead emphasized the importance of human contribution to God's plan. These revisions to the millennial agenda presumably encouraged Perfectionists to assume a more active engagement—more than passive faith dictated—in the enterprise of building a Zion on earth.

And indeed, after a year of living communally and practicing sexual communism, the Putney Perfectionists thought they had achieved perfect holiness and, in effect, jump-started the Millennium. Imitating life in heaven, they had succeeded, they felt, in drawing heaven to earth. On June 1, 1847, they declared that a resurrection state had come to exist among them. The Putney townsfolk were outraged by the pretension and shocked, as well, by the practice of group marriage. Forced by negative public opinion to flee Vermont, Noyes and his followers relocated to central New York between Utica and Syracuse. There, on a bank of Oneida Creek, they joined their fortunes to those of a small Perfectionist band coalescing on the property of one Jonathan Burt.

Figure 4: The earliest Perfectionist settlement on Oneida Creek, painted from the boyhood memory of George F. Cragin, about 1915. Prominent in the left foreground is Jonathan Burt's sawmill, then (to the right), the Burt house, an Oneida Indian log cabin, and–partially visible on the right edge—a blacksmith shop.

Utopian Success

When the Vermonters of Putney united with the New Yorkers, the settlement comprised a motley assortment of already existing and hastily built structures. (**Figure 4**) Faced with the necessity of housing some ninety persons before winter, they acquired the property across the creek which boasted a small farmhouse, two barns, and the only topographic relief in the neighborhood: a knoll offering an extensive view of the surroundings. At the base of that knoll, they built the "Mansion House," America's first communal dwelling in which males and females were not compartmentalized into monogamous pairs or nuclear family units as custom prescribed. (**Figure 5**) During the course of carrying out this project, Oneida Community members forged a sense of themselves as a cohesive group.

Childcare was collectivized early on. Initially the raising of children was separated from parental supervision and segregated from the adult world during the day with the construction, in early 1849, of a Children's House. Distinct residences for adults and youngsters meant the physical concentration of household labor and childcare. When performed cooperatively, the result was less work. The arrangement revolutionized the domestic sphere by lightening household drudgery regarded as feminine. Separating children from their parents during the day required parental acceptance of the arrangement. Oneidans, of course, loved their children as much

Figure 5: Early Mansion House complex, about 1851. A drawing by Charlotte Miller depicts the original Mansion House of 1848, a three-story structure (center) that grew quickly with the addition of two wings and a woodshed. The Children's House of 1849 is visible behind the Mansion House. An earlier farmhouse can be seen to the right.

as parents anywhere. The emotion, however, was institutionally discouraged if it became "sticky"—that is, exclusionary in its focus. When that happened, it was considered a sin called "philoprogenitiveness"—loving one's own progeny more than those of another.

Noyes proposed, in early 1848, that men and women should mingle in their daily pursuits. Such an activity was physically impossible for women so long as they wore the stays, crinolines, petticoats, and ground-dragging garments then considered fashionable. While building their communal residence, the women invented a new costume permitting them to work with men both indoors and out. The revolutionary Oneida short dress with pantalets may have been the prototype for the "Bloomer costume" of the incipient women's rights movement. (**Figure 6**)

Another innovation that came out of building the 1848 Mansion House was the custom of working in "bees"—extemporaneous groups of men and women formed to accomplish a task, usually outside. (**Figure 7**) By the early 1850s, the practice of men, women, and children working together became profoundly intertwined with the Community's interest in what they called "horticulture"—tending fruit trees, berry bushes, and vegetable gardens.

In a very short time, the Oneida Perfectionists had completed the country's first phalanstery, invented a new fashion in clothing for women, and transformed the environment of home and work. This new commune surely would have been hailed as the poster child of world communitarianism—had anyone noticed. But no one did and the Oneidans were not much given to boasting.

Sexual and Gender Relations

During the early years, Community members also worked out the emotionally challenging terms of sexual communism. They did so well enough to establish a system of group marriage (perhaps the world's first) that worked. Sex at Oneida was supposed to be a pleasurable and spiritually fulfilling experience in which the partners recreated and drew nearer to God. Community members were expected to enter into the holy ordinance of group marriage ("pantogamy") in which

Figure 6: Young women show off their characteristic apparel (short dress and pantalet), 1865.

heterosexuality was assumed, monogamy was forbidden, celibacy was discouraged, and free love was encouraged. Each individual was to love all family members of the other sex as a spouse and without jealousy or selfishness. There was to be no exclusiveness in love that would encourage the formation of couples. This did not mean that one could not find particular enjoyment in one partner—so long as it nourished love for all. If it did not, it was classified as a relationship exclusive to two egos focused solely on themselves. Contemptible and selfish, that kind of bond was a sin called "special love."

An Oneida man was expected to suppress ejaculation in order to relieve his partner's fear of pregnancy and to heighten her enjoyment. An Oneida woman, in consequence, was freed from unwanted pregnancy and marital bondage—at least more so than in the outside world. Incredibly, Oneida sexual practices transformed what Aldous Huxley called "a wild, God-eclipsing passion into a civilized act of worship, a prime cause of crime and misery into a source of individual happiness, social solidarity and good behavior."[9]

Figure 7: The Oneida Community gather for a bee to hoe and rake, 1867.

There were, however, hierarchical regulations at work in the Community's sexual arrangements. Noyes and his inner circle monitored romantic couplings to discourage amative selfishness and to head off socially disruptive affairs. The system of ascending fellowship encouraged the young to have sex with older partners. But strictures of control were softened and ameliorated by a deeply engrained notion of justice: sex in the Oneida Community required the consent of both partners. No compulsion, the Perfectionists claimed, was permitted in love.

As the Oneidans worked out new relations of sex, they also were pioneering new relations of gender. By the early 1850s, the practice of men, women, and children working together outside became bound up with the Community's interest in tending fruit trees and berry bushes. Noyes never elaborated a real scheme for subsistence from garden produce, nor did he propose that such a lifestyle could elevate the standing of women. Nevertheless, that is what happened when a horticultural regime was developed in real life. Oneidans discovered that bringing men and women together in outdoor work was socially satisfying, spiritually enriching, and fun. It pleased them to realize they were advancing female standing in practical ways.

"The amelioration of woman's lot in our manner of life is too manifest not to be seen by all" was a sentiment frequently expressed in Community writings.[10] It was true. In the Oneida Community, women supposedly were liberated from the bondage of marriage in the nineteenth century. Almost certainly, they were relieved from propagative and domestic drudgery to an extent unmatched in the outside world. Going further, the Community redefined the ideal of gender relations around the practice of bees in which men and women cooperated happily in horticultural pursuits. In that fashion, mingling of the sexes paved the way for practical advances in female standing and for the development of gender relations that were astonishingly progressive by the standards of their day. Relations between the sexes were more truly equitable in the Oneida Community during the 1850s than they were elsewhere in Victorian America.

The Early Years

The Oneida Community grew to about two hundred members by the end of 1849, the level at which it stabilized for most of its existence. Most joined as heterosexually married couples. Most were of the "middling" sort although some came from truly disadvantaged backgrounds. The majority were small-town New Englanders and New Yorkers comfortable with physical toil. They tended to be modestly schooled. And, although few had any knowledge of Fourierism, they brought with them a veritable storehouse of practical knowledge about farming, building, domestic industries and mechanical contrivances

They were serious, professing Christians from conventional Protestant sects: Congregationalists, Methodists, Baptists, Presbyterians. But they were also dissatisfied with the customary preachments, distressed by religious uncertainty, and searching for answers. They were convinced that they had found the light in Noyes's Perfectionist teachings. As devout believers, they joined Noyes in his purpose and, in so doing, dedicated themselves to what they considered to be the highest possible cause. They were, in their own minds, subordinating themselves to God with the recognition that Noyes was "the chosen representative of Jesus Christ, and the ordained one who is to set up the kingdom of heaven in this world." A Community member frequently "confessed" or publicly avowed Noyes "as my head, and the medium that shall modify me and organize me into Christ's body." Such homage was rendered voluntarily. Furthermore, it seemed proper to acknowledge Noyes as paramount because he radiated a magnetism that made people happy to be in his presence.[11]

As soon as the Mansion House was finished, Noyes left to take up residence in Brooklyn in order, it was vaguely said, to be able to concentrate and write. He remained in New York City for the better part of six years. Throughout that time,

Noyes would recommend various courses of action which the Bible Communists in Oneida endeavored to operationalize. Early on, for example, Noyes proposed a doctrine of spiritual ranking, an ascending fellowship with himself at the apex. At Oneida, they took the measure of the concept, then administered its logic to one another. In general, the Oneida Bible communists worked out the essentials of communal existence themselves.

A distinguishing feature of the commune was its fashion of worship or, more accurately, the almost complete absence of formal ritual. Noyes never insisted on much in the way of participatory religion. His followers, for their part, harbored a general mistrust of engaging in any behavior that might seem ostentatious or pretentious. They did not like public displays of emotion. They avoided anything smacking of "idolatry"—outward signs of formulaic belief, including such material symbols as crosses. A strain of ideological indifference to cant may have resulted from a religious outlook in which every act was an expression of faith.

Two institutions characteristic of Oneida were "mutual criticism" and the evening meeting. In mutual criticism, a committee drew an individual's attention to anything objectionable in that person's character and conduct. Effectively combining peer pressure with self-examination, the purpose of the exercise was self-correction. A practice perhaps more crucial to communal stability was the evening meeting, a daily gathering of the adult Perfectionists. These events were strongly stamped with the democratic character of a New England town meeting in which anyone—or, at least, any man—had the right to speak his mind. At Oneida, "all important questions are brought before the Community for decision," they said, "and in the general assembly every person, male and female, has a voice and a vote." They claimed that nothing at Oneida was attempted without first obtaining general consent in the evening meeting.[12] Although both mutual criticism and the evening meeting delivered participatory satisfaction akin to church services, neither was regarded as primarily a rite of worship. Both were viewed as social events essential to harmonious group life throughout the existence of the commune.

Always the Oneidans valued and promoted intellectual improvement. In addition, they crafted a system for labor in which committees assigned tasks on a rotating basis and working brought contentment. They laid the foundation for future economic developments by learning how to make metal animal traps. And they established a mostly vegetarian diet and formulated a visitation policy which welcomed tourists. Oneida Perfectionists built Eden from the ground up.

Meanwhile, Noyes's establishment in Brooklyn became the first of several Perfectionist communities outside of Oneida. Collectively styled the "Associated Communities," they were small groups residing in Manlius, New York; Cambridge, Vermont; Newark, New Jersey; and Wallingford, Connecticut; as well as the Oneidans who had moved to Brooklyn with Noyes and a few who had reoccupied their original location in Putney, Vermont. These communities seemed to accrete haphazardly when a handful of people, staying where they lived, declared allegiance to Noyes's movement, or when people joined established communities and gifted their farms to the Association. The largest of these was the Wallingford property of Henry and Emily Allen, which was donated to the cause in 1851. None of these smaller centers was self-supporting. The maintenance of Brooklyn, which must have required thousands of dollars, was an especially heavy drain on the original association in central New York.[13]

The untimely death of the Association's treasurer, John Miller, brought Oneida's period of communal development without Noyes to a close. Oneida Perfectionist Harriet Worden credited Miller with "the successful management of our finances, and the toleration gained for our movement in this State."[14] His death—ascribed by some to overwork and worry—focused attention on the organization's financial health because, under his stewardship, Oneida had born the weight of the Associated Communities. With Miller gone, an anemic income, and assets rapidly dwindling, the Association could no longer deny the folly of supporting Brooklyn and the other colonies. The time had come, Noyes conceded, to contract and consolidate. Accordingly, Perfectionists closed the various outposts in 1854-1855 and assembled at Oneida to concentrate on fiscal responsibility. Noyes himself returned at the end of 1854. The only satellite community allowed to operate was the one at Wallingford. It continued its parallel existence with Oneida for nearly as long as Oneida lasted.

Traps and Industrialization

Focusing on fiscal viability, the reassembled Bible communists pinned their hopes on manufacturing metal animal traps. One of the early joiners at Oneida, blacksmith Sewell Newhouse (**Figure 8**), had developed a hand-forged model of trap superior to anything then available. When the Oneida Community took over trap making, they invented devices to mechanize virtually every step of the manufacturing process. As soon as the new machinery was installed in their mill (1857), they were able to make 26,000 traps—more than in the first five years combined (21,000). Thereafter, the Oneida Community generally manufactured 45,000 to 95,000 traps annually until 1863. Then, swamped by orders, they made 226,000 in 1863 and 275,000 in 1864. The frantic pace of production was made possible by the hiring of some fifty non-Community workers. The Bible Communists said that they became employers to fill their orders and keep their customers satisfied. A new factory for trap making, built in 1864, was the largest such manufacturing facility in

Figure 8: Sewell O. Newhouse (1806-1888), blacksmith and inventor of the Newhouse Trap.

the United States.

Oneida's new industrial center was situated a mile north of the Mansion House to take advantage of waterpower available there and to be close to the nearest pool of outside labor—a small settlement along the Seneca Highway called Turkey Street. In 1865, the Oneida Community bought the Wilson foundry on Sconondoa Creek near the trap works. Plows and other agricultural implements were, for a time, manufactured at that facility. To supervise operations at the factory and foundry, about thirty members of the Oneida Community moved north to the Seneca Highway to establish a branch commune called the Willow Place Community (1867-1876).

Traps financed a second factory industry: the manufacture of "Machine Twist," silk thread for the Singer Sewing Machine just then (1866) coming into widespread use. Since both traps and thread were industries based on hired labor, the Community was now committed to a mode of factory production requiring employees. By the 1870s, there were about two hundred adult Perfectionists with about an equal number of hirelings doing factory work but also employed in a wide range of nonindustrial tasks including laundry and farming.

But reconciling their new roles as labor bosses with their belief in egalitarian Christianity posed an ethical problem the Bible communists never entirely resolved. In compensation, perhaps, for the awkward position they found themselves in as employers, they formulated generous personnel policies. They paid well, instituted an eight-hour workday, provided decent working conditions, and furnished housing when needed. The Perfectionists were, in their time, exceptionally good employers.

In addition to financing thread production, traps paid for a second Mansion House built in 1862. The ingathering of Perfectionists in 1855-1856 had created a housing shortage at Oneida. In consequence, planning an expanded family home became one of the commune's favorite pastimes during the ensuing years. Eventually the group agreed to build it in the "Italian Villa" style popularized by the leading architectural theorist of the day, A. J. Downing. The result of all those years of discussion—the Mansion House of 1862—remains today an impressive manifestation of collective will. (**Figures 9-10**)

Factory production of traps and threads ushered in financial prosperity and material plenty, and those conditions altered the Oneidans' outlook. For one, the Perfectionists spoke less about bringing heaven to earth and more about being in heaven on earth. By 1865 they were saying that the business of Oneida was to present to the world "a working model of Communism, and leave its effect on others to the silent action of truth and the Providence of God."[15] In 1872, they said "the sole end and aim of the Oneida Community is to make a happy home for reconciling man and woman to each other, and by reconciling both to God." Such goals were enunciated with reference to having an audience, and the Perfectionists began to encourage the world to come to them.[16]

The world complied. At least 1,500 dropped by on July 4, 1863. Over the

Figure 9: Photograph of the main Community buildings in 1865. Visible (left to right) are the first Mansion House (1848), the Children's House (1849), the permanent Mansion House (1862), and the "Tontine" (1863).

next five years, the Community welcomed some 45,000 guests. Many more came when a train line was constructed across the Community's land in 1868. In exchange for a free right-of-way, the Midland Railroad built a depot about one hundred yards from the Mansion House. One train on a single day disgorged 1,300 visitors to pour through the Perfectionists' home and over its grounds. The Oneida Community

Figure 10: Print of the main Community buildings, about 1865. This view illustrates how the Perfectionists wanted their home to be perceived by the outside world. It probably was rendered from a photograph, very possibly the one given as Figure 9.

entertained more visitors than any other utopian community in America, probably more than all the others put together.[17]

The Perfectionists had never been averse to making money from their horticultural pursuits, initially from the sale of produce and nursery trees. Inspired by the canning precedents of the North American Phalanx (a Fourierist association in New Jersey), they turned to developing the technology of vegetal preservation. In 1856, the Oneida Community test-marketed tomatoes preserved in cans and jars. What came to be called the fruit business began in earnest in 1858 with retail sale of tomatoes, strawberries, cherries, and grapes in hermetically sealed glass jars. This enterprise was discontinued after a decade, however, when the Oneidans discovered that their work might more profitably be directed toward making more traps.

Although they resumed fruit canning several years later, it was never again an undertaking valued for its spiritual benefits in mingling men and women in work. On the contrary, the enterprise was carefully planned out and funded to the tune of $9,000—by far the biggest expense in the 1872 budget. The money was allocated to developing a massive state-of-the art fruit-preserving facility staffed by hired help. The later fruit business was a commercial venture about dollars and cents.

Closing Years

The Community's final years were marked by a daring eugenics program called "stirpiculture" based on a Latin word meaning rootstock or family branch. Selective breeding was a topic widely discussed at the time and, as students of Darwin and Galton, the Perfectionists hypothesized that spirituality might be genetically transmissible. If so, specialists in religious perfectibility would be highly qualified to develop and pass the trait along. Their idea was to produce a spiritually elevated group of people who would benefit humankind.

During the first twenty years, Community women had born about thirty-five children, a birth rate they thought was very low. Many, perhaps most of the children were regarded as intentionally conceived. If a policy existed for having children, it was that they would raise a pair of children annually, "just enough for playfellows."[18] Some births may have been authorized by the Community in cases of women wishing to have children but approaching menopause.

Now contemplating the stirpicultural program and feeling prosperous enough to raise children as responsible parents, they added a new section to the Mansion House for their intended offspring: the South or Children's Wing (1869-1870). Then they turned to the business of reproduction. During the stirpicultural decade (1869-1879), 58 children were born to 41 mothers and 40 fathers.[19] A second wing, called the "New House," was added to the Mansion House in 1878 to house Perfectionists fleeing Wallingford, their satellite commune in Connecticut beset with malaria. A skeleton crew remaining at Wallingford started up the manufacture of silverware, which would long sustain the Community's successor organization, a manufacturing enterprise.

Figure 11: John Humphrey Noyes (1811-1886), about 1863.

The stirpicultural program proved to be the single greatest cause of the Community's breakup because it unleashed individualistic tendencies long harnessed to the cause of Bible Communism. Internal problems were exacerbated by inappropriate actions by Noyes at this time, including the appointment of his eldest son, Theodore, an agnostic unskilled in leadership, to head the Community. Simultaneously, Noyes promoted the idea that a state of high sanctification was carried in his blood. (**Figure 11**) The effect of such policies was to elevate Noyes's family to a position of aristocracy within Oneida while revealing the limitations of Noyes's judgment.

At the same time, the 1870s were the heyday of Victorian domestic values in which unconventional sexual arrangements were widely regarded as intolerable. In the end, the Community voluntarily gave up all its practices known to be unacceptable to the outside world—beginning with complex marriage and ending with communism. By vote (199-1), the Community transformed itself into a joint stock-holding company called the Oneida Community, Ltd. on January 1, 1881. The company was to continue the successful industries of the Oneida Community to provide its stockholders, former members of the Community, with an income.

The company was not, at first successful. Barely surviving its first fifteen years, it was saved, at the eleventh hour, by the return of the Oneida Community's now-grown children. The younger generation refocused the firm on manufacturing high-end tableware. Toward that end, they developed a new process for silver-plating and new techniques for marketing that would influence the advertising industry of the twentieth century. In 1910, silverware became the company's leading product, and the older businesses were phased out. The Oneida Community, Ltd. (later shortened to Oneida Ltd.) became renowned for quality silverware.[20]

Notes

1. See Edward Deming Andrews, *The People Called Shakers: A Search for the Perfect Society* (New York: Dover, 1963, originally published 1953); and Henri Desroche, *The American Shakers: From Neo-Christianity to Presocialism* (Amherst: University of Massachusetts Press, 1971, originally published 1955) for introductory works to a vast Shaker literature.

2. Lawrence Foster estimates maximum Shaker population to have been between four and six thousand. See Foster, *Religion and Sexuality: The Shakers, the Mormons, and the Oneida Community* (Urbana: University of Illinois Press, 1984, originally published 1981), 23, and *Women, Family, and Utopia: Communal Experiments of the Shakers, the Oneida Community, and the Mormons* (Syracuse, New York: Syracuse University Press, 1991), 7. For Shaker settlement pattern, see Chris Jennings, *Paradise Now: The Story of American Utopianism* (New York: Random House, 2016), 56-57; and Louis J. Kern, *An Ordered Love: Sex Roles and Sexuality in Victorian Utopias: The Shakers the Mormons, and the Oneida Community* (Chapel Hill: University of North Carolina Press, 1981), 56.

3. John Humphrey Noyes, *The Berean: A Manual for the Help of Those Who Seek the Faith of the Primitive Church* (Putney, VT: Office of the Spiritual Magazine, 1847), 434.

4. Robert Allerton Parker, *A Yankee Saint: John Humphrey Noyes and the Oneida Community* (New York: G.P. Putnam's Sons, 1935), 155-

17; Arthur Bestor, *Backwoods Utopias: The Sectarian Origins and the Owenite Phase of Communitarian Socialism in America, 1663-1829*, 2nd enlarged ed. (Philadelphia: University of Pennsylvania Press, 1970, originally published 1950), 44.
5. Jonathan Beecher, *Charles Fourier: The Visionary and His World* (Berkeley: University of California Press, 1986), 274-96; Carl J. Guarneri, *The Utopian Alternative: Fourierism in Nineteenth-Century America* (Ithaca, NY: Cornell University Press, 1991), 18-19, 122-34, 181-82l; Edward K. Spann, *Brotherly Tomorrows: Movements for a Cooperative Society in America, 1820-1920* (New York: Columbia University Press, 1989), 77-78, 102-6.
6. Albert Brisbane, *Association; or, A Concise Exposition of the Practical Part of Fourier's Social Science* (New York: Greeley and McElrath, 1843); Guarneri, The Utopian Alternative, 32-34.
7. Guarneri, *The Utopian Alternative*, 475, 480.
8. Anthony Wonderley, ed., *John Humphrey Noyes on Sexual Relations in the Oneida Community: Four Essential Texts* (Hamilton College Library, Clinton, NY: Richard S. Couper Press, 2012), 113.
9. Aldous Huxley, *Tomorrow and Tomorrow and Tomorrow, and Other Essays* (New York: Harper and Brothers, 1956), 29.
10. "Community Journal: Oneida," *Circular*, July 11, 1870, 182. Historian Spencer Klaw rightly suspected that Oneida, was the most successful attempt ever made "to build a society in which men and women could live together as brothers and sisters, sharing with absolute equality the fruits of their common labor" (1993, 7).
11. *Daily Journal*, January 14 and 29, 1866. See also William M. Kephart, *Extraordinary Groups: The Sociology of Unconventional Life-Styles*, 2nd ed. (New York: St. Martin's, 1982), 145; Pierrepoint Burt Noyes, *My Father's House: An Oneida Boyhood* (New York: Farrar and Rinehart, 1937), 297-98; and James B. Herrick, "In luminatuo lumen videmus," Quadrangle 1, no. 2 (May 1908), 11.
12. Oneida Community, *Hand-Book of the Oneida Community: Containing a Brief Sketch of Its Present Condition, Internal Economy, and Leading Principles*, No. 2 (Oneida, NY: Oneida Community, 1871), 34-35. See also Charles Nordhoff, *The Communistic Societies of the United States: Harmony, Oneida, the Shakers, and Others* (New York: Harper and Brothers, 1875), 183.
13. Foster, *Free Love in Utopia*, 93-94, 291; Constance Noyes Robertson, *Oneida Community Profiles* (Syracuse, NY: Syracuse University Press, 1977), 65-105, Oneida Community, *Third Annual Report of the Oneida Association, Exhibiting Its Progress to February 20, 1851* (Oneida Reserve, NY: Oneida Association, 1851), 17-18.

14. "The successful management" quoted from Harriet M. Worden, *Old Mansion House Memories, by One Brought Up in It* (Oneida, NY: Oneida Ltd., 1950), 77. See also Parker, A Yankee Saint, 202.
15. Oneida Community, *The Oneida Community: A Familiar Exposition of Its Ideas and Practical Life, in a Conversation with a Visitor* (Wallingford, CT: Office of the Circular, 1865), 19.
16. "Community Journal: Oneida, *Oneida Circular*, November 4, 1872, 357.
17. See *Circular*, July 9, 1863; June 22, 1868; and January 11, 1869; American Socialist August 29, 1878; Robert S. Fogarty, *Special Love / Special Sex: An Oneida Community Diary* (Syracuse, NY: Syracuse University Press, 1994), 4; William Alfred Hinds, *American Communities and Co-operative Colonies*, 2nd rev., 3rd ed. (Chicago: Charles H. Kerr, 1908, originally published in 1878), 185.
18. "An Oneida Journal, *Circular*, May 26, 1859, 71; see also Robertson, *Oneida Community: An Autobiography*, 336; Richard DeMaria, *Communal Love at Oneida: A Perfectionist Vision of Authority, Property, and Sexual Order* (New York: Edwin Mellen, 1978), 192.
19. Hilda Herrick Noyes and George Wallingford Noyes, "Oneida Community Experiment in Stirpiculture," *Eugenics, Genetics and the Family* 1 (1923), 377-78; Parker, *A Yankee Saint*, 253-61; Klaw, *Without Sin*, 204.
20. Wonderley, *Oneida Utopia*, 162-205; Maren Lockwood Carden, *Oneida: Utopian Community to Modern Corporation* (Syracuse, New York: Syracuse University Press, 1998, originally published in 1969), 113-212.

Chapter 2. Histories

Part One: "One of the Four," by Harriet Skinner

In his *History of American Socialisms* (1870), John Noyes took the opportunity to review the history of the Oneida Community. But the chapter on Oneida contained little more than the personal story of Noyes, his time in Putney, and a few pages of Community financial summaries. What Noyes wrote there was far from a full historical account. Later, his sister, Harriet Skinner (**Figure 12**), became interested in placing Oneida in historical perspective. She recorded the past from the perspective of the Community's later years because, as she explained, "the second generation of the Community ask for it."[1] In this section are two groups of historical sketches by Skinner, together comprising the most substantive attempt

Figure 12: Harriet Noyes Skinner (1817-1893)

by a Community member to preserve knowledge of what came before. A third, by Charlotte Miller, is excerpted from one of Skinner's historical accounts. These sketches provide unique, firsthand information about the Oneida Community.

In Putney during the early 1840s, John Noyes recruited his siblings, including younger sisters Harriet (then nineteen years old) and Charlotte (sixteen) to join him in his efforts to establish a new community. Both would prove to be important collaborators in Noyes's publishing and proselytizing efforts over the years. Both were revered in the Oneida Community, "They could criticize without personal animus," Jessie Kinsley remembered fondly. "They could reconcile a sore heart to see its faults; they could stimulate ambition to rise out of littleness of Spirit, both for itself and others. They were great hearted and made you feel great hearted." Both sisters were accorded the title of "Community Mother"—one who served as a house supervisor and was looked up to as a font of guidance and sympathy.[2]

Figure 13: John L. Skinner (1803-1889)

Early on, Harriet gave up the possibility of obtaining a teaching position when she accepted her brother's religious program. Subsequently she married John Skinner (**Figure 13**)—a Quaker school teacher who became one of Noyes's earliest converts. Thereafter, Harriet Skinner staunchly supported John Noyes and, just as staunchly, waged war against sin and worldliness. She described herself as:

> tall, red-haired, impulsive, more or less combative, possessed of an intellect of masculine strength, and of a keenness of instinct which her brother John used to say was almost omniscient. She was not handsome, but there was something in her sunny hair and in the clear depths of her large grey eyes which in certain moods gave a touch of the angelic to her countenance.[3]

Her nephew, Pierrepont Noyes, remembered her as beautifully homely "with many freckles, sandy hair and almost masculine features."[4] The quality of being "masculine" often was applied to her, possibly because she looked like her older brother. Like him, she was a systematic thinker with an eye for practicalities. After studying the Oneida Community diet, for example, she turned the knowledge to account in the form of a cookbook tourists could buy.[5] The most organized of the siblings, Harriet was effectively the Community manager.[6]

Harriet Skinner could provide a complementary and even corrective spin to the views of her older brother as she did, for example, on the subject of croquet. Introduced in 1866 as an occasion for recreational mingling, the game quickly became the Community's sport of choice—and inspiration for Perfectionist philosophizing. After one match, Noyes announced "that he had got a new view of the subject of competition." If God is on both sides in every fight, he reasoned, competition is legitimate and good. "By loyally recognizing God in the game, and that he controls the result and gives the victory to whom he pleases, we may enter it heartily and exercise our utmost skill and power to win."[7] Soon after, Noyes's sentiment was papered over by that of his sister:

> One secret of the popularity of [croquet] evidently is its adaptation to both sexes. Then the question arises, how can the men best preserve this social and civilizing feature—the partnership of the women? First, I should answer, let the gentleness and moderation of the women, modify the tendency to excess and competition in the men. The violent way in which many of the men croquet their opponent's balls, seems very directly calculated to spoil the attractiveness of the game, especially for the women...The toning down of the eagerness and excess of the masculine element, would, in the humble opinion of one at least, add very much to the attractiveness of the game, and serve very much to perpetuate it, as a pleasant and improving pastime.[8]

In this fashion, Harriet Skinner redefined a competitive spirit as an occasion for men and women to enjoy each other's company.

Skinner was a prominent member of the Oneida Community throughout its thirty-two years of operation. Afterwards, she took up retirement residence with her brother and several other elderly, old-guard Perfectionists. After leaving Oneida in 1879, John Noyes had ended up on the Canadian side of Niagara Falls where, in 1880, the Community purchased a house for him. The Stone Cottage, as it was called, was large enough to accommodate a reconstituted association of Perfectionists wishing to rejoin their longtime leader.

"One of the Four" was a column of nineteen installments which ran in the *Oneida Circular* (**Figure 14**) from March 8 to July 19, 1875. The "four" of the title presumably refers to the Noyes siblings (John, Harriet, Charlotte, and George).

**Figure 14: The *Oneida Circular*
Photo by Jim Demarest**

Histories 23

The point of the work is to pay tribute to recently deceased Charlotte Miller. Although she probably succumbed to malaria, the Oneida Community ascribed her death to a liver infection.[9] The series is unsigned. Several individuals, including a male writer, could have contributed to it. Nevertheless, I attribute it to Skinner because her narrative voice predominates. Further and as of 1875, only she could have provided the information about the Noyes siblings given here. The series is a worshipful, a frankly hagiographic tribute to Miller. But it is also an important source of early Community history available nowhere else. It provides, for example, contextual information about the revival fervor of 1831 and its effects on Putney, Vermont, and how that affected John Noyes and his Perfectionist theology. The piece is especially strong in the details given about the Putney years and the initial period of the Oneida Community. There is also much about the Brooklyn and Wallingford branches. Miller's religious earnestness is demonstrated throughout as is her zeal for the cause of John Noyes, for Bible communism, and for the welfare of the commune.

In the series, we also learn much about the office and responsibilities of a "Community Mother." Conceivably the series title refers to the fact that, as of 1875, there had been four Mothers who, in addition to Charlotte Miller and Harriet Skinner, included Mary Cragin and John Noyes's wife (also Harriet). Such an individual kept a daily journal of the commune and contributed to the publication of Oneida's periodical. Further, and in Charlotte Miller's case,

> she had a general care for the Community...[She] had in particular to look after the spiritual, intellectual and social interests; took part in the daily routine of labor, washing and ironing with the rest of the women, and ever foremost at "bees" for outdoor labor; was in demand at criticisms, private and public; was a member of multitudinous committees of consultation; was expected to see and converse with the notables who called at the community; [and] had many correspondents.[10]

A Community Mother may have been the female counterpart of John Noyes in initiating or vetting men into the Oneida system of complex marriage. Oblique references to such a duty may be found in Miller's comment that God chose her "from my companions to be a lover of Christ, and a helper in establishing his social gospel."[11] "One of the Four" makes it clear that the subject of rights for women was of interest to the Oneida Community and of particular interest to Charlotte Miller who:

> fully sympathized with the object sought by the advocates of these "Rights"—the enlargement of woman's sphere in respect to labor and education. Her influence was always felt on this side of the question in all the discussion of the Community; and

practically she did much to bring about the present status of women in the Community, which makes them free to speak and vote on all questions affecting the common interest—to engage in any pursuit for which they have an attraction—to superintend and conduct any business for which they are qualified.[12]

Women of the Oneida Community and advocates of women's rights were aware of one another. In 1852 Miller conversed with "one of the most prominent advocates of Women's Rights in the country, who had called at Oneida." This unnamed visitor, Miller reported, "freely admitted that if we had found a way to avoid unwilling maternity we certainly had made great gain. I assured her that we had, and that every woman practically acquainted with our principles felt that Mr. Noyes had done more than any other man for the redemption of woman." Miller assured the visitor that "the problem of women's deliverance from the curse of undesired maternity and unnatural bondage to man had here been solved."[13]

The following texts are taken from "One of the Four: Memoir of Charlotte A. Miller," as they appeared as nineteen installments in a series in the Oneida Circular that ran from March 8-July 19, 1875.

Text 1: [The Noyes Family in Putney] "One of the Four: A Memoir of Charlotte A. Miller, I," *Oneida Circular***, March 8, 1875, p. 75.**

The pioneers of every good cause live in history. They become concrete manifestations of the cause itself. Louis XIV said, "L'état, c'est moi." With equal reason may these pioneers say, "I am the cause." How inseparable, for example, are Luther and Reformation, John Wesley and Methodism, George Fox and Quakerism.

But while the chief interest centers in the leader or originator of a movement, his first and most trustworthy associates elicit an interest only second to that which attaches to their principal. Melancthon's name will not die while that of Luther lives; Charles Wesley is as intimately associated in our minds with John Wesley as the brothers were in labor and love; and it is difficult to speak of George Fox without at least thinking of William Penn. So while John H. Noyes will always command the attention of the students of Perfectionism and Bible Communism, the names of his first faithful co-laborers will ever receive a share of the interest given to him and the cause itself.

John H., Harriet H., Charlotte A., and George W. Noyes—these formed the original nucleus of Putney Perfectionism. Others were soon added, perhaps equally faithful to their chosen leader, and equally useful to the cause—notably Harriet A. Holton who became the wife of John H.; John L. Skinner, who married Harriet H.; John R. Miller who married Charlotte A.; the Cragins, Leonards, and others; and still later many more scarcely less worthy of mention.

The object of this sketch is to bring together some of the events and experiences in the life of Charlotte A. Miller, one of the original four; but that life was at first so intertwined with that of her sister and brothers, and subsequently with that of the Community of which she was so many years a conspicuous member, that it will be necessary in tracing it to include much relating to other members of the Noyes family and to the general Community.

The little village of Putney, sequestered among the hills of southern Vermont, was in no way remarkable forty years ago. The blue Connecticut ran along its eastern boundary, and the scenery far and near was characterized by the variety of woodland, low mountain-ranges and sparkling, zigzag, pebbled brooks, so peculiar to the New England landscape. Brattleboro, a town of some notoriety as a fashionable summer resort, was within a two hours' drive; but no shrill whistle of railway locomotive awoke the echoes of the slumbering hills.

The two leading men of the town were "Squire" Noyes and Judge White, both members of Congress during a part of their careers. In a large, handsome, old-fashioned house, situated on a graceful eminence overlooking the village on the south, dwelt "Squire" Noyes with his wife and children. A group of locust trees of uncommon height and luxuriance gave to the place the name of "Locust Grove."

Mr. Noyes was a native of Atkinson, N. H., and though brought up on a farm he very early showed such a propensity for learning that, by school-teaching and hard study, he managed to fit himself for college. He graduated at Dartmouth, was tutor for two years and then studied divinity; but his health failing he was advised to engage in more active employment. He obtained a situation in the store of an acquaintance in Brattleboro, and found an attractive boarding-place at the house of Rutherford Hayes. Being then nearly forty years of age he had acquired much knowledge on all subjects, science, philosophy and literature. He was a rare conversationalist, and Polly Hayes, the eldest daughter, a tall, slender girl of nineteen, was a delighted listener, and as he was fond of communicating, he soon found in her that kind of attention which would make them never tire of being together, and accordingly after several years of acquaintance they reverently jointed hands in the path of life.

After the birth of their eighth child, Mr. Noyes, having become quite wealthy for those days, determined to retire from business and remove to some place where he could find better educational advantages for his family. After considerable deliberation Putney was fixed upon. Here, then, at the time our story opens, he has resided for twelve years, absent a part of the time at Washington, but engaged principally in educating his children, sending his boys to college and his girls to the best boarding schools.

Mr. and Mrs. Noyes were what we should call in these days of stirpicultural experiment a "splendid combination." Mr. Noyes was a man of learning, a scholar, a thinker and a most methodical, accurate person in whatever he did; he was a great reader, and possessed of one those plastic memories on which facts leave an indelible imprint, enabling the owner to make an apt quotation either in verse or statistics, wherever occasion required. Education was one of the most important words in his vocabulary. Notwithstanding his conversational powers were such as to entertain by the hour the guests who gathered at his table, he was extremely reticent in regard to whatever concerned himself, never alluding in any familiar way to the thoughts and feelings connected with his affections. An extraordinary self-control and reserve governed all his actions. He inspired a profound respect, and you would not more than once wish to meet the reproof of his eye. Although he showed in many practical ways how deep was his regard for his wife and children, yet he never lavished on them those little endearments by which most fathers express their affection. He was wise, upright and of unblemished integrity in business, but he was not a religious man.

Mrs. Noyes (**Figure 15**), generous, high-toned, open-hearted, had one of those inspirational natures which are so many-sided as to attract friends from all classes of society. She was remarkable for the breadth of her sympathies, which were bounded neither by rank nor sect nor nation. Children and young people felt the stimulus of her love, which was salted with that rare wisdom which incites its object to be and do all that its nature is capable of. But stronger than this human interest was her love for God. This love was her governing passion. It was easy to see that God was no mere abstraction to her; he was her dearest and nearest friend, and she realized his personality much as did the prophets of old. She taught her children above all things to *fear the Lord*, and events have proved that this was indeed with them the "beginning of wisdom." She was more anxious that they should please God than that they should obtain any earthly applause. "She was ready to spoil our chances for worldly advantage, rather than that we should forget God," writes her daughter Harriet. The Bible was her daily and hourly companion, and she nourished her little ones with its truths from the moment they could lisp the sweet words of her favorite David.

Figure 15: Polly Hayes Noyes (1780-1866) in her later years.

Mr. Noyes, though not a religious man, had great respect for the piety of his wife and left the spiritual education of the children entirely to her care. Notwithstanding their inability to work together in this field of vital interest, their mutual reverence and delicate deference in their personal treatment of each other made the household one of perfect harmony so that the boys and girls grew up with undoubting loyalty to the divine institution of marriage. No harsh words or jarring arguments ever rent the veil of romance in which the world from time immemorial has wrapped conjugal bliss.

Mr. Noyes never administered corporeal punishment to but one of his children, and then, most characteristically, with birch in hand, he whipped the truant boy all the way to school. Mrs. Noyes gave each of the children when quite young a sound chastisement for telling a lie, and after that was sure to govern them quite easily without resorting to the rod. Truthfulness and reverence she considered of greater value than any accomplishment. She never allowed any class distinction to stand in the way of moral rectitude. If one of the girls had shown disrespect to Bridget, she sent her to the kitchen to ask forgiveness, and this was often one of the severest punishments that could be inflicted. But prayer was her most important means of family discipline. She not only taught her children to pray, but she prayed with them, taking advantage of every event which was softening to the heart, to kneel with them and turn their thoughts to God as a being whose presence could be felt. Yet there never was a more playful, approachable woman than she, nor one who drew the enthusiasm of children more genuinely. Thus the young Noyeses grew up in an atmosphere which stimulated the broadest development of the heart and brain.

Text 2: [Childhood in Putney] "One of the Four: A Memoir of Charlotte A. Miller, II," *Oneida Circular*, March 15, 1875, p. 83-84

There were nine children born to Mr. and Mrs. Noyes; but when the youngest, who was christened William, was a baby, George W., a boy of ten years, died after a short illness. Little William was consequently re-named and became the George W. so well known to all who have followed the fortunes of the pioneers in Christian Communism.

During the period of child-bearing Mrs. Noyes was prepotent in transmission. She was a large-framed woman, of a somewhat spare figure, considerably above the medium height, with a strong nose and a head high above the ears. She was red-haired and had the mercurial temperament belonging to this much-reproached hair which has caught a measure of the sun's brightness. An admiring nephew writes: "It is but as of yesterday, when her stately, queen-like form (for I looked on her in my early days as a good specimen queen) passed before us, and her silvery voice rang through our circle joyously and persuasively, when we gathered around her and sought for youthful amusement. Her step was light, her countenance rich in thought, her language pure, her dignity graceful, her hospitality unbounded. She was at once mother and friend. I shall never see her equal, as she looms up in my recollections of the wise, beautiful, and dignified."

Mr. Noyes, scarcely reaching five feet ten, was inclined to more robustness of contour. He had dark-brown hair and large eyes of hazel blue, if the paradox is allowable. His mouth was small and indicative of fastidious refinement. That feature in the faces of both was a marked one in beauty of outline and coloring.

Of the children, seven were red-haired and two brown-haired; all except two also were above the average size of men and women. The brown heads were among the daughters, the third and eighth in the line, respectively Elizabeth and the subject of our sketch.

At the time our memoir opens the three youngest children, Harriet, Charlotte and George, were all that lived at home. Mary, Joanna, and Elizabeth were married, and John and Horatio were at Yale College.

There was but a year and eight months between the ages of Harriet and Charlotte, and consequently they grew up side by side, knowing each other most intimately. They were quite opposite in appearance and temperament. Harriet was tall, red-haired, impulsive, more or less combative, possessed of an intellect of masculine strength, and of a keenness of instinct which her brother John used to say was almost omniscient. She was not handsome, but there was something in her sunny hair and in the clear depths of her large grey eyes which in certain moods gave a touch of the angelic to her countenance. Charlotte was of a more delicate mould. People called her beautiful, and we can believe them, for when past fifty the traces of youthful loveliness were easily discernible. The father was prepotent in her composition. Her hair, which was of great length and thickness, she wore in a lustrous crown on her well-balanced head; her eyes were large, of a grayish blue with flecks of hazel in the iris; her nose straight and feminine; but her mouth was her most beautiful feature—the matching of the lips perfect, and delicately curved upward at the corners, with an expression of touching sweetness. She was gentle and self-possessed in all her ways, and her demeanor was characterized by extreme amiability and evenness of disposition. Her temperament was artistic, having very early evinced a marked talent for sketching.

Many beautiful things have been said of the affection and unbroken harmony which existed between these sisters. They never quarreled even in childhood, and when, in the bloom of their youth, they turned from the world, and joined their brother in an unpopular cause, their love for each other took the deeper character of spiritual unity and fellowship as members of Christ. In thus deviating from the time-honored customs of society and attaching themselves to a movement which was destined to lead the van of the forces of progress, it would not have been strange had there been temptation to envy between these sisters and some of that strife to be greatest which we call diotrephiasis; [14] but the records of those days and the testimony of people who then knew them, bring us evidence of nothing of that kind. They seem to have adapted themselves without a struggle to the true order of the duality; Charlotte always looking upon Harriet as the dynamic member, and likely to be the safer guide in matters of eternal interest, and Harriet deferring to Charlotte's taste and sense of beauty in external things. Charlotte, when speaking of her sister only last summer, said she could not recall one unpleasant word that ever passed between them, and thus the relation continued until the day of her death. At the last hour neither was troubled with the sickening remorse for unkind words or unsisterly treatment which embitters many a death bed; but Charlotte, true to the life-long bond, put out her hand in mute appeal to Harriet to strengthen her faith in making the transition, and Harriet, though her heart was breaking, gave that sympathy which exalts the spirit above the flesh and enables the soul to meet the untried world with unshaken confidence in its Creator.

Charlotte was an insatiable reader; histories, biographies, travels, poems, were devoured with such an absorbing interest that her mother often had difficulty in arousing her to attend to other duties. Curled up in a corner of the sofa or seated in a shady nook of the open terrace, she spent hours in the companionship of Walter Scott's heroes and heroines or among the kings and queens of foreign lands. Milton and Shakespeare were favorites, and the papers and magazines subscribed for by her father she read from beginning to end. She was very fond of history—particularly English history—and was an excellent teacher to the young in that branch of study. One of the last things she did for the class of growing girls in the Community was to put them through a course of English history. Her retentive faculty being nearly equal to her power of absorption, this early course of reading was of great value to her in after life. In connection with this subject we are reminded of an incident which occurred at W. C. [Wallingford Community] eight or nine years ago. G. W. N. [brother George Noyes], who had charge of the meetings, took from the library one evening the Biographical Encyclopædia and put out questions concerning the characters hap-hazard as to who they were and for what they were remarkable. The names of many persons were read, about whom most of us could only claim a knowledge of their existence and of some of whom we could not even boast as much information as that; and we well remember with what surprise and admiration we listened to Charlotte while she related in the femininely suggestive way of hers, events of interest in the lives of each one mentioned, showing that none were to her among the mass of nobodies and anybodies of which the world is generally composed.

Mrs. Miller became one of our most able and discriminating critics, and as it is always interesting to discover the germs of things, we will make a few extracts from simple "sketches" of her school-mates, written when attending Miss Fiske's seminary at Keene, N. H., at the age of fourteen. The two last are descriptions of her sister Harriet and herself:

"H. A.—Dark hair and eyes, complexion rather dark; a high, intellectual forehead; universally acknowledged to be the best and most sensible scholar in school.

"F. B.—She is decidedly above my comprehension; simplicity, wisdom, fine mind, sweetness and affection. The latter trait seems to predominate. Very plain; black, brown or hazel eyes, which she is too fond of raising to the plastering. I can't imagine the use. Like her as much as I can.

"E. B.—Handsome face and form. As for the jewel within I have not a very great or good opinion of it.

"E. C.—A pretty Miss. Disposition rather good. I have heard it hinted that she was—meaning that she had little ears; can't say how true it is.

"H. N.—A fine girl; sensitive and well-informed for her age and much respected by Miss Fiske and Miss Kent. Disposition generally good though obstinate. She is a very good girl, however. She is going to Hartford next summer, and I hope she will improve a monstrous much. Orthodox to the bone.

"C. N.—A most disagreeable, sour-disposed girl; continually pottering in school and spending her time to no advantage. Black hair and skin, grey eyes, snub or retroussé nose, decently large mouth, bends backwards, and is very affected in her walk and manners. Intellect nothing at all. Can't say as to how people think of her; disposed to be very conceited of nothing at all. She will, I hope, mend manners and mind."

Another incident which we find in this old book of school-scribbling gives a glimpse of youthful proclivities:

"One evening seated alone beside a cheerful, blazing fire
I laid aside my work and took up an interesting book. I had just commenced reading aloud—
"Let not Ambition mock their useful toil,
Their homely joys and---"

when my attention was arrested by the sound of footsteps on the carpet. I raised my eyes and beheld an old and withered dame seat herself without the least ceremony on a vacant chair by the fire with her back to me. I will not attempt to describe her, for my surprise was so great as to who she was, what she was, and how she came there, as to quite confuse me. I knew this, that her confidence was astonishing. A thought came into my head: 'This room in which I am sitting with my strange visitor has long enjoyed the enviable reputation of being haunted, and ghosts never speak without being spoken to.' Being no believer in such apparitions I determined to speak to her. I a-hemed and was about to speak when the good dame rose, turned toward me, and lifted her arm. My eyes were fixed on her, but her arm fell, and a low suppressed titter met my ear. I jumped up, and with little reverence twitched off her tight red cap, and revealed the laughing face of my sister Harriet. Several of my companions now ran up to us enjoying the joke, and I enjoyed it too. They told me that knowing that I intended to pass the evening alone, Harriet persuaded them to join in the plan to punish my unsociability. The repulsive and deceitful garb was laid aside, and with the assistance of a plenteous distribution of fruit and the conversation which naturally ensued, the evening passed very pleasantly and without any further calamity."

In thus briefly referring to the school-days at Keene we must not overlook one event in the life there, which, had it not been for its providential termination, would have put our present effort among the things never contemplated.

One winter evening Harriet and Charlotte went to take a bath in a room fitted for the purpose. The stove being out of order the servant brought in a small furnace of glowing charcoal and left the girls alone. In the midst of their ablutions a strange sensation of suffocation sent Harriet to the window to get a breath and then again they both put their mouths at the aperture to taste the pure air. The room had rapidly filled with the fumes of the burning charcoal, but the effect was at first so insensible that the girls were not in the least aware of the danger, and were soon groping about the room and stumbling over the furniture without a thought of their terrible condition. Charlotte lay down exhausted, but just then Harriet was seized with one of those instincts of self-preservation which sometimes compel people to save themselves although they are conscious of no alarm, and catching her clothes she somehow got outside the door, crept up the back stairway to her own room and pushing open the door fell on the floor utterly unable to speak, and greatly frightening two of her schoolmates who were sitting there. As soon as she got her breath she gasped, "Go and get Charlotte!" They ran instantly to the bath-room and arrived not a moment too soon, for Charlotte was fast approaching the last stages of suffocation, and was beyond all power to help herself.

The school authorities felt very much criticised by the affair; but Harriet and Charlotte have often told the story to their children as a striking example of the miraculous interposition of Providence to save them when they were all oblivious of danger.

Text 3: [Education] "One of the Four: A Memoir of Charlotte A. Miller, III," *Oneida Circular,* **March 22, 1875, p. 90-91.**

Although Mrs. Noyes was a very unworldly woman and cared far more to have her children kept in training for the life to come than to have them obtain honor of man for any qualities commanding superficial admiration, it was inevitable from the position of the family that they should mingle to some extent in society. Every person of note who stopped at Putney was expected as a matter of course to accept the hospitalities of the Noyes mansion, and thus the girls formed many agreeable acquaintances which enlarged their minds and stimulated their interest in the "pomps and vanities;" and then, as education was as essential in the estimation of Mr. Noyes as religion was in that of his wife, they were sent to school abroad where they met the gay and fashionable. Mrs. Noyes, who was a woman of great originality and some eccentricity, never allowed herself to become so burdened with household cares but that she could shake herself free every summer and set out in her own carriage on a several weeks' tour of cousining. She always took one of the girls with her, and as she traveled sixty miles or more from home, going through such towns as Deerfield, Amherst, Chesterfield, Granby and so forth, they had a chance to see considerable of the New England world. Harriet and Charlotte took great delight in these trips, which were sure to be enlivened with adventures that would furnish topics of conversation for weeks after the return. We asked Harriet if her mother never lost her way in guiding herself over such long distances. "O yes," she answered, "but then she never cared if she did, she could find it again." There was a romantic charm about this independent mode of traveling which makes railway transportation seem in comparison monotonous and unsocial. The climate of central New England is so even that there are often days together of uninterrupted sunshine and balmy softness, and the steady old horse jogged easily along over the firm, dry roads peculiar to that region. Mrs. Noyes was never in a hurry, and the girls were full of interest in all they saw, and thus the days were long with the variety of new scenery and happenings at taverns and watering-places.

In 1833, when Charlotte was fourteen and her father nearly seventy, the railroad between Lowell and Boston—one of the first built in the country—was completed. Mr. Noyes was a man who always kept up with the times, and though so much advanced in years he had not lost any of his interest in the progress of events. He did not feel able himself to endure the journey, but he wanted to have his children see this novelty which he knew would prove to be among the greatest inventions of the century, and he accordingly sent Horatio, Harriet and Charlotte to Boston by stage to take a trip to Lowell and back by rail at the opening of the road. Horatio, the eldest, was but eighteen, and we can imagine with what bounding pulses the youthful trio left their country home, to see the wonder of the age. Being generously provided with money they made quite a dash for those days, taking lodgings at the first hotel in the city, ordering the best of every thing for dinner, and running through more than a hundred dollars in about a week.

Joanna, one of the older daughters, was married the same summer to Mr. Hayes, American Consul at Trinidad, West Indies. Beautiful, strong and independent, she was one of those women who leave their mark on those with whom they associate. She had a great effect on the characters of her younger sisters, who looked up to her as a model in almost all respects, so that her leaving home was a great event, and particularly sorrowful because she was to go so far away. Her tastes were exceedingly fastidious, and the younger brothers and sisters were often mortified by her criticisms. Proud and worldly-minded, she had considerable difficulty several years later in accepting her younger brother as her spiritual leader, though she finally did so. He tells us of a long argument he had with her one day which he ended by offering himself to her merciless scalpel, and he assures us she did not spare him; but he obtained lasting benefit from the ordeal, and was able thereafter to recommend the practice of mutual criticism from a personal knowledge of its good effects.

Charlotte spent her seventeenth summer at a superior boarding-school in Hartford, Conn. Among her papers we find a bit of autobiography which throws some light on this early part of her life which, to every memorialist is enveloped in considerable obscurity unless he be writing the history of a well-known contemporary. Being in the bloom of maidenhood she was affected by those fascinations which often mislead the young and attractive. She says:

> "I studied with success at Hartford and cultivated my taste for drawing. To this last pursuit I devoted myself as one of my greatest pleasures and most desirable accomplishments. My society was almost entirely that of gay, fashionable girls of my own age, and I

was soon imbued with their spirit about dress and admiration and the allurements of horizontal fellowship. To this day I have a keen sense of what an all-powerful principality this love of dress and admiration is, from what I remember of the character and spirit of the society I met in that school. At the end of six months I went home, and for several weeks continued the course in regard to worldliness I had pursued at Hartford."

Text 4: [Importance of Religion] "One of the Four: A Memoir of Charlotte A. Miller, IV," *Oneida Circular,* **March 29, 1875, p. 98.**

Putney, the home of the Noyeses, appears to have long been a center of religious influence. It was the scene of many revivals. We are told that there was a wonderful awakening there as early as 1819, "which spread in the neighboring towns and swept through all classes, taking possession of even children by the hundreds." There was another great revival in Putney in 1826, and a third in 1831, which, ere it terminated, converted the subject of our sketch and nearly all her brothers and sisters. "And the same power which wrought such conversions in the Noyes family," Charlotte says, in her "Backward Glancings," [has written], "pervaded the whole country and produced everywhere important results. It was remarkable, not only for its range and energy, but also for the character and standing of its converts. In our immediate neighborhood it took possession of the best families and enlisted their brightest and most talented young men and women." "New Measures, protracted meetings and New York evangelists had just entered New England," says J. H. N. [John Noyes] in his *Religious Experience* [1849], "and the whole spirit of the people was fermenting with religious excitement. The Millennium was supposed to be very near." It is difficult at the present time to conceive of the intense earnestness that then prevailed. To save sinners was the one supreme duty. It was the constant theme of conversation. Those who were converted rested not till every means had failed to turn the hearts of all whom they could reach to God. Charlotte lived, as we have seen, at one of the centers of this religious fervor, and her character must at that time have received an impress not subsequently effaced. Her mother was always fully alive to the interests of religion, and her eldest son [John Noyes], having been taken captive, left the study of the law, and resolving to devote his life to God had entered the Theological Seminary at Andover, whence he wrote frequent letters to his friends at home full of zeal. The following to an unconverted brother, not only reveals his state of mind at that time, but will serve as a good illustration of the spirit which possessed the converts of the revival of 1831-32. It was written when that fearful scourge, the cholera, was threatening to sweep over the country, having already visited Montreal and other northern cities. It is an appeal to the fear of a dread hereafter rather than a presentation of the attractions of Christian life; but that was the style forty years ago:

DEAR BROTHER:--Amidst all your studies and amusements, your bright, flattering prospects of distinction and pleasure in the dim, distant future, and your merry forgetfulness of the storms which await you, it may be a good thing for you occasionally to look away from the bright visions which haunt the imagination of youth, and give yourself up to sober reflection on matters of gloomier aspect. For a wise man must think on all subjects connected with his existence; and surely you have lived long enough to know that sorrow and trouble enter largely into the composition of human existence. Let me then disturb for a few moments the accustomed course of your ideas by such thoughts as your situation naturally presents to my mind; and think not that my habitual meditations are gloomy, for I assure you I am very happy; but consider that gloom must rest upon every idea connected with the impenitence and consequent peril of a brother.

When I look back and think how little exertion I made to convince you of the necessity and value of religion when an opportunity was forced upon me, I shudder at my unfaithfulness. If you ever feel the worth of the soul you will shudder too, and wonder at my indifference. Do you think there can be too much anxiety about endless consequences of life or death? Think on that word *eternity*, and you can not help starting back with horror as from the brink of a bottomless abyss. Now, I have made up my mind to devote my life to thinking on that and similar subjects, and to making preparations to meet the final reality; and the more I think the more I wish you to think, because I see more and more that every thing which does not center on this one object of getting ready to die is vanity and a delusion. If we ever get to heaven, and much more if we get to hell, we shall look back and think ourselves the veriest fools for expending so much thought and anxiety on the concerns of that little span of three-score years and ten, while we almost forgot from day to day the interests of ages unnumbered!

Oh! Do be wise *now*. There is thought and truth enough in that one word *eternity*, to bow the most stubborn soul that dwells on this rebellious earth if that soul would look. A four days' meeting is not necessary in order send conviction to the heart, if the sinner would only uncase himself from the triple armor with which he defends his heart. Dare you to suffer your thoughts to linger around the word? If not, your case is pitiable—afraid to think of that which you must need to think of! As if a man, to be tried soon for his life should not dare to think of the court-house, or prepare his case. Of course, all comparisons fall infinitely short of their prototype when infinity is concerned. Have you any lurking hope that a death-bed will give you time for thought and preparation? Consider how many there probably are at this moment in Montreal in the agonies of a dreadful death who have lived upon the same hope and are entering eternity without God. It is dangerous for the seamen to wait till the tornado is upon them before they shorten sail or tack the ship, amid the terror and confusion of the storm. There is a bare possibility that matters may be set aright, but the vast probability is that the first blast will sweep the deck, and the first wave will sink them in the yawning deep. The contingency is one of fearful hazard. I would not mention the cholera to excite unnecessary alarm, and yet when there is danger it should be spoken of. God now holds up before us new and energetic motives to prepare to meet him; and if we are ever to prepare, *now* is the time. The destroying angel may not be commissioned against us, but wisdom bids "be ready." If the cry shall be heard amongst us as it is in the cities of the North, "Bring out your dead"—who will then dare to enter upon the labor and anxiety of attending to the subject of religion? *Now* is the time—I beseech you improve it.

All I desire specially to recommend is that you obtain an unshaken confidence in God, which is the best preventive of the cholera, and the *only* preventive of that disease which spreads wider and more terrible desolation than the cholera, and which commences its fiercest ravages when the cholera has done its worst, even sin. I feel as if we were entering a battle, and there is a chance we may be found among the slain. Let us then gird up our loins and set all things in order, and then we may look to Calvary for an example of dying conduct. Jesus died for us by a death more violent and horrible than any form of the cholera, and shall we not follow in his footsteps without faltering? When we can say, 'Lord, not my will, but thine be done,' we may walk through the valley of the shadow of death and fear no evil.

Good bye,
    Your affectionate brother,
        J. H. Noyes.

Text 5: [Religious Revivals and Perfectionism] "One of the Four: A Memoir of Charlotte A. Miller, V," *Oneida Circular*, April 5, 1875, p. 106-107.

The revival of 1831-2, though more widespread and powerful than the revival which preceded it, had the same defects. It accomplished great good in arousing men from the lethargy of unbelief and the cant of the churches, but its work was nevertheless superficial and transitory. It saved people from the grosser forms of worldliness, but did not cleanse their hearts from sin; it converted them to a legal, ordinance-observing religion, but did not give them the grace and security of the gospel.

We are not therefore surprised that Charlotte, looking back at her early conversion, should say, "Though I was converted at the age of thirteen in the old-fashioned way and joined the church, my interest in religion was not very deep, and consisted mostly in attending meetings, keeping the Sabbath, and reading the Bible daily." Nor is it surprising that with her natural attractions and the temptations which surrounded her she should lapse into worldliness.

But if the general effect of the revival was superficial there were some noteworthy exceptions. In a few it kindled a fire that should not go out. J. H. N., the brother of Charlotte, was of this number. "Seeing no reason why backsliding should be expected, or why the revival spirit might not be maintained in its full vigor permanently, I determined," he says, "with all my inward strength, to be a young convert in zeal and simplicity forever. My heart was fixed on the Millennium, and I resolved to live or die for it." This purpose led him to study the Scriptures with almost unparalleled earnestness, and finally landed him in new and radical views on several important subjects—especially on that one of transcendent importance, salvation. He came to the conclusion that the New Testament language is to be taken literally—that Christ did indeed come into this world to save men from sin, from all sin, now and forever. The news of Mr. Noyes's conversion to Perfectionism went rapidly over the land, even in those days of stage-coaches, and a power accompanied it which shook the churches and made the sincere everywhere examine anew the foundations of their faith.

Charlotte was then only fifteen, but she says, "I remember reading the Testament through during the summer of 1834, with my eye upon the proof of the Second Coming of Christ eighteen hundred years ago. I noted each text where it spoke of the coming of the 'Son of Man,' 'the coming of the day of the Lord,' etc., and in what a blaze of light this doctrine shone out on every page almost of the Testament when I got through. In the same manner the doctrine of salvation from sin seemed written as with a sunbeam in every chapter. In short, under the powerful illumination shed by the testimony of the New Haven believers, the whole Bible became a new and unsealed book."

Mr. Noyes soon had a band of co-laborers, some of whom, like Boyle and Dutton, were men of eloquence and power; and they proclaimed the new truths as with authority. It seemed as though Perfectionism would triumph speedily. The Free Church in New Haven yielded to its influence, and here and there other churches acknowledged its truth; but soon the cry of heresy was raised, and then it became evident that Perfectionism would not be a popular religion—that it must grow by the principle of selection—by taking from the churches and the world those who were prepared for this highest standard of religious experience. As Charlotte herself says: "The great revival of 1831-2 had sounded abroad the near approach of the Millennium, and had raised high the standard of personal holiness. In nearly every church could be found a select few, more sincere and earnest than their fellows, who waited and prayed like Simeon of old for the dawn of this great salvation. Such persons were found in Cambridge, Fletcher and adjacent towns in Northern Vermont, and in Westminster and Putney of Southern Vermont. They were scattered more or less through all the New England States, and were found in considerable numbers in Newark, New Jersey, and in Central and Western New York." To such persons the new doctrines were indeed glad tidings of great joy; and *The Perfectionist*, a paper started in New Haven in the interest of the new truths, was sure, as Charlotte says, to fall into the hands of these persons. "Often it seemed that a Providence more certain and subtle than any device of man directed the papers to them. They were passed from hand to hand and from neighborhood to neighborhood. Everywhere they awakened earnest thought and discussion. The more spiritual and sincere of their readers said, as did a lovely and cultivated lady of Putney, Mrs. T. Crawford, "This is what I want; this is such a Christian as I should like to be."

Though believers in Perfectionism were scattered throughout New England and New York, it had its centers of interest, and Putney was one of them. Here had been, as we have seen, a favored revival ground; here Mr. Noyes was personally known, and his family was held in great respect; here the *Perfectionist* was freely circulated; here Mr. Noyes had been converted in the revival of 1831, and had himself labored for the conversion of sinners: and here would naturally be the greatest desire to hear him preach. Charlotte tells how he was received there in the winter of 1835:

> "Curiosity and the craving to hear and tell new things were mingled with much genuine hunger for gospel food. The regular pastors did not show any cordiality, or open their churches to him, but the people came eagerly to hear him in school-rooms, in tavern-halls and in private houses. The leading physician of the place, Dr. A. Campbell, and his wife (at whose hospitable home Rev. O. A. Brownson, before his conversion to Catholicism, was often a guest), became deeply interested in the new doctrines, and opened their house for evening meetings. The example was followed by Mr. J. Crawford, a lawyer. He and his refined and intelligent wife had never professed religion before, but having 'tasted of the good word of God' as preached by J., now manifested all the simplicity and enthusiasm of young converts. The company which assembled at these meetings embraced a variety of classes and denominations. Some were members of the most orthodox and influential families in town. Others were Universalists, Methodists and Nothingarians.
>
> "The meetings were generally very informal, not given to vocal praying or much singing. J. usually took the Bible and discoursed upon some text or topic, treating it in an original, soul-

searching way, and interspersing familiar conversation and questions. The interest growing out of these evening discourses was intense and lasting. Many persons who had never before cared much for the Bible began to love and study it, and felt that with the new weapons furnished by J. they were able to meet and confound ministers and church-members. Some who had been seeking religion for years, but who were chilled and disappointed by the low, unsatisfactory hopes held out by the churches, heard the glad tidings of a full salvation with joyful surprise, and became steadfast followers of J. through evil report and good report.

"From the village the interest spread to the borders of the town. The 'East Part,' as it was called, was a sort of neutral ground, where all religions and no religion by turns held sway. It was now the head-quarters of Methodism; but that church was not in a very flourishing or harmonious state, and could hardly be said to hold the place. Mr. L. Pierce, who belonged to no church, but thought J.'s doctrine the best he ever knew, invited him to preach at the 'East Part,' in the Methodist church. A revival followed this preaching. Several of the most religious and substantial families became interested and opened their houses for meetings. The converts, in most cases, were remarkably whole-hearted and steadfast. The rumor of these events reached the neighboring towns, and invitations to preach came in from Westminster, Dummerstown, Fayetteville and other places almost daily. My sister and myself generally accompanied J. to the meetings in town, and occasionally to those out of town; greatly to the consternation and grief of our fashionable friends. To forsake our regular church meetings and assemble with a miscellaneous company in some out-of-the-way school-house, or at some remote and obscure private house, was a grievous derogation from the family rank. Loss of caste was held up to us as a threat and a warning; but we pursued our course, caring little for the remarks of those who would keep our attention upon considerations of that kind."

Text 6: [Early Preaching Career of John Humphrey Noyes] "One of the Four: A Memoir of Charlotte A. Miller, VI," *Oneida Circular*, **April 12, 1875, p. 113-114.**

Our last chapter left J. H. N. at Putney, preaching with success at various places in that and the neighboring towns. His sisters Harriet and Charlotte, though not fully converted to his views, yet usually accompanied him to these meetings, considering it a great privilege to hear his words and share his fortunes. His spirit was full of victory and hope. He wrote to his friends at New Haven: "The Lord is opening for me a wide door for the preaching of the gospel, and is giving me power that prevails against all adversaries. The day of Pentecost has not yet come in our house, but the Lord of peace is here. This village was never in such a state of agitation as it is now. Publicans and sinners hear me more gladly than the Pharisees, and many of them are receiving the truth into good and honest hearts. A general and most intense desire to hear more prevails. I shall preach as often and long as the Lord permits. I have full and blessed employment. The fields around are white unto the harvest, and the Lord says, 'Thrust in the sickle.' He gives me great liberty in declaring the truth, and complete victory over the devil in every encounter. I am in the midst of a perpetual battle, and yet have perpetual peace."

But this experience was the precursor of unmeasured trial and suffering. In the course of a few months great defection occurred in the ranks of Perfectionists; some of the brightest lights ceased to burn; many persons went back to the churches; Boyle, chief editor of *The Perfectionist*, quarreled with Mr. Noyes and refused to publish his contributions; a separation took place between Mr. Noyes and Charles H. Weld, an ex-minister and prominent leader among Perfectionists; "discord and dissensions within and reproach from without rendered the desolation of Perfectionism almost complete." Mr. Noyes says of himself, "I was perhaps never in a more desolate condition as to outward friendship than now." At the same time he had to measure conscientiously his "own responsibility for the disastrous consequences which seemed to follow the doctrines of Perfectionism." In a substantial sense, he says, "I stood before the judgment seat of Christ; my works were tried by fire." The defection went on—some returning to the churches, others to the world—until Mr. Noyes was left almost alone. His own individual experience was at the same time of a character tending to wean him from all outside attachments. He wrote, "Earthly relations and friends can never again hold me in bondage. I am as free for God's service as if I had never known father and mother or brothers and sisters." Apparent misfortune had strengthened the conviction of many that he was indeed crazy, according to the report put in circulation after his first confession of holiness. Even some of his own near relations were ready to question his sanity. Not so with Harriet, Charlotte and others in his father's house. "We knew," says Harriet, "that he was an earnest, spiritually-minded man, and our confidence was in God that he would protect and guide him." It is easy to imagine how much concern must still have been felt by the Noyes family while, destitute of employment and money, he traveled from place to place, impelled by a voice within. There was the practical, worldly-wise father, who could have regarded his son's unsettled course with no sort of complacency; the earnest, God-fearing mother, who sympathized with her son's high religious aspirations, but must often have been tempted to wish he could have worked with the nominal church; George W. in the midst of his preparations for college; Charlotte, admired of all and susceptible in a high degree to the attractions of worldly society, and just then at a boarding school in Hartford, where, as we have seen, she was surrounded by gay, fashionable girls of her own age, and much affected by worldliness; and Harriet, who, though possessed of the fullest confidence in her brother's integrity, had not fully committed herself to his faith, and was moreover subject to such worldly inducements as presented themselves at Saratoga, and in an invitation to become a teacher in a popular seminary and offers of marriage. Joanna, the eldest sister, whose husband was in the West Indies, spent this summer of 1836 at home. She is described as a person of great strength of character, very attractive and much beloved by all. "Though a church member, her tastes and ambition" says her sister Charlotte, "led her toward worldly success. She saw and felt instinctively that her brother John's influence over us tended to make us unfashionable as he was. This, seen from her point of view, was to make life a failure." Joanna's influence at that time must have been a powerful one to distract the family from the cause of Holiness; Charlotte confesses that "for the time being it looked as if we should all drift away with the tide."

The summer of 1836 was unquestionably the darkest time ever seen in the history of Perfectionism. The leaders no longer working in harmony—many gone back to the churches; many devoting themselves to antislavery, temperance and minor reforms; some disgracing Perfectionism with their fanaticism, others using its liberties to serve their lusts. Mr. Noyes going from place to place, scarcely knowing where to rest his head; his friends at home subject to temptations and distractions—so far as outward appearances go, the days of Perfectionism seemed to be numbered.

But that darkest night soon gave place to day. Mr. Noyes returned to Putney; and that event he has always regarded as the turning-point of his own experience and that of the cause of Holiness. "From this time," he says, "is to be dated the commencement of the change which transformed the center of operations to Putney...I returned from Newark to Putney, and remained at my father's during the following winter. At this time I commenced in earnest the enterprise of repairing the disasters of Perfectionism, and establishing it on a permanent foundation; not by preaching and stirring up excitement over a large field as we had done at the beginning, nor by laboring to reorganize and discipline broken and corrupted regiments, as I had done at Prospect, but by devoting myself to the patient instruction of a few simple-minded, unpretending believers, chiefly belonging to my father's family. I had now come to regard the quality of the proselytes of holiness as more important than their quantity; and the quality which I preferred was not that meteoric brightness which I had so often seen miserably extinguished, but sober and even timid honesty. This I found in the little circle of believers at Putney; and the Bible-school which I commenced among them in the winter of 1836, proved to be to me and to the cause of Holiness the beginning of better days."

Mrs. Miller refers to the same event in her "Backward Glancings" as follows:

> "Late in the fall John returned home. He came unannounced as usual, but was received with joy. Mother was a frequent invalid at this time, and kept her chamber. In her room John felt most at

home. The Bible was always her favorite study, and her interest in true religious experience was never cold. I do not know exactly how it commenced, but soon my sister Harriet began to spend her evenings in mother's room listening and reading with them. Her whole soul was hungry for salvation—for an experimental acquaintance with God. While she was thus pressing forward she had one great drawback; it was the thought that she must leave me behind. If I continued indifferent, she and I, who had been inseparable from childhood, must here part. To give me up cost her many tears. How did I know it? Nothing had been said to me of her struggles, but I felt in my heart that Harriet had left me, that she had set out in earnest to be religious. This broke up my indifference. My heart melted toward God. I must go with her. She had opened the way and I would follow with all my heart. I joined her in spending all my leisure time in the 'upper chamber.' George came too. This was the beginning of a new era in our family. John commenced his Home-Talks there with mother, Harriet, George and me for listeners. It was a revival on a small scale that lasted all winter. We studied the Bible in a practical, self-applying way. The truth that had been before held as a theory was laid to heart. John watched the process of conviction, and warned, exhorted, and encouraged us, and led us along step by step."

In an unpublished manuscript of Charlotte's we find a paragraph relating to the same period, in which she says:

"The school that commenced then I always look back to as the most important event in my life. The study of the Bible and conversations on spiritual subjects became the most interesting business of the day and evening. The fashions of the world, my passion for drawing, and desire for success in fashionable life, all came up for criticism, and the separation from the world, which had been only partial before, was now thorough. In the course of this winter Harriet, George and I made a public confession of Christ, and thus forever destroyed the bridge behind us.

"Thus passed the winter of 1836-7. It was the pleasantest winter I ever spent; though we had many trials in separating ourselves from our unbelieving brother, and from the family spirit in several ways, yet it was a time of fresh and genuine growth of the heart, and the commencement of true interior fellowship with God and Mr. Noyes. His spirit and words became the food of life to us, and for unity with him we could easily forego the society of others whether young or old. Our position was now well understood by the world, and we went on independently, and were less affected by the censures or attractions of society. The small circle of believers furnished all the social enjoyment we desired, and those who attempted to lure us out of it by worldly love and offers of marriage found that our confession of Christ and fellowship with Mr. Noyes was a wall of fire round about us."

Text 7: [School in Putney, 1836] Excerpts from "One of the Four: A Memoir of Charlotte A. Miller, VII," *Oneida Circular,* **April 19, 1875, p. 122.**

The school started at Putney in the winter of 1836, which Charlotte pronounces the most important event in her life, and her brother says proved to him and the cause of Holiness the beginning of better days, had great influence on the character of its students. Its success was unquestionably due to J. H. N., its founder. He inspired those who engaged in its studies with his own enthusiasm, which never abates in the pursuit of truth. He is like a miner who has struck a rich vein and throws out the golden grains at every spade. That school read the Bible and history and events with a new light. Charlotte has already told us how the great truths declared by her brother *shone out* on every page of the New Testament and seemed written *as with a sunbeam* in every chapter. The same illumination went with them in all their studies. They believed they should be guided unto all truth—that they had, in fact, the key which unlocks the history of the world. With positive pleasure Charlotte and the rest plodded through such tomes as *Prideaux's Connection of the Old and New Testament*s, and investigated such profound questions as these:

> On what ground can we claim the promises of God?
> What is justification?
> What is the bible testimony concerning the duty of believers in relation to baptism?
> What is the nature of condemnation, and in what does it consist?
> What time is meant by the inspired writers when they speak of the last days?
> Is the punishment of the wicked after death total destruction or everlasting torment?
> Have the prophecies relating to the restoration of the Jews been fulfilled? If not, what remains to be fulfilled?
> What does the apostle mean by saying, "He that hath suffered in the flesh hath ceased from sin?"
> Is the death of the body the consequence of sin?
> What are we to understand by Gog and Magog spoken of in Revelation?
> What is the nature of the rest that remains for the people of God?
> Can the efforts of believers hasten the coming of the day of the Lord?

What benefit is the Second Coming of Christ to us?

The school was specially engaged in Bible studies, having its morning Bible-class, first at the "upper chamber" of the house at Locust Grove, then at the new house of J. H. N., and finally at a chapel erected by the Perfectionists in the center of the village for the convenience of the believers who lived in scattered houses; but its attention was by no means confined to Bible studies. It watched with lively interest current events, and discussed all the great questions agitating the public mind. I have before me a journal begun July 1849 [which includes Charlotte's description of daily life]..."We spend the first half-hour after getting up in the morning in studying the Bible; the rest of the forenoon is occupied in printing or some other outward employment; the afternoon is devoted to studying the Scriptures and the cultivation of the spiritual, intellectual and moral departments—thus instituting a semi-daily Sabbath; this plan raises the soul from the attitude in which the love of money places it and gives it an opportunity of proving that it is the noblest part of man." . . .

Text 8: [Early Publishing Career of John Humphrey Noyes] Excerpts from "One of the Four: A Memoir of Charlotte A. Miller, IX," *Oneida Circular*, **May 3, 1875, p. 137-38.**

When John entered on his publishing enterprise at Putney, in the fall of 1838, he began in the simplest manner. Neighbor Cutler, a kind of tinker by trade, and one of those stony-ground believers in whom the love of the truth wilts and dies the moment trouble comes, lent him the use of a small room up stairs in his saw-mill. John sent his younger brother George (**Figure 16**) to Keene for three weeks to get a smattering of the printing business, and then commenced with prophetic calmness his life-work. Meanwhile his wife, Harriet A., and his sisters Harriet and Charlotte, were left pretty much alone at the house. They associated little with the families in the village, and having no more to do than ladies usually have, they began to feel very lonesome with John gone all day. Finally one morning after putting the house to rights, and leaving Sally with directions about the dinner, they started out to see what John was about. They found him distributing new type into cases. After watching him a few minutes, they caught the fever of industry, and their quick and careful fingers were soon employed in putting the shining types into the little boxes. The next day they went again to the saw-mill, and assisted John, who was "setting up" "The Way of

Figure 16: George Washington Noyes (1822-1870)

Holiness," by glancing ahead at his copy and setting a word at a time to hand to him when he reached it. As he was but a novice in the art, his progress was thus considerably accelerated. These young ladies were full of zeal, and liked their new employment so much that they determined to continue it every day. Mrs. Freeman, a woman of some devotion to the cause of Perfectionism in the earlier stages of its development, volunteered to look after house-keeping matters. Accordingly, we might thereafter have seen the two Harriets and Charlotte starting for the saw-mill every morning, returning to dinner at noon, then back again for several hours in the afternoon. For a considerable part of the time they kept factory hours, going and coming with the bell. "We used to remark," said Mother Noyes the other day, "that we had become quite like the working-people who went to and from the factory at the same time we did." By and by, Mr. Cutler let them have a better room in the story above, and this they carpeted and made quite attractive in other ways. When winter came, they carried their dinner in a pail, and had cozy times sitting beside the little stove, munching the cold viands and chatting enthusiastically of future schemes. From this simple beginning, sprang the system so common in the Community, of the combination of the sexes in labor.

After finishing "The Way of Holiness" they continued the publication of *The Witness*, a paper begun at Ithaca, and issued at odd times for six years…

Text 9: [Noyes and Partnership with John R. Miller] Excerpts from "One of the Four: A Memoir of Charlotte A. Miller, X," *Oneida Circular*, May 10, 1875, p. 145-146.

John R. Miller was the son of a well-to-do farmer living in Westminster, a village about six miles distant from Putney. His youth was spent at school and in assisting his father on the farm; but not being physically adapted to this employment he injured himself when eighteen years of age, and considered it unwise thereafter to continue the heavy duties of farm routine. For two years he led the life of a rover, not going beyond the limits of New England, yet encountering men and events in sufficient variety of aspect and circumstance to expand his mind with new views of the world and a fund of information and anecdote which were afterward to prove very useful. Returning home, he obtained a situation as clerk in a store in the village.

When Mr. Noyes began publishing *The Witness* Mr. Miller and a young lady friend, Miss Maria Clark, were among the first to take an interest in the new doctrines he presented. They subscribed for the paper, and occasionally invited Mr. Noyes to preach in their village. This course threw Mr. Miller into disfavor with his employer, who summarily dismissed him, and he accordingly went to New York City, where he occupied a good situation as clerk for several months; but his chief interest in life lying nearer home he soon returned and was received again by his old employer, who established him this time in a store which he owned in Putney. Here he could observe more closely the movements of the Perfectionists. Not long afterward he formed a partnership with Mr. Wheeler, a merchant in Putney.

During a revival which came upon the village Mr. Miller's interest in Perfectionism became a conviction which ripened into an enthusiastic devotion. He possessed one of those magnetic, genial, diffusive natures which attract friendship from all classes of people. Intensity, sympathy, ardor, and a rare ability to enter into and rapidly execute the plans of others, made him a valuable coadjutor. Though continuing to be a firm believer in Mr. Noyes's doctrines, he had had no intimate acquaintance with the Noyes family. Of his first introduction to the Noyeses he thus wrote some years later to his friend, James Crawford, Esq.:

> "I often think of the happy hours I spent with you and your wife when I first came to Putney to live. Well do I remember the first time you invited me to your house to spend an evening. You came into the store and told me that Horatio, Joanna, Harriet and Charlotte Noyes were at your house, and asked me to go in and spend the evening. As we entered the room you turned to the company and said, 'This is our friend.' I shall never forget the scenes of that evening. I remember the conversation as well as if it were but yesterday. It was upon the subject of holiness, a subject which has been dear to me ever since. That is a bright spot in my past life, which I shall always look back to with pleasure. I presume you do not remember that time so vividly as I do, nor have you the same reason; for I never had had an opportunity before to associate with more than one or two who believed in the doctrine of holiness. Although at that time I had not received the doctrine into my heart I saw it and loved it, and thanks be to God, he has never allowed me to desert it. In 1839 I knew what it was to confess Christ in me a Savior from sin. I then began to meet with opposition; for so long as I was called a 'Perfectionist' and did not live the truth, the world and the world's church cared little about it; but when one can say he knows that Christ is a present Savior from all sin he may arm himself for conflict with the church and the world."

In 1840 Mr. Noyes proposed to Mr. Miller to dissolve his business partnership, abjure political aspirations, and come to his house to board and study theology. Mr. Miller accepted this advice, and putting aside personal ambition unhesitatingly united his fortunes with those of Mr. Noyes. On the seventh of September in the following year Charlotte gave herself in marriage to Mr. Miller. There is nothing particularly romantic to tell about the courtship; and indeed, it could hardly be called a courtship, though Charlotte's beauty and goodness from their earliest acquaintance appealed to a tender spot in Mr. Miller's heart. But those were earnest days, and those engaged in the movement felt like soldiers enlisting for battle, so there was little time for sentiment. He was a pandour, and she a *fille du regiment,* and love was an incentive to the conquest of legends. Charlotte had previously received a number of brilliant offers which would have placed her in the most select circles of the land; but these she declined as temptations of the adversary to draw her away from a sacred cause; and though Mr. Miller, socially considered, was somewhat below her in station, the marriage proved a very happy one. Charlotte adapted herself to the position of wife with instinctive grace. Although naturally fitted to be an appreciative and entertaining companion to men of culture and learning, there was not a suspicion of strong-mindedness about her. She gave man his true place as head of woman, and felt no suppression or infringement from his superiority. Yet though always affectionate and amiable she did not dote on her husband, or try to wheedle or manage him by feminine arts. You would have said she was a true woman in all her functions in life, and yet she would not have provoked your envy.

The eight years succeeding the marriage of Charlotte were full of interest to her and the Putney school. Many chapters might properly be devoted to this period; but as a history of it is in preparation by Mrs. Skinner (of which our readers will in due time have the full benefit), we must be content with the briefest statement in this connection of some of its important events.

During this period the members of the Putney school were considerably increased, so that at its close it numbered nearly forty persons, and included many who have since been prominent members of the Oneida Community. Besides the Noyeses there were Mr. Miller, Mr. Skinner, Mr. Woolworth, the Cragins, Leonards, Bradleys, Bakers, Burnhams and others.

During this period the Bible was the daily study of the Putney school. They literally fed upon its truths. The Bible-classes referred to in previous numbers were kept up in one form and another during these eight years. It was their constant aim to familiarize themselves with the Scriptures, and to invite its spirit into their hearts. This was the preparation and seed-sowing, which in later years produced the Oneida Community and its Pentecostal form of society.

In this period J. H. N. began his series of Home-Talks. Seated around him in the large parlor at the Upper-House or at the Lower-House or at the Chapel, his disciples eagerly received his words, finding therein something which satisfied their hearts.

During this period the Putney believers ceased to say "mine" and "thine" respecting houses and lands and goods. The spirit which followed the teachings of their leader and their New Testament studies swept away the claims of selfish ownership as it did with the early Christians, and no man said "that aught he possessed was his own." They tilled their farms, worked in their shops, carried on mercantile operations, and published a paper, and prospered in all their undertakings, like a band of brothers and sisters having one interest.

The same spirit which swept away property distinctions stayed on in its course till even the selfish claims of marriage were also swept away. These changes were in no sense arbitrary, but the legitimate, natural effect of the Pentecostal spirit which had taken possession of the Putney school.

In this same period mutual criticism became a Community ordinance. In the midst of their revolutionary changes in respect to property and marriage, sincere, earnest, heart-searching criticism held sway; and the members were eager to avail themselves of the benefit of this ordinance, so strong was their desire for personal improvement.

During this period Harriet A. Hall was cured by faith, and other manifestations of miraculous power occurred, which were noised all over the land.

During this period, the remarkable testimony was given by the Putney believers, that the Kingdom of God had commenced in this world.

As the school grew in unity and numbers its publications were more widely read and appreciated, and by this means the little band at Putney became an acknowledged power in the land. The jealousy of the churches was aroused; others through mistaken zeal or from some less worthy reason coöperated with the church-members, and so a hot fire of persecution was raging. In a few months the prosperous, happy Community was scattered—some going to Northern Vermont, some to Connecticut, some to New York, some to other States—leaving Mr. and Mrs. Miller and a few others only, to look after their common property, and face the wrath of their persecutors...

Text 10: [Departure from Putney to Central New York] Excerpts from "One of the Four: A Memoir of Charlotte A. Miller, XI," *Oneida Circular*, May 17, 1875, p. 153-154.

In June, 1849, Charlotte and the rear-guard of the Putney Perfectionists reached Oneida. This Community was then in its infancy, building houses, clearing land, planting trees, and doing its best "to make a living" from its farm and saw-mill, while disciplining and organizing its members. There was much rude work to be done. No mechanical contrivance anywhere lightened labor, save perhaps at the saw-mill. The kitchen work and all else indoors, farming, teaming, and all else outdoors, had to be done by the pioneer Communists. The sexes mingled much in labor, the men taking part in the washing and kitchen work, and the women assisting them to lath the new house and keep the gardens in order. Grand "Bees" of all the members were often called, for making picket and board fences, husking, etc. Criticism was much in demand; and that and many other measures were often called in requisition to keep the raw recruits of Communism harmonic. Thirty or forty children of all ages also had to be instructed and guided into true paths. Altogether there was no rest for the "tried soldiers," as the Putney members were called.

Charlotte arrived in time to participate in these pioneer labors. Mrs. Noyes, Mrs. Cragin and Mrs. Skinner were then regarded as Mothers of the Community, but Charlotte's influence and example were none the less effective; and though there was nothing in her that would assume or seek any such position for herself, she naturally and irresistibly gravitated toward it, and soon took her place as a Mother and leader of the Community, not however in any way to displace the others mentioned. The four worked in perfect harmony...

Text 11: [Life in the Community: Children and Women's Rights] "One of the Four: A Memoir of Charlotte A. Miller, XII," *Oneida Circular*, **May 24, 1875, p. 165-66.**

As mentioned in our last chapter, Charlotte was given the care of the Community children in the summer of 1850. Her letters...show how important she regarded her new responsibility. A letter now before us, dated, September, 1850, shows that it was not long before she began to reap the reward of her labors. In it she says: "I see that the peaceable fruits of righteousness are beginning to appear among the children. I am much strengthened and encouraged, 'knowing that our labor is not in vain in the Lord.' The testimony of J. L. in meeting this evening made me say in my heart to Mrs. L., 'Happy mother.' She was grateful beyond the power of words to express." A few months later Charlotte penned the following, which more fully expresses her ideas of the influence and measures that should be brought to bear upon children:

> "It is generally known that our Community consider the children's department one of the most important and interesting fields of labor that Christian Association presents. We find that the discipline and experience of our children is a miniature copy of our own; and that we stand in relation to them more as the monitors in a large school to the small classes placed in their charge by the principal teacher, than as independent and irresponsible governors. We believe, in short, that in proportion as obedience, sincerity and other fruits of the Spirit are wrought in us, to the same degree we shall be able to instill and infuse these principles into them. We understand now, as never before, how to fulfill Paul's injunction to parents, to bring up their children in the *'nurture and admonition* of the Lord.' It is a cause of heartfelt gratitude to those of us who are parents, that we have ourselves been placed in a school where the combined powers of love and criticism have been steadily employed in cultivating the good and weeding out the evil in our natures. God has furnished here, in the ruling spirit of the church, all the elements of nurture and admonition too. The same influences are employed upon our children; and in giving our children to the church unreservedly we place them where they can have the full benefit of both. We know in our own experience that we should never fully see our faults unless a perfectly disinterested person held up the mirror of criticism to us.

So with our children, who are part of ourselves—they need the love and criticism of impartial guardians, to make them healthy and pure in their spirits and bodies."

In one of the letters included in the last chapter, Charlotte describes the interest excited at Oneida by a Home-Talk by J.H.N. at Brooklyn on the subject of Woman's Rights. This subject was ever a live one with her. She fully sympathized with the object sought by the advocates of these "Rights"—the enlargement of woman's sphere in respect to labor and education; her influence was always felt on this side of the question in all the discussion of the Community; and practically she did much to bring about the present status of women in the Community, which makes them free to speak and vote on all questions affecting the common interest—to engage in any pursuit for which they have an attraction—to superintend and conduct any business for which they are qualified; and yet there was nothing in her manner, voice or spirit reminding one of the self-asserting masculinity that too often offends in many advocates of Woman's Rights. She neither asked nor sought for herself or others of her sex independence of man. She believed that in the unity of the sexes could be realized the greatest liberty as well as the greatest happiness of woman. Esther and Judith, Miriam and Deborah, Rahab and Ruth, and other patriotic and wise-hearted Jewish women, were her ideals of feminine excellence.

"While reading the story of Judith lately," she wrote in 1851, I received a new and vivid impression of the character of the Jewish women. It appeared to me to be of a very different type and greatly superior to any that the Gentile world can show, either ancient or modern. The trait I was peculiarly struck with was their patriotism; and patriotism in true Jews was something different from what it is among the Gentiles; it was one and the same as loyalty to God as their King and Husband.

I have often thought of the expression, 'Every woman that was wise-hearted.' It is applied in Exodus to those who wrought in furnishing the sanctuary, and is, I think, particularly descriptive of Jewish women. They appear to have been, from Sarah down, marvelously endowed with wisdom and beauty. And here we see their wise-heartedness, and the great distinction between them and their Gentile sisters; instead of perverting these gifts to the ignoble arts of making themselves centers of worship, they, with manly faith and purpose, made their gifts cunning ministers to the advancement and glory of the Theocracy. Esther and Judith are especial examples of this kind of patriotism. Miriam and Deborah, and those daughters of Israel by faith—Rahab and Ruth—the mothers of Samuel and Sampson, Abigail and the Shunamite, are noble specimens of loftiness of soul, heroic faith and loyalty to God, and utter exemption from the pitiful vanity and narrow-mindedness which a false religion and false education have tolerated and encouraged in modern women.

It is evident that these Jewish women were thoroughly imbued with the national spirit; and so God could safely lavish upon them beauty and understanding. With hearts full of national love and going out in all its power toward such noble objects, they were not liable to the disgusting disease of egotism.

They were, as far as we can trace, a 'smaller pattern of man;' and are worthy of study as examples of what woman has been under the training of God, and what she will be again, as fast as the Spirit of Truth, which comes to us from the New Jerusalem, is received into her heart.

In another place Charlotte expresses herself with equal enthusiasm about Hannah, the mother of Samuel. "In the case of Hannah," she says,

> Philoprogenitiveness has been severely disciplined and reduced to complete subordination to the will of God before the birth of Samuel. When she arrived at that stage of experience where she could with her whole heart dedicate her first-born son to the Lord all the days of his life, her prayer was granted. She was no more sad, but became in due time the joyful mother of a son. She named him Samuel, that is, asked of God, recognizing from the beginning her covenant with God. From what we have seen of her heart, we can well imagine that the duties of a mother were peculiarly endearing and attractive to her. But it is impossible to detect the least wavering or lingering in fulfilling her vow to the Lord. As soon as the usual period of nursing was over she carried him herself to the house of the Lord, that he 'might abide there forever.' Her song of rejoicing and praise composed on the occasion evinces a large heart, one that was wholly satisfied with God's goodness to her and with the disposal of her son. She sympathized with God's far-reaching purposes concerning his people. She felt that a place in God's house and among his special servants was better for her and her son than to have his society, or see him grow up rich and prosperous in worldly possessions. This exalted faith was consistent with the tenderness which mothers feel in providing for the comfort of their darlings, for it is said 'she made him a little coat and. Brought it to him from year to year, when she came up with her husband to offer the yearly sacrifice.' Her character shows a beautiful blending of faith, tenderness and devotion, without any jarring conflict between the claims of spiritual and natural love.

Her wise and enlightened motherly affection procured the highest advantages of education for her son, and a glorious destiny as he grew up to manhood. At a very early age God commenced personal communication with him, and 'let none of his? Words fall to the ground.' As he increased in years, 'all Israel from Dan to Beersheba knew that Samuel was established to be a prophet of the Lord.'

But while these Jewish women were Charlotte's ideals of womanhood, and while religion was always to her the crowning excellence of character, it would be very unjust to think of her as in any sense limited in her scope by the religious element. The fact that one had given his heart to God was to her the best of reasons why he should develop himself in every possible way; and so, while she desired for her children and her associates that the spirit of worship and loyalty should possess them which shone so beautifully in her historical ideals, she would at the same time have them gifted with every accomplishment; she would have them love music, art, literature and all that makes society and home attractive; she would, in short, have them perfect men and women.

Text 12: [Death of Mary Cragin] Excerpts from "One of the Four: "A Memoir of Charlotte A. Miller, XIII," *Oneida Circular* **12, No. 22 (May 31, 1875), p.170-171.**

In saying that it required much criticism during the first years at Oneida to keep the raw recruits of Communism harmonic, we did not intend to convey the idea that the "raw recruits" alone had the benefit of that ordinance. There was little partiality shown; every one was expected to occasionally pass the ordeal. The records show that the leading members had their full share of criticism, and the "tried soldiers" of Putney were expected to set the example of both receiving and giving it in the right spirit. Charlotte had to take her portion with the rest; and, though her faults were not conspicuous nor offensive, she had to meet and overcome the temptations that beset one so externally attractive and so appreciative of every form of outward beauty. Especially were her fellowships a source of distraction to her and a subject of criticism on the part of others. The "trying experience" mentioned in one of her letters…was in respect to a fellowship which had proved unprofitable. One of the best things that can be said in her praise is, that she conquered her temptations to seek happiness in outward things and became an example of sincerity and spiritual-mindedness.

The years 1850, '51 and '52 were years of extreme trial to the Community. First, the conflict with internal evils, such as insubordination, disloyalty and pleasure-seeking, culminated in the withdrawal of several families, and seemed at times to jeopardize the very existence of the Community. Then we had no profitable industries and, except to the eye of faith, there was little to encourage in our financial prospects even before the destruction by fire on the 5th of July, 1851, of a store, printing-office, shoe-shop, stereotype-foundry, etc., involving a loss of $3,000. Three weeks afterward the sloop Rebecca Ford on the Hudson was capsized and sunk, carrying down two members beloved by all -- Miss Eliza Allen and Mrs. Mary E. Cragin. Words can not depict the impression made upon the Community by this last event. Mrs. Cragin at that time was honored as no other member save Mr. Noyes. Every heart was stricken and driven to God for consolation. Our cup of trials seemed full to overflowing; but immediately following these sad events came persecutions from without, and of so bitter and unreasonable a character that the Community considered the question of seeking a new location. Happily the better part of our neighbors took the matter into their own hands and resolved that the Communists were peaceable, industrious and good citizens, and should have liberty to remain and work out their experiment unmolested. But the trial to the Community was as great as though it had actually sold out its possessions and sought a new abode.

Charlotte returned from Brooklyn to Oneida immediately after the death of Mrs. Cragin, and filled the office of Community Mother during that most eventful period . . . .

Here, under date of May 10 [probably 1852], is an account of the disaffection and insincerity of one of the members; of his private and public criticism; of his determination to withdraw with his family; of their loyalty and earnest wish to remain; of his surrender; his renewed disaffection, and final withdrawal with his wife and children...[15]

Text 13: [Women and Childbearing] Excerpts from "One of the Four: A Memoir of Charlotte A. Miller, XIV," *Oneida Circular,* **June 7, 1875, p. 178.**

. . . "DEAR MR. MILLER [in Putney, Charlotte is writing to her husband]:--Your last letter produced a good deal of sympathy with you, yet my heart was able to trust in God and believe in his guardian care over you and the interests of his truth in Putney. But I was very indignant at Mr. ----'s assertion, that "every decent man looks upon our principles with horror and disgust!" If I thought that were a deliberate expression of his own heart I should have very little hopes of him, for I am certain he has seen and heard enough of our spirit and doctrines to know that we are pure and sincere and better than the world; and then good men, of large hearts and progressive minds all over the country, have regarded our principles with hope and candid admission that we are far in advance of present society. I know that all decent men and decent women are and will be in sympathy with us just in proportion as they understand our principles and objects, and above all, the heavens over us are our pattern, and are themselves introducing these new ways into the world. This is my belief, which is firmer than ever; and I shall insist that Mr. ---- will believe it when he looks into his deepest heart and not through the eyes of hard-hearted worldliness"
. . .

In a letter dated Sept. 22, 1852, she reports her conversation with one of the most prominent advocates of Women's Rights in the country, who had called at Oneida. "This lady," says Charlotte, "freely admitted that if we had found a way to avoid unwilling maternity we certainly had made great gain. I assured her that we had, and that every woman practically acquainted with our principles felt that Mr. Noyes had done more than any other man for the redemption of woman." And then Charlotte went on to discourse upon the necessity of scientific human breeding. Not only is it great gain to avoid unwilling maternity, but of unspeakable importance that human propagation should be controlled by intelligence and science as well as the propagation of plants and animals. What pains are taken to improve every vegetable and fruit and to produce superior breeds of animals, while human propagation is left to the control of chance and ignorance? It is high time, considering the great improvements and discoveries of the present time, that some great social discovery should be made—such a discovery as will be found in the principles of the Community. She affirmed to her visitor that the problem of women's deliverance from the curse of undesired maternity and unnatural bondage to man had here been solved.

Part Two: "A Community Transplanted" by [H.H.S (Harriet Noyes Skinner]

This series of articles appeared in nine issues of the *American Socialist* (**Figure 17**) from August 14 to October 9, 1879. The articles are amusing to read but difficult to follow because Skinner frequently veers off into unexpected directions. The articles open with descriptions of landscape detailing the settings of Putney and Oneida. While each has its beauty and advantages, Oneida comes off better. It seems to follow that those conditions favored the Oneida Community. With God's providence, everything was conducive to the Community's well-being in New York.

Good historical content is provided on Putney: what the village was like, how its society was altered by financial disaster and revival excitement, and how those altered conditions proved to be the fertile ground for Perfectionism. Original information is given on the social prominence of the Noyes family and on young John Noyes and his Bible study group.

**Figure 17: The *American Socialist*
Photo by Jim Demarest**

"We came to Oneida," Skinner recalls, "without any view to the land. Mr. Burt, who invited Mr. Noyes to come here and gather the Putney family in a new home, had a saw-mill for material basis." Skinner emphasizes how the Perfectionists were never tempted to make their living as farmers. "Most useful for fruit-raising,"

Oneida acreage "has been given up to the gardeners, the vine dressers and fruit raisers, for whose productions the land is peculiarly adapted." "Carried on by 'bees' in which both sexes and all ages worked together," the horticultural regime "was a communizing drill of the best kind."[16] Sewell Newhouse and trap production are described in some detail as is the manner in which the Oneida Community escaped the draft during the Civil War.

A passage about the local Oneida Indians is pointed toward the conclusion that Indians and Perfectionists had in common the communal ownership of land. The notion is then advanced that the unconventional religious views of the Oneida Community are perfectly at home in a region characterized by revival fervor, spiritualistic excitement, and intellectual ferment.[17]

Text 14: [Early Life of the Community in Putney] Excerpt from "A Community Transplanted. From Putney to Oneida, I," *American Socialist*, August 14, 1879, p. 261-262.

It is known that the Oneida Community is the second growth and expansion of a Community originally started in Putney, Vermont. The reasons for the translation, or the circumstances which led to it, make quite a story. A small religious sect take for their ambition the total abolition of selfishness. They live in communism of property for several years, and still preserve the ordinary arrangements of separate families, as well as the strictest forms of New England morality. But their object leads them finally to combine households and adopt a new social order, and this advance offends the other churches in the place, and results in the dispersion of the Communists. Providentially a new home is waiting for them in another State, and in less than a year from their being scattered to the four winds they have regathered, and their number is doubled by additions from different quarters, of friends holding the same religious faith. The story of the development of the Putney Community, the village excitement and proceedings--ecclesiastical and civil--the dispersion and the regathering at Oneida is in manuscript; but its full publication would be untimely now. It is in parts, however, that are more or less complete in themselves, and the first part at least, which is preliminary to the real story, is not liable to any misconstruction by parties watching for occasion against us. It is a showing of the advantages gained by the enforced migration. This part, at the request of the editors, is given to the *Socialist* by the writer, H. H. S.

Chapter I

When the Jews of old would teach their children the fear of the Lord, they rehearsed to them the story of Israel's deliverance, the story of Moses and Pharaoh, of the Red Sea, of the journey through the wilderness, and the conquest of the promised land. They went back to the glorious manifestations of that time for the measure of God's power and for the justification of their hereditary faith. The miracles of that pilgrimage were memorized and their impression perpetuated in every possible way; by feast days, by songs, by relics and by monumental stones. The written history could not be put into the heads of the young as it may be now, but memorials continually presenting themselves, excited the curiosity of the childish mind, and induced the natural questions, What is this? What mean ye by this service? And so one generation repeated the story to another. The Passover was an anniversary feast; the Ark of the Covenant was a cabinet of relics; Joshua's pillar in Gilgal was set up for a sign, that when children should ask their fathers, What mean these stones? They should be told how the children of Israel came over Jordan on dry ground. The lesson of every memorial and every story was, "The hand of the Lord is *mighty*."

There is a passage in the history of the Oneida Community which we remember as the Jews remembered their translation from Egypt to the land of Canaan. It is the translation of the Putney family to Oneida. The story of this translation is a story of miracles and providences, not so stupendous in a physical sense as those which marked the journey of the Israelites, but more adapted to the present stage of human cultivation, making the same impression and teaching the same lesson. We rehearse them to ourselves when we would magnify the power of God, and tell them to our children when we would teach them his unsearchable ways. The story of the Putney migration has never been written out in consecutive detail, and now the second generation of the Community ask for it. Readings which we have had lately in our evening meetings from letters and diaries written at that period have excited special interest, and the young folks are eager to gather and save all the reminiscences extant, whether in manuscript or in the minds of those personally concerned.

The story deserves a dramatic pen of the highest order--not, indeed, to color its scenes and incidents, but to do justice to their transcendental character. As to the pen which has been chosen, it is only capable of a "plain, unvarnished tale;" but will do, perhaps, until the predestined poet among our scions of stirpiculture shall discover his epic genius. Meanwhile, the writer can adopt the hackneyed claim, "All of which I saw, and part of which I was," and at the same time is not dependent on her own memory or that of others, but has a pile of old letters and private journals which should give her facts and scenes some of the freshness of "a sketch taken on the spot."

The Oneida Community was started at Putney like a plant in a conservatory; but that was not the place for it to grow in till it became a tree; and the gardener took it up at the proper time and planted it in a location prepared, where its roots would have room to spread wide and strike deep in a soil rich with the elements of growth, and where it could attain all its fair proportions under the sunshine and rain and dewy influences of the open sky. We can conceive what an unexpected and what a chilly, disagreeable operation it must be to a plant to be taken from its cozy shelter and put into strange circumstances of exposure, and so it was in our case. We were not consulted. What gardener does consult his plant? It seemed like the hand of violence, but it was really the hand of care, that rooted us up. It seemed like the wrath of man, but it was really the goodness of God, that drove us away from our early home. A better place had been prepared for us. How much better--indeed, what extraordinary advantages were gained by the change--we will go on now to show, and then tell the story how it was brought about.

And first, some description and retrospect of the conservatory. Putney is a small town in the southeastern corner of Vermont, sheltered by hills shading off from the Green Mountain range on the west, and separated from a New Hampshire town by the "blue rolling Connecticut" on the east. It was approached, at the time of our story, 1847, by no railroad within forty miles. Brattleboro, an incorporated village ten miles south, was its metropolis. It had a woolen factory, two paper mills, three stores, two churches.

Its business was never important, but twenty years earlier it had a society of considerable pretensions. There was one street, or part of a street, familiarly called Congress Row, because two gentlemen residing on it had represented their State in the national halls. These gentlemen, Judge White and Squire Noyes, were neighbors and friends, their lands joining, and their politics happily agreeing. Both had large families. Both at that earlier time had three girls just out of boarding-schools, accomplished and gay. The oldest daughter of the first family, a dazzling beauty, accompanied her father to Washington, and not long after was carried out of town as the bride of an M. C. from Maine. There were several other high-bred families in the town. The minister was a "gentleman of the old school," more learned than devout, an enthusiast in the laboratory rather than in the pulpit. There was a Captain Green, whose family was very proud, and their style of living quite elegant for those days. The daughters were educated at Mrs. Willard's seminary in Troy, and the only son was sent to college. The minister and the two M. C.'s had sons in college also, and a college education was an aristocratic distinction at that time. There was a General Leavitt, who should have been a Southern nabob for his love of luxury and show. He was the uncle of the late Rev. Joshua Leavitt of editorial fame, who was himself a lawyer at Putney in 1825. These families, and others that we need not mention, frequently increased by agreeable visitors from abroad, made a brilliant society in Putney for a brief period between 1822 and 1827. Music and dancing, jewels and plumes, fine horses and martial parade, come up in the memory of one who was a child at that time.

But this *régime* was short; it lasted only about five years, when there came a great general change--a French revolution. In one hour this gay society came to naught. A financial crisis broke it up suddenly and totally. Many of the leading men *failed*. There was dismal news at the breakfast table in those days. One morning you heard that Captain Green's property had been *attached*. Midnight was the sheriff's hour for such work in old times. Not long after, you heard that Gen. Leavitt had been unpleasantly waked up, and so on. To fail was then no indifferent affair; it was a mortal disgrace. It meant poverty and blight. Messrs. White and Noyes sustained the pressure, but unfortunately for the pleasant relations of the neighborhood they were among the *creditors*. The social breaches were dreadful. The fathers at war made sorry times for the young folks. It was a reign of estrangements and separations. Pleasant windows were darkened and every courtesy chilled. The Greens and Leavitts soon left the town.

In 1831 another change came over the place--a new control, as we should say in Spiritualistic parlance. Its conditions were prepared, no doubt, by the preceding years of humiliation and distress. In that year Putney was visited by the great Finney revival, and a more powerful control cannot be imagined. It made a new society wherever it went. It abolished caste; it raised up the low and humbled the proud; it changed the customs. Vain show of dress and beauty was all forgotten in the solemnity of its presence. The dance gave way to the prayer-meeting, and for a time religion was supreme over business. It was the talk in barrooms and stores as well as in the churches.

Those who had figured in the *régime* of fashion were now mostly married off and gone to other parts. The younger members of the same families entered society under very different reigning influences. Abby White, the youngest of her family, instead of being educated at Troy and appearing as a belle at Washington, was educated at Mrs. Grant's Seminary at Ipswich, a great center and nursery of the revival spirit, and made her *début* in Putney as a young convert, with eyes uplifted to heaven and only one thought on earth, the salvation of souls. Her musical gifts were rare; she was an accomplished pianist and singer, but she despised the admiration of the world, and her voice was only heard in sacred song. She found her best companion in the mother of the Noyeses, who, through all distractions, led a life of prayer, and whose sympathy with young converts was always fresh. There were other young folks of both sexes who emulated her devotion, and the whole society was leavened with the same spirit.

J. H. Noyes and two younger sisters were subjects of this revival. He was twenty years old and one year out of college. His sisters' ages were fourteen and twelve. Six weeks after his conversion he went away for a three years' course of theological study, giving up the law which he had chosen for his profession, and devoting himself to the ministry. The two girls were taken under the care of the church, and the sobriety of their youthful life was in great contrast with the fashionable round in which their older sisters had passed the same age. . . .

The pure afflatus of this revival was soon spent, but its effect on the social customs was lasting. The dance, for instance, was scarcely reputable in Putney down to the time we came away in 1847, and the merchant and lawyer and town officials of all kinds, found it for their interest to belong to the Church and sustain its institutions.

Text 15: [Perfectionism in the Early Community] Excerpt from "A Community Transplanted. From Putney to Oneida, II," *American Socialist*, August 21, 1879, p. 269-270.

In 1834 J. H. Noyes received the gospel of Salvation from Sin. In this gospel was wrapped up the Oneida Community as the tree is wrapped up in the seed. Putney was the quiet nursery prepared for its early growth. This gospel was fully preached there by J. H. N. in 1835, and while it fell into some good and honest hearts, it found no aristocracy and no strong religious dynasty to interfere with its inception. The offensive bluntness of the second minister had cost him his place, and his successor was a man of very different temper. Controversy was odious to him. He could not bear a "muss." He kept a quiet pastorship of the same church till he was entirely superannuated. We have to thank him for giving us very little annoyance, though it may be a doubtful compliment to his ministerial faithfulness. Enlightened tolerance is one thing, and supine love of peace is another. We ascribe his inaction to the last rather than to the first. Perfectionism was excommunicated from his church with all due formality, but its doings outside were generally ignored. The Methodists, who were finally instrumental in our expulsion, had no meeting-house in the village at that time; their center was in a distant part of the town, and though several of their best members forsook their fellowship for ours, they gave us no trouble for many years.

The respectability and general popularity of the Noyes family was one of the prepared conditions for the safety of the Community germ. Though it was the wealthiest family in town, it was one which always attracted the good-will rather than the envy of the less fortunate. It was unostentatious, approachable, hospitable. Everybody who knows anything about the founder of the O. C. knows that he finds his own happiness in making others happy; and that his appreciation of merit is without respect of persons. Something of the same spirit characterized the Putney stock. The father was in his element as host and patron, and the mother took into her heart with her own children all the boys and girls of the neighborhood. The father was scholarly, the mother was spiritual. Every lecturer that came into town, every artist or cultured notability of any kind that stopped in the place, was a guest in the mansion of the Noyeses. It was the house of clergymen in particular, but whether they were more attracted by Mrs. N.'s spirituality or Mr. N.'s varied knowledge and conversational power, it was not easy to tell. The open door, cordial hand and generous board entered into the charm no doubt. Mr. N.'s business integrity and the moral purity of the whole family were unblemished.

The character and social distinction of H. A. Holton, wife of J. H. N., added much to this favorable prestige. She was long engaged to a gentleman who, when he heard that she had joined her fortunes with the vagabond he supposed J. H. N. to be is reported to have said, "Poor Harriet! she has thrown herself away. I would have carried her to Washington." He was then a member of Congress. An eminent clergyman of New York City labored hard to cure her of Perfectionism, with motives which were understood to be personal, Her grandfather, Hon. Mark Richards, by whom she was adopted, was Ex-Lieut. Governor of Vermont and her uncle, Hon. Wm. C. Bradley, would have been Governor many terms, if the Democratic candidacy were ever anything but nominal in that State. He was a widely known lawyer and savant. These friends had the magnanimity of true rank, and did not disinherit her as to her share in their property or their affections on account of her religious eccentricity, and except for that she had the highest esteem of everybody else who knew her.

The Putney Community had another fortunate outside connection in the family of an older sister of the Noyeses. Her husband, the Hon. L. G. Mead, was a popular lawyer in the county, and both had a wide social influence which they benignly exerted in favor of their odd relatives.

The personal character and family reputation and family connections of those who formed the nucleus of the Community made it their true policy to settle where they were best known, as there they had the least to fear from the shafts of calumny and contumely. Nevertheless, this policy was instinctive rather than calculating.

Perfectionism at that time bore the reproach of Christ, and the devil too, as one might say. A sect in New York State taking the name had disgraced it by mysticisms and fantastic barbarities of manner and speech, and not a few of them by sexual irregularities, spiritual-wifery, etc.--and the Putney Perfectionists bore their reproach. When Mr. Noyes's social theory came before the world, it was not strange that persons who did not make sure of the truth, and especially those who were willingly ignorant of it, should confound the two people, although the fact is that for eight years after that theory was published the Putney believers continued to walk in all the commandments and ordinances of common morality *blameless*. There was probably, never a people where the law of chastity was more inviolate or its spirit more respected.

. . .

Text 16: [Community Organization in Putney] "A Community Transplanted. From Putney to Oneida, III," *American Socialist,* **August 28, 1879, p. 277.**

The town interfered at last, but not until it would have been treason to the State not to have done so. We had declared ourselves under a higher jurisdiction and had moved into a social order which was not lawful in Vermont. The first shock of the disclosure raised a tumultuous excitement which compelled us to seek a new location. Nevertheless, we kept the homestead, J. H. N.'s house, where our school began, and within three years after our dispersion and settlement at Oneida we had a branch Commune in Putney of fifteen or twenty members. This number was kept good for five or six years, and as frequent interchanging is the custom between our Communes, probably not less than a hundred members from the O. C. had a chance to visit the Mecca of their faith. The relations of this family with the village were perfectly peaceful, our social principles being graciously ignored. And if we had been "mindful of the country from whence we came out," we might, probably have had opportunity to have returned as a whole; but now we desired a better country, and we *had* a better, and in 1859, under a policy of concentration, we sold out entirely in Putney and left no interest there except what we had in the hearts of a small circle of outside believers.

When the faith of Holiness was first preached in Putney, it gathered of all kinds. Universalists and Nothingarians helped to crowd the halls and school-rooms where J. H. N. with the Polyglot Bible in his hand did little more than read and collate the testimony on the subjects of the Second Coming of Christ and Salvation from Sin. It sufficed for these classes that the truth he brought out confounded the Orthodox sects. Their interest in Perfectionism was like that which Julian Avenel, a lawless Scotch baron in one of Walter Scott's novels, had in the Reformation. "We of the laity," said he to a preacher of that order, "care not what you set up, so you pull merrily down whatever stands in our way. Call your doctrine what you list, to me it is recommended because it flings off all these sottish dreams about saints and angels and devils, and unhorses the lazy monks that have ridden us so long and spurgalled us so hard." But three years after, in 1838, when J. H. N. married his wife and came to Putney to live, from which we date the beginning of the Community, the chaff had been winnowed from the wheat, and he found a little band of disciples ready to gather around him as the twelve did around Christ, and give themselves in whole-hearted devotion to what he was about.

The organization took the form of a *School* at first. Instead of keeping the Sabbath in the usual way, we gave a seventh, yes, two or three sevenths, of every day to the study of the Scriptures, and our meetings were more like a Bible-class than any other form of gathering. The school continued several years, and then developed into "The Corporation," by which name we were known when our business interests were publicly united. After two or three more years, when our households were combined, we were called "The Association." And lastly, when we entered into our new social order, we stood forth a confessed Community. It was in this stage of development that Putney became too strait for us, and destiny brought on the birth-throes which cast us into new circumstances with improved relations and enlarged opportunities.

Our number at the time of the dispersion was thirty-one, twenty-one adults and ten youths and children. The adults were all between the ages of twenty-five and thirty-five, except three, one the mother of the Noyes's, and two others less by two years than twenty-five. Eleven of the adults and most of the children, were born in Putney or adjoining towns. The rest came from different parts and at different times, three from New York City, two from Northern Vermont, two from Belchertown, Mass., one from Meriden and another from New Haven, Conn., one from Newark, New Jersey; in all of which places Perfectionism appeared as one of the fruits of the

Great Revival, and Mr. Noyes's writings had many readers.

The Putney Community was never self-supporting. It had a farm, a store, a printing-office, and twelve or fifteen thousand dollars in the bank. It had no mills or factories; nothing that ran by "power." Its press was a hand-press, hardening the muscles of J. H. N., which were indifferently developed by his earlier training. The inevitable saw-mill, which you see in the first purchase of almost every Associative attempt described in "American Socialisms,"[18] was wanting in the Putney property.

The nearest we came to having a saw-mill in Putney was the fact that our first printing was done in a loft over a saw-mill. We got a press and type before we had built an office, and a friendly neighbor offered us the use of a roughly-finished room over his mill, which we occupied several months.

The farm fell to us in the settlement of the Noyes estate, but none of our men were farmers. They were scholars, tradesmen and mechanics. And there was no money in the farm for the best of farmers; at least a New York man would say so. It supplied our table with milk and butter, vegetables and nice garden stuff, with apples, nuts, etc., and filled our barn with hay. It had several dwelling-houses on it which were convenient for our families. It furnished eligible lots for our store and chapel. It was a blessing in many ways; but we never could have afforded it if we had not felt rich.

We published a paper in the printing-office. There we had an industry, a pleasant family industry, but not a productive one. Our paper was then, as it is now, an enterprise of benevolence, and stood in our accounts on the debit side.

The store was a source of income. It was a popular store, notwithstanding some crotchety arrangements. It kept no intoxicating liquors, and was closed at 8 P. M., that hour being then, as in all our Communes since, sacred to the family meeting. As much as the profits of our store came short of our expenses, which was considerable, so much we sunk of our money in the bank. But we were like a boy in his minority going to school. We knew our father was rich and would set us up in business when we were old enough; and meanwhile we were not afraid to spend the pocket-money which he freely gave us.

We had a scheme in our heads and a prophecy in our hearts of a grand Phalanstery and an enormous business. The Phalanstery was to be on "the plain," a sunny plateau on one part of our hilly farm, and the business a great printing establishment, like the New York Bible-House, or Methodist Book Concern, for the publication of Community doctrines and literature. We have realized the Phalanstery, and the vision of the printing establishment, though it has tarried long, has not faded out of our hearts. The dam at Wallingford may be one hand or one foot of its incomplete "materialization." (Editor's note: When this was written, five years ago, the Wallingford Community had recently built a valuable dam, which a promising printing business was beginning to utilize.) The vision of the Phalanstery was realized, but not in respect to its place. It is for us to show now how much better place Oneida is than Putney would have been.

Text 17: [Beauty of Central New York Location] Excerpt from "A Community Transplanted. From Putney to Oneida, IV," *American Socialist*, September 4, 1879), p. 285.

. . . .

Mr. N. once compared our transfer from Putney to Oneida, in view of all its perilous chances and the manifest care of Providence, to falling out of a balloon a thousand feet high and landing on the ground safely, and afterwards he added, "not only landing safely but in *the very garden of Eden*." His language about this place was not more extravagant than what our visitors frequently report. A student from Clinton writes to the Utica Herald as follows:

> "There are many points in these central counties which afford fine rural views, but for a sport to call forth the superlatives and make proud the heart of a free citizen of these domains, commend us to the top of the tower at the Oneida Community. The Community is famous for its views--peculiarly famous for some of them--but when one stands upon this tower and looks about him he forgets his previous and intended discussions of Communistic questions and feasts his gaze. We did thus yesterday. The landscape looked like the garden of Eden, or if it didn't the garden should have looked like this scene."

Dixon says:-- "Few corners in America can compete with the swards and gardens lying about the home of the Oneida family, as they arrest the eyes of a stranger coming upon them from the rough fields even of the settled region of New York."[19] Another English tourist, Rev. Mr. Bevan, said in our evening meeting last summer: "I admire your place--the best compliment I can give is to say it reminds me of an *English landscape*. If you want to see a fine country scene, come to England. We have no Yosemite nor Niagara, but we have some of the sweetest little landscapes you can imagine." A correspondent of the New York *Tribune* says: "The location is the most beautiful in the land." A writer in the New York *Herald* calls it "a beautifully chosen spot." Another newspaper describing the place says: "587 acres of land as fine as any in the Empire State, gently rolling, watered by clear spring brooks, etc. Certainly the person who selected this as the home of a large family was a man of taste and discrimination." This is true, but he takes just as much credit to himself for selecting this location as if he had fallen on it from a balloon, or as Robinson Crusoe might have taken for the discovery of his solitary island.

We might multiply similar quotations, but these will suffice. As to what we hear in our Reception-Room every day, it is more extravagant even than the newspaper reports. "You live in Paradise," is a stereotyped expression, and "garden of Eden" is a favorite hyperbole.

We did not fall into this garden, already made. We fell into its *possibilities--*

possibilities which were far from existing where we came from. Putney had a native beauty; its scenery was romantic. But it was not garden-like, and no cultivation could have made it so. Communism can do almost anything; but we cannot conceive of its clothing a hill farm in Vermont with the rich verdure, the luxuriant vegetation, the affluence of flowers and fruits, the scenic loveliness, which are possible on this soil. And this leads to an agricultural view of the location here or rather an horticultural view, as it is in the way of fruit-raising that our land has been most useful.

. . . .

Text 18: [Work in the Early Days at Oneida] "A Community Transplanted. From Putney to Oneida, V," *American Socialist*, **September 11, 1879, p. 293-294.**

We came to Oneida without any view to the land. Mr. Burt, who invited Mr. Noyes to come here and gather the Putney family in a new home, had a saw-mill for material basis, but not ten acres of land. Chances for buying small lots around the saw-mill soon offered—very providential chances, as we thought—and chances for buying adjoining farms continued, till in 1870 we had purchased nearly seven hundred acres. Our later policy, however, has been to contract rather than to enlarge in this kind of property, and we have at present less than six hundred acres. For goodly as the land is on which we have fallen, it has never tempted us into farming for a living. According to facts in the "History of American Socialisms,"[20] "land mania has been the bane of Associations. Many of those who started in the great Fourier excitement, thirty years ago, were literally "wrecked by running around." "Land, land, land," says Mr. N., "was regarded by them as the mother of all gain and comfort." Our greatest number of acres was less by three hundred than the average number possessed by the forty-five Phalanxes which started in that excitement. We have never tried to raise even our own bread-stuffs or make our own butter. Reserving pasture and meadow sufficient for a never-failing supply of milk to our large family, the greater part of the remaining acres has been given up to the gardeners, the vine dressers and fruit raisers, for whose productions the land is peculiarly adapted, and whose success has brought us some gain and any amount of home comfort.

Strawberry Culture has been a bright thread in the woof of our industry. We commenced it soon after coming here, and carried it on with great enthusiasm for several years, till the growth of manufactures absorbed our forces. It would not be easy to tell all the profit we got out of it. It brought us some gain, as we have said, when other resources were wanting. Indeed, it was profitable enough to tempt all our neighbors into trying it, and with what success appears in the fact that Oneida Depot sends away more carloads of strawberries in their season than any other station on the Central. We had to create our market for the strawberry; in all this region at least. The popular taste was quite uneducated when Mr. Thacker, the father of our fruit-growing, sent his first dozen quarts of Early Scarlet to Oneida village. It was in '49. He offered them for a shilling a quart, but half his venture came back. The

Wallingford Commune, which has some years harvested nearly a thousand bushels, had the same experience in the beginning, not being able to sell more than fifteen or twenty quarts in the neighboring city of Meriden.

Carried on by "bees" in which both sexes and all ages worked together, the strawberry culture was a communizing drill of the best kind. Then the free use of strawberries on our own table educated our taste for fruit in general as a staple article of diet. Again, visitors were first attracted to the Community by its strawberries. It was far from our intention, on first raising this ruby fruit, to offer any such bait to the public, but strawberries were very rare in this region, then, and, persuaded once to furnish them with sugar and cream to a party who called, we could not withstand the stream of importunity, and by that means were actually drawn into the great system of entertaining visitors which has since been such a feature in our daily life. This system has thrown our life open to the light, as nothing else could, and we owe to it in a great degree the toleration we enjoy. Finally, the cultivation of the strawberry led to the establishment of our fruit-preserving business, which is already third in importance to our other businesses, and bids fair to equal that of the trap and silk manufactures.

The woods on the Putney farm were much finer than any we have here. The romantic among us have sometimes regretted the forest pleasures of our mountain home, but for other uses we have not missed the woods. Coal is the only fuel for a Community, and especially a manufacturing Community, and here we find ourselves on the great coal routes. A furnace and hot-air pipes were introduced into the family mansion in 1854, and we have used but little wood for warming since. Who does not know that the use of coal is a great step forward in making a pleasant home? How long we should have gone without it living Putney we do not know; when we came away coal was a mineralogical curiosity in that place. As to lumber, the saw-mill for several years gave us plenty of that, and the railroads since have left us little reason to regret the lack of forests on our own domain.

Paul uses the paradox concerning himself, "an unknown, yet well known," and it may be said of the site of this Community that it is a place hidden and yet set on a hill. We are more secluded here by Oneida Creek than we were at Putney. There we were under the surveillance of a village—a very conservative New England village. Here we are a mile from any village, and except our own tenantry have very few neighbors within that distance in any direction, and what we have are free from any sectional pride, contented that we should raise the price of real estate around us, and use up our own reputation at pleasure. But our seclusion is not a wilderness. The ceaseless rumble of the New York Central reaches our ears, and by that thoroughfare we connect with the great world in the most direct and eligible way. The cities of Utica and Syracuse, one on our right, the other on our left, are both within two hours' ride by rail. And Oneida Depot, four miles distant (or in time now on the Midland, seven minutes), is a fast-growing place and large enough at present to serve many business purposes.

When the Midland was first projected, though it was desirable to have it run by us as a business convenience, it seemed undesirable as an invasion of our retirement. But we have suffered very little annoyance from it in any way. It touches us, and goes off like the tangent to a circle. Its course through our domain is not parallel to our buildings, but diagonal, and diagonal to their rear, coming nearest to the southwest corner, or what would be called our back door. The depot, thirty rods from this corner, marks the spot where the track touches the circle and strikes off both ways. North, the track is hid by a cut only a few rods from the depot. South, at about the same length, it runs on to a high trestle, greatly to the delectation of our children (whose wing of the house overlooks the scene), and is lost to view at the end of the trestle about one hundred rods distant, so that a train makes as little disagreeable sensation as possible.

But what is still more favorable to our quiet, this railroad, so far, has not proved to be the heavy, noisy route—the rival of the Central and Erie—which it was expected to be. It has not been the servant of New York City and the interminable West, but rather of midland New York. And as a local accommodation it is a great blessing to the Community. For two or three summers it flooded us with picnics and pleasure excursions, occasionally dropping six or eight car-loads of visitors at once. Sometimes we would have been glad to decline these "surprise parties," and the profits financially were decidedly doubtful; but we knew that when the whistle of their returning train called away the scattered company from our gardens and arbors, from our Hall and tower, from every part of our house and grounds, they would go less prejudiced than they came, and we were contented to get our "pay" in that way. They came perhaps with frowns, but they went away with smiles; and waving handkerchiefs, testifying their good-will, whitened the train till it was out of sight. The same spectacle greets us now whenever an excursion passes by here, which is a frequent occurrence—one week to Oneida Lake, another to the Thousand Islands, and another to New York City.

The Midland brings coal to our door, which formerly we had to draw from the canal, a distance of five miles. It brings our raw material, and takes off our manufactures, which was once done by teams between here and Oneida.

It is part of our good luck in connection with this railroad that just where it touches the circle, or just where we wanted a depot, its grade happened to be on exactly our level, while many villages south of us are left far below its track on the hillside.

The point to observe in what we have said is this: while the success of our social experiment required that we should be sequestered from the world, and irresponsible in a certain sense to other society, it was important to our business interests that we should be near railroads and cities, and the two conditions are found in our situation here.

Text 19: [Water Power and the Community] "A Community Transplanted—From Putney to Oneida, VII," *American Socialist,* **September 25, 1879, p. 309.**

To get back to the saw-mill: the water-power which carried it, though not large—ten-feet fall—has been a fortunate possession to us first and last. It was large enough for the infancy of our manufactures, and when they outgrew its capacity, and, as good luck would have it, other water-powers fell into our hands, it still remained invaluable to us as a home convenience, carrying our laundry machines, odd jobs of which are coming up every day, not to mention the boxes used by thousands in the fruit-packing rooms near by.

The trap business was utilizing this power to its fullest extent at the time (1861) we proposed to build the permanent brick edifice in which we now live, and as this business was carried on by our own industry, the advantage of being near our works influenced our choice of a site for the family dwelling. Other places were considered—places more sightly, and further back from the public road—but we have always been glad we chose as we did; and so far as the old saw-mill water-power influenced our choice its worth to us cannot be estimated.

It should be said that Mr. Noyes selected this spot for our first Community dwelling in 1848, and broke the ground himself, leading the van of men, women and children who dug the cellar and laid the foundation-walls of the cheap wooden structure we used to call the "Mansion House." The new house was built hard by the old, and finally by the addition of a south wing displaced the old altogether. Here the witch-hazel pointed from the first, and now we will mention some of the advantages of the site:

It is quite central as to the home domain, the successive addition of half-a-dozen little farms, since this site was first selected, not throwing it much out of this position. It is on a plateau of about three acres in extent, nearly circular, and sloping gently on every side. We need not say that sewerage is a great problem in such an institution as this. See it solved for us by our elevation and by a bend in the creek. That thoughtful stream, flowing by us or rather around us at a distance of a hundred rods, takes a sudden turn in front and comes almost straight toward us, to within thirty rods off the plateau, where it receives all the drainage of our many sinks washed by a constant flow of fresh water through a cement pipe one foot in diameter, the duct being buried under our cellar floor, and twelve feet below the turf of the lawn.

But though we are high enough for good drainage, we are fortunately low enough to receive water from a spring on our domain, west half a mile, the only good spring of running water in the neighborhood. Its level is two feet higher than the second floor of our major dwelling, calling the kitchen or basement floor, the first; not high enough for every convenience without the supplement of an engine by which the water is pumped into the attic, and from there distributed through the house, the engine, however, serving many other domestic uses. Our arcade, horse-barn and laundry and other subordinate buildings around us are supplied by the same spring, being on a lower level.

The soil of the plateau is the choicest on the domain, or at least the best for home grounds—a rich sandy loam—giving early verdure to the lawn and brightness to the summer foliage and flowers.

No other place on the domain would have matched the route of the Midland so well, and if we had gone off from the public road to an elevation east that offered some attractions we might have missed another wonderful chance, which we will turn aside here to mention.

In time of the war the Community escaped the draft simply by reason of the location of its dwellings. There was but one draft in this county, and that we escaped. We did not want to go to the war. Fighting is not in the line of our genius. We choose to show our bravery and patriotism in another way. There is many a reckless soldier who would turn a cowardly back to the batteries we face. But let that pass. We did not see how we were going to be cleared. We had confessed ourselves the subjects of the Prince of Peace, and we expected he would interfere; but how we could not see. The chances were a thousand to one that some of our men would be drawn. Our proportion would have been ten or twelve. But behold when the names were published there was not a Community man's among them. What was the matter? We did not know ourselves; we were profoundly ignorant of the cause. "They have bribed the enrolling officer," folks said. No, we had not seen the officer; he had skipped us through his own stupidity, or, to speak more charitably, under the confusion of circumstances. The creek is the line between Oneida and Madison Counties. We live in Madison County, but our nearest neighbors right and left, on the public road which passes directly in front of us, live in Oneida County, and the water-power and mill we have lately spoken of are in that county. Think of the road as the chord of an arc, made by the creek east of us taking the great curve we have elsewhere mentioned. We live near the middle of the chord, and the road crosses the creek both sides of us, north and south, about a quarter of a mile each way. The enrolling officer of Oneida County comes to the bridge north and sees that we live in Madison County. "All right," he says, "I have nothing to do with them." The enrolling officer of Madison County passes along in the way of his duty on the road west of us about half a mile, and looking over here supposes we are in the same county with our neighbors on each side, that is in Oneida County, and says to himself also, "All right; I have nothing to do with them." Not very sharp, indeed; but then you must admit that there was some excuse for this confusion. At all events we were not to blame, and there was no bribing, as everybody saw when the matter was explained. "Community luck," was the word that went round then. A call for a new enrollment was made, which we did not oppose, but those of the enrolled who escaped being drafted would not consent to the risk of a new drawing, and so there was no help for it; we went free.

"Community luck" was notable a year or two after this affair, in the acquisition of the fine water-power on which we built our new factory. It was offered for sale on acceptable terms just as the demand for the "Newhouse traps" obliged us to enlarge. It was a mile further from our home than the old shop, but a half-mile nearer to Oneida Depot, where we received and shipped freight at that time and for several succeeding years. The factory was built directly on the Seneca turnpike, which fifty years ago was the grand thoroughfare between Albany and the West. A house which we subsequently bought and occupied, for the convenience of the Community men who worked in the factory, was a tavern at that time, and old inhabitants remember seeing twenty stages stopping there at once. A little neighborhood surrounded the power, and that was a good point, as we were just beginning to employ outside help. The trap manufacture did not fill the new building. There was room for a spacious machine-shop and a blacksmith's-shop, still leaving an unoccupied wing. That did not wait long for our silk manufacture, which soon filled all the extra space, and, growing fast, pushed in wherever the trap machinery was contracted by improvements. The silk-works, for several years, required from eighty to a hundred girls, and the villages of Oneida and Oneida Castle, connected with the works by the turnpike most of the way, constituted an arrangement for supply which could not be much improved. The ride to and fro was pleasant and healthy for the employees, and there are some advantages in having a factory a little out of a large town.

Text 20: [The Community and the Oneida Nation] Excerpt from "A Community Transplanted--From Putney to Oneida, VIII," *American Socialist*, October 2, 1879, p. 317.

To go back to the saw-mill once more. The original establishment owned by Mr. Burt was known all about here by the name of the *Indian* saw-mill. It belonged to the Oneida Indians. In grading the ground for the enlarged structure which was put up in its place we came upon what must have been an ancient burying place of the tribe, as several skulls and other bones were turned up by the plow. The first house we bought was an Indian hut, but is remembered fondly as a shelter from a howling storm of persecution, and as the scene of many glad reunions that summer of 1848 when the scattered Putney family were gathering here. We revert to the saw-mill and log-hut as a cue to something we would say about the historical interest attaching to this locality.

Here was the home of the Oneidas, the most sagacious, most eloquent, and most gentle of all the Iroquois tribes, which tribes again were distinguished above all the other aborigines of this continent for their intelligence and prowess. A neighboring county took their name, but it was in Madison County that the Oneidas had their principal villages, and when after the Revolutionary War this tribe ceded from time to time other sections of their original Reservation, they kept the town of Lenox in which we live to the last, only giving that up when they emigrated as a body to the West some forty years ago.

A late visitor, taking a walk before breakfast through our orchards and meadows, came home delighted with what he saw, ready to believe, as we do, that we had miraculous guidance to this place. When we told him it was formerly part of an Indian Reservation, he said: "There, that is the secret; the Indians knew where to pick; they knew where the sunny spots were; I thought of that very thing when I was walking, and wondered if this was not an Indian Reservation." The town of Lenox was, it appears, a town twice picked, or the Reservation of a Reservation.

We virtually took the land, or at least several of our first purchases, from the hands of the Indians themselves, for the white settlers had not paid their debt to the State when they passed their titles to us. And so this soil scarce knows the touch of private ownership, for the Oneidas held their lands in common. We find an interesting mention of this fact in an old Circular. J. R. Miller, in a sketch of a visit he made to a remnant of the tribe still living here, writes as follows:

> "We called at the home of Sconondoa, a great grandson of the celebrated Indian Chief of that name, to whom is attributed the inimitable trope; 'I am an aged hemlock, dead at the top: the winds of a hundred winters have whistled through my branches.' The descendant, about forty years of age, has a wife and four or five children. He is quite intelligent and speaks the English language fluently. We asked the present number of the Oneida tribe. He replied: 'We have here only about one hundred and eighty. At Green Bay, Wisconsin, there are eight hundred and ninety-two, and there are nearly five hundred in Canada.' He said: 'When we all lived together the land was common, but when we sold out to the State in 1840 those who did not choose to accept their share of the public funds and go West with the tribe, had separate farms set off to them which they now occupy.' I told him that the Community held the land in the way his fathers did, and that we had no separate interests, which seemed to please him much. He said: 'We had a great deal better time when we owned our land all in common than we ever have had since with our little private patches. Then we could plant our corn, sow our wheat and pasture our cattle in the best places. If we wanted a stick of timber we could cut a tree anywhere that was convenient. We were not obliged to build fences to protect our rights. We were free to go where we pleased; but now we cannot step over our own line without trespassing. There was more peace and harmony among us then than there is now; having separate farms makes a great deal of trouble, makes folks quarrel.' 'You like the old way best then,' said we. 'O yes,' he replied, 'I like it much the best to have our chiefs and own our land together; it is so much more friendly.' Sconondoa the fourth owns a good farm, lives in a frame house, and has money at interest.
> . . . .

As to the remnant in this neighborhood, we have always found them friendly and harmonious—nothing about them vicious or annoying. They preserve the gentle character of their fathers, and are, like them, in respect to easy fraternizing with the whites. The squaws come to our back door almost every day, not as beggars, but offering their baskets and beadwork in exchange for pieces from the table; and they are always pleasant; never seem suspicious nor morose. The men are good, peaceable citizens. Their settlements, of which there are two, both about two miles distant from us, are an attractive feature of the neighborhood, and make occasion for many a pleasant excursion to our visitors, especially on Sunday, when the Indians have regular meetings and you may see them together and hear their resonant music and liquid speech. Thomas Cornelius, their minister, is a native specimen well worth going to see. [A local history] says of him: "His remarkable physical presence, which his size, dignity and grace make up, together with his noble Christian spirit, impresses one with a sense of his magnificent individuality."

The phenomena of American Spiritualism are remarkable for a strong aboriginal element. Indians figured in the "manifestations" which the Shakers had some time before the Rochester knockings; they figure in the notorious "Eddy manifestations," and mediums all over the country have had Indian familiars. If we admit the ideas which some people entertain that spirits hover over the localities which they once inhabited, like the mists of evaporation, then, as the American continent must be overshadowed by dense clouds of Indian spirits—a thousand red faces to one pale face—it is but natural that the red should rush in first when a door is opened. We have never heard of any apparitions of that color among us, but we count ourselves happy to be surrounded by the shades of the Oneidas rather than those of more savage tribes, and hope if we ever do have any Indian visitations they will be from some of the nation whose ancient hunting-grounds we enjoy.

Text 21: [The Community and Other Religious Movements] Excerpt from "A Community Transplanted--From Putney to Oneida, IX," *American Socialist*, **October 9, 1879, p. 325.**

But later associations and reminiscences of this region are more interesting than the aboriginal. Central New York was the special seat of the famous Finney Revival, as New England was of the "Great Awakening" in the time of Edwards. Finney commenced his career sixty miles north of here, but his great fame as an evangelist and medium of the Holy Spirit first went out from Oneida County, where his preaching in 1825-6 aroused a religious enthusiasm which is spoken of by the Presbytery of that county in some report, as "without parallel in this country, and seldom discovered in the history of the Church." In the Life of Dr. Lyman Beecher mention is made of this Revival as follows:

> "The year of Dr. Beecher's removal to Boston (1826) was signalized by powerful revivals in different parts of the land. Among

these, none were more remarkable than those in Central New York, particularly within the bounds of the Presbytery of Oneida. From week to week the columns of the Boston Recorder and other religious journals contained glowing accounts of the wonderful outpourings of the Holy Spirit. Whole towns in some instances were said to be converted. In other cases all the professional and leading men were gathered in. The mightiest opposers and unbelievers were in some places changed to friends, or stirred up to wrath. 'It does seem,' says one (Feb. 21), 'that there never was a time like the present since Pentecost—such wonderful displays of divine grace, such multitudes flocking to Christ.'"

We select a few items from an account of this Revival published in the Utica *Herald* a few years ago. Of the work in Rome it is said: "Special religious meetings were continued through a period of six weeks. It was a season of the greatest revival probably ever known, meetings being held every day and evening, not in the church alone, but in the court-house, hotels and private dwellings." "The year of the 'Great revival' is spoken of among us to this day. Rome was comparatively a small village then, but the number of conversions was over five hundred, and there was scarcely a family which was not visited." In Whitesboro "the interest was general, and the factories stopped to give operatives a chance to attend meetings; business was neglected for more important matters." In Utica "the influence was felt by all classes. Rich and poor forgot the distinctions of social position, and bowed together as equals. Gamblers, drunkards and Sabbath-breakers forsook evil ways and company."

If the Indians left their nimbus here, we trust much more that the spiritual atmosphere continues to be affected by the influence of that religious afflatus. The Oneida Community has always claimed to be the child of Revivalism. What better home for it than here in the old revival field?

The State of New York has distinguished itself by hospitality toward spiritual novelties. The mental condition of the population seems to attract them. Rochester and the region round about was the focus of the great Fourier excitement in America. Of a Socialistic Convention held there in 1844, T. C. Leland writes in language curiously descriptive of the revivals which had preceded this movement, as follows:

> "The turnout was astonishing; nearly every town in Genesee County was represented. Many came from five to twelve miles a-foot. Indeed, all of Western New York is in a deep and shaking agitation on the subject. Nine Associations are now contemplated within a mile of this city."

Mormonism and modern Spiritualism both had their rise in a county between here and Rochester. Gerrit Smith and his radicalisms have distinguished our own county. New York Perfectionism was born in this immediate vicinity. We live very near the center of the district burnt over by that fire. And it was not all Tartarian fire; there was a good deal of celestial heat in that excitement. There was a good deal of the true love of God in its beginnings and in individuals. In fact, the excesses by which it was at last scandalized and extinguished were not different from what have followed every revival in a greater or less degree. Mr. Burt, one of the fathers of the O. C., was a New York Perfectionist; also Mr. Ackley and the brothers Nash—strong men among us; but it is just to say that none of these were involved in the scandals of the sect.

Mr. Noyes was evidently following the star of his destiny when he came out to this region in 1836 (two years before he settled in Putney), and commenced the publication of the *Witness*. His constituency—what he had then—was in New England; but he saw a light in Central New York—to borrow an idea from Spiritualism—and here he came, a total stranger, on foot and without money, stopped in Ithaca, hired a printer, and sent out his paper. If there was more instinct than calculation in his erratic course, he still gives a reason, thus: "I regarded this region as the birth-place of some of the mightiest moral and political movements of the time, and as a place where the largest liberty of speech and of the press is allowed." He published three numbers and then went back to Putney and staid ten years. But this period was really episodical. It was the period of the nursery or first growth of the Community. The close New England air was good for that; but when the plant was ready for its permanent place, it was transferred to Central New York—the region which Mr. Noyes had first instinctively chosen for its home.

. . . . .

Part Three: Childhood Friends by Charlotte Miller

During the Putney years preceding Oneida, Harriet's younger sister, Charlotte, married fellow Perfectionist John Miller (**Figure 18**), a Putney storekeeper who, for a decade and a half, would serve as the Community's treasurer and head accountant. Artistically inclined Charlotte (1819-1874) would be looked up to as adviser to the girls and youthful women of the Oneida Community. She inspired the most lasting memories of warmth. It was "Aunt Charlotte Maria—beautiful Aunt Charlotte who, on one of my first homesick days [away from Oneida] took me in her arms and comforted me,"

Figure 18: John R. Miller (1813-1854)

Figure 19: Charlotte Noyes Miller (1819-1874)

Pierrepont Noyes recorded years later.[23] Jessie Kinsley's recollection of Charlotte was "of a gentle teacher who made English History delightful—a loving friend who always made criticism seem like love, and a gentlewoman who wanted me to keep my hands clean and to stand straight, sit erect and 'breathe deep.' There was unspeakable reverence for the beauty of her character in my heart. I wanted to be like her."[24]

When Noyes returned to his hometown to recruit his own cadres, he enlisted—in addition to Harriet—another younger sister, Charlotte (1819-1874) (**Figure 19**), then sixteen years old. In the course of those Putney years, Charlotte married another zealous member of their Bible-study, printing-crew group, John Miller, a Putney storekeeper who, in future years, would serve the Oneida Community as treasurer and head accountant. In the Oneida Community, Charlotte Miller was looked up to as advisor to the girls and youthful women. She taught Community youngsters history and drawing. Along with Harriet Skinner and Harriet Noyes, she was accorded the title of "Community Mother." Charlotte Miller probably contracted malaria at the Community's branch commune at Wallingford, Connecticut.[2]

The following is taken from the column "One of the Four," Part 18, a part of the series in the *Oneida Circular* published during 1875, which was mostly written by Harriet Skinner. Skinner introduced this column with the following note: During the time that Mrs. Miller was mother of the Wallingford Community, she held a weekly composition class with the girls, writing something nearly every week herself. Among her productions we find the following [entitled] Retrospect." In it, Charlotte reminisced nostalgically about school-childhood friends. I include it here because it contains some interesting demographic material pertaining to the women of the generation of the Noyes children. Most in that cohort, it turns out, were devoted to finding a husband, raising a family, and avoiding the stigma of being an "old maid." Sadly, of Miller's eleven named friends, most (seven) died young. This, then, is a little cameo of female existence demonstrating that life was hard and hazardous.

Text 22: "[Childhood Friends]" by Charlotte Miller, "One of the Four: A Memoir of Charlotte A. Miller, XVIII," *Oneida Circular*, July 12, 1875, p. 222-23.

I have been interested in recalling to memory the names and various fortunes, so far as I became acquainted with them, of the playmates and school-fellows of my childhood and youth. My circle of acquaintances was not particularly large, nor were their histories very peculiar. Yet, gathering them all together, and tracing their different paths as they emerge from childhood to youth and womanhood, enough, perhaps, of interest may be found to entertain our circle a few moments. Three or four of my early friends, at the age of fifteen or sixteen, went South as teachers and governesses. Wealthy Southerners seemed to think these New England maidens great prizes, and they were soon married, some to lords of slaves and cotton bales, and if now living are involved in the fate of war in Alabama and Tennessee. One lovely girl, Ruth S., whom I and all the girls looked up to as almost a saint—she was so religious and so good even when a child—moved out West while still young, married there and soon died.

Laura G., whose home was quite near mine, belonged to a very consumptive family. The symptoms of this disease began to show themselves in her when about eighteen; yet she was so ambitious, so determined to make a good figure in society that she concealed and ignored as much as possible her situation, and finally became engaged to be married while privately taking anti-consumptive medicines. She attained the object of her ambition, a fashionable wedding, a husband and a good position in society. In about a year she became the mother of a feeble infant, lingered a few weeks, and then died, and her baby was buried with her.

Kate X. lived in the next house to Laura, and was for some years my most intimate friend. She was an intellectual, well-educated girl, quite independent and self-reliant, and one that always won respect; but she evidently had a very different ambition from Laura. She never married, but remained at home the comfort of her parents, and the "good aunt" to her sister's children. Her mother was an invalid, and Kate, cheerful, industrious and intelligent, was the solace of her mother in her decline; and she is now at the age of forty-five, an old maid--the friend and consoler of her father, and esteemed by all who know her.

Across the street from Kate, lived Lavinia G. She was an orphan and lived with her uncle and aunt. The family was extremely strict in all the outward forms of religion, and very pious in their way; but narrow-minded, pharisaical and devoted to mammon. When about eighteen a rather mysterious malady seized Lavinia; she died, and a rumor reached us, whether true or not I never knew, that she loved a clerk in her uncle's store, and that her uncle opposed their love because the young man was poor. Her life always seemed to me to have been blighted by a false and unnatural education.

When I was old enough to go away from home to school, I formed a new circle of acquaintances. Isabella S and Amanda B. were room-mates with my sister and myself, at a boarding-school. Isabella was left an orphan very early, with considerable property and grew up proud, secretive and suspicious. She made but few friends, but those she loved almost to idolatry. Her lack of good parental training, and her unbroken will, without religion to soften and enlighten her heart, made her ill prepared to meet the demands of life. She often seemed unhappy, and died a few years after we left school. Amanda B. was aristocratic in birth and education, but had not wealth or accomplishments equal to her ambition. She was lively and friendly, but full of fashionable ideas about beaus and admiration, and used to talk of not marrying short of a hundred thousand dollars. But alas! Her charms of person and mind were not powerful enough to secure her the husband she thought worthy of her, and she has been for many years an old maid, rather notorious for gossip, poor health and an uncomfortable temper.

At another boarding-school, I was surrounded by another group of friends. I know the fate of but few of these. One sweet girl, a universal favorite, Frances W., a native of Pensacola, Florida, was an orphan, but connected by birth and marriage with the Washington family, and with the family of Murat, ex-king of Naples. She died young, of consumption. Another, a dark-eyed brunette, Maud G., was evidently an octoroon. She had a mysterious history before she came to the school, became wild and uncontrollable while there, and after leaving, went to Paris. From there she eloped with an English officer, and when last heard from was leading the life of a courtesan in Montreal. A third school-companion and a cousin of mine was a sister of Mr. R., Helen E. She was a pious, thoroughly educated New England girl, the opposite in every respect of the octoroon. After teaching a few years she married and went out West. My other room-mate was Maria F. She was something of a poetess, attractive but eccentric, vain and fickle. She jilted Mr. R. two or three times and finally married a merchant in Hartford, and according to report makes a queer sort of life. For instance, once when her husband was expected home after a few days' absence she dressed up the bolster in her cap and gown and put it in the bed and hid herself under the bed meanwhile, to enjoy his surprise and disappointment.

My list closes with two young ladies from Brattleboro just my own age. Ida G. was a belle; lively and handsome, and of wealthy parentage. She was not distinguished for intellect or scholarship, but was a fine musician. She married soon after she left school. In a few years she returned to her father's house a widow with one little boy. She lived in her old home till five or six years ago, when a short and sudden illness carried her to the grave. Lissette H., my other Brattleboro friend, was a very amiable and lovable girl. She was an orphan and depended on her friends for support and education. She endured many humiliations from her sister's children and other proud and money-loving relatives on account of her dependence. Her lack of fortune made her chances of a suitable marriage less than many of her companions, though her gentle and amiable temper made her much beloved. A young gentleman of a wealthy family, to whom she had been much attached, who apparently loved her, and had long paid her special attention, from some slander or injurious remark about her, suddenly left off his attentions, and heartlessly exposed her attachment to ridicule. This was a blow too much. Lissette was taken sick, soon after, as I was told, and died of a broken heart. Her beautiful corpse, most splendidly arrayed, and enclosed in a costly and elegant coffin, was brought home from New York to Brattleboro. This was all that remained of poor Lissette H.

In thinking over my own career since leaving school, I can truly say that God's goodness to me has been very great. I have not had great wealth or honor as the world esteems wealth and honor, and I have had what the world deems afflictions in the loss of property, reputation and husband. Yet the fact that God chose me from among my companions to be a lover of Christ, and a helper in establishing his social gospel, is in my eyes a blessing and honor that that outweighs every other consideration. Nothing would induce me to exchange the experience and the hopes that are mine by my connection with Mr. Noyes and the Community. Life has not been to me a lottery with a blank for my portion, but has been a sure and satisfying progress from good to better, and will bring me to the best at last. I have had with the other good things promised to those who forsake all for Christ—a degree of health that I am sure is owing to the faith that separated me from the world.

Notes

1. John Humphrey Noyes, *History of American Socialisms* (Philadelphia: J. B. Lippincott, 1870). For Skinner, see *American Socialist*, July 14, 1879, 261-262, and in this volume within "A Community Transplanted," chapter I.

2. Jane K. Rich, ed., *A Lasting Spring: Jessie Catherine Kinsley, Daughter of the Oneida Community* (Syracuse, NY: Syracuse University Press, 1983), 86; Oneida Circular, October 5, 1874, 321.
3. *Oneida Circular*, March 15, 1875, 83.
4. Pierrepoint Burt Noyes, *My Father's House: An Oneida Boyhood* (New York: Farrar and Rinehart, 1937), 28.
5. J [James Herrick]. "Harriet Noyes Skinner," *Quadrangle* 1, no. 8 (December 1908), 10-12. See Skinner's writing on food in Chapter 5, Part Six and in *Circular*, July 12, 1869, 134.
6. Robert Allerton Parker, *A Yankee Saint: John Humphrey Noyes and the Oneida Community* (New York: G. P. Putnam's Sons, 1935), 95.
7. Anthony Wonderley, *Oneida Utopia: A Community Searching for Human Happiness and Prosperity* (Ithaca, New York: Cornell University Press, 2017), 144.
8. *Daily Journal*, September 12, 1866.
9. Information about her final illness and death appears in the *Oneida Circular*, October 5, 1874, 321-322 and July 19, 1875, 226-227.
10. *Oneida Circular*, June 7, 1875, 178.
11. *Oneida Circular*, July 12, 1875, 223.
12. *Oneida Circular*, May 24, 1875, 165.
13. *Oneida Circular*, June 7, 1875, 178.
14. Defined by Noyes as the "who-shall-be-greatest mania," "diotrephiasis" was an Oneida Community neologism. It was coined to mean an unhealthy preoccupation with doing things better than other people (Spencer Klaw, *Without Sin: The Life and Death of the Oneida Community* [New York: Allen Lane, Penguin, 1993], 117, 229).
15. The early Oneida Community, we are told in this section, experienced internal trouble, disaffection, insubordination: "The years 1850, '51 and '52 were years of extreme trial to the Community. First, the conflict with internal evils, such as insubordination, disloyalty and pleasure-seeking, culminated in the withdrawal of several families, and seemed at times to jeopardize the very existence of the Community." And then, specifically, "under date of May 10, is an account of the disaffection and insincerity of one of the members; of his private and public criticism; of his determination to withdraw with his family; of their loyalty and earnest wish to remain; of his surrender; his renewed disaffection, and final withdrawal with his wife and children." Yet, nothing relevant follows. The advertised account, presumably referring to 1851, seems to have been deleted. Who was insubordinate? Lawrence Foster suggests it was George Cragin (*Religion and Sexuality* 1984: 113-15; *Women, Family, and Utopia* 1991: 112-13). But this passage suggests

otherwise. The actions and circumstances that are mentioned do not correspond to those of that individual. Could the insubordinate one have been Abram Smith? In the end, we are left to wonder.

16. In addition to the excerpts provided here, see *American Socialist*, September 4 and 11, 1879, 293-294.
17. Cf., Carl Carmer, *Listen for a Lonesome Drum: A York State Chronicle* (Syracuse, NY: Syracuse University Press, 1995, originally published 1936); Whitney R. Cross, *The Burned-Over District: The Social and Intellectual History of Enthusiastic Religion in Western New York, 1800-1850* (Ithaca, NY: Cornell University Press, 1950); and Jocelyn Godwin, *Upstate Caldron: Eccentric Spiritual Movements in Early New York State* (Albany: SUNY Press, Excelsior Editions, 2015).
18. J. H. Noyes, *History of American Socialisms*. For the Putney Community, see Anthony Wonderley, ed., *Writings from Wallingford: The Connecticut Outpost of the Oneida Community* (Hamilton College Library, Clinton, NY: Richard W. Couper Press, 2020), especially 59-62.
19. William Hepworth Dixon, a prominent English literary figure who visited the Oneida Community, recorded his impressions in several books including a best seller of 1867 called *New America*.
20. Although Noyes expresses reservations about owning too much land, I can't find this specific statement within the pages of his *History of American Socialisms* (see note 1).
21. P. B. Noyes, *My Father's House,* 31.
22. Rich, *A Lasting Spring*, 36.
23. P. B. Noyes, *My Father's House*, 31; Rich, *A Lasting Spring*, 36; and "Death of Mrs. C. A. Miller," *Oneida Circular*, October 5, 1874, 321-322.

Chapter 3. Doctrines

The members of the Oneida Community were bound by a set of doctrines and practices, carefully outlined and published in the pages of the numerous pamphlets and books written by John Humphrey Noyes as well as in the pages of their newspapers and other publications. The most important were communal living, selflessness, self-improvement, and adherence to God's laws, all in the interests of creating a kingdom of heaven on earth. Of central importance was the concept of complex marriage, the idea that all adult member of the Community were spouses to one another. This was a central tenet of the Community and one that was explained in a variety of ways. The Community also believed strongly in what today might be called lifelong education, believing that all members had a responsibility to be informed and continually improving themselves. "Mutual Criticism" was a frequent practice in the evening meetings, designed not only to improve individual members but to reinforce the central principles of the Community. The texts in this chapter provide insight into the ways in which Community members articulated their beliefs and standards for living.

Part One: The Bible Argument

In the upstate New York home of Jonathan Burt (**Figure 20**) in February 1848, John Noyes contemplated the nature of the association about to coalesce on the banks of Oneida Creek. First published in the Oneida Community's *First Annual Report of 1849, as Bible Argument: Defining the Relations of the Sexes in the Kingdom of Heaven*, the treatise was a blueprint for the coming association. In 1853, it was included in *Bible Communism; A Compilation from the Annual Reports and Other Publications of the Oneida Association and its Branches*.[1] In it were reasoned out most of the important principles that would become reality in the Oneida Community. This writing was Noyes's first public defense of group marriage initiated a short time before in Putney. It was also his first substantive explanation of what would become Oneida's doctrine of free love and, as such, his magnum opus on sex. In the passages given below, Noyes conveys his ideas about group marriage (although the term "complex marriage" is not used), sexual attraction, and sexual intercourse.

Figure 20: Jonathan Burt (1806-1886)

Also introduced is "male continence," the Community's distinctive form of birth control (although that term, as well, is not employed). Noyes explained it by analyzing sexual intercourse as a package of two components. One, the amative function, comprises sexual attraction, desire, and the sex act itself. The other, the propagative function, includes male ejaculation, conception, and reproduction. These functions can be separated by prohibiting male climax.[2] And they should be separated until children are wanted and can be properly cared for. There were supposed to be, in addition, other benefits to having the male suppress or withhold ejaculation. "Our method," Noyes elaborated, "simply proposes the subordination of the flesh to the spirit, teaching men to seek principally the elevated spiritual pleasures of sexual intercourse."[3] Further, this technique of birth control will open the door to "scientific propagation," or eugenics. Here Noyes predicted "stirpiculture," a program of selective breeding which the Oneida Community would undertake twenty years later. "We believe the time will come when involuntary and random propagation will cease, and when scientific combination will be applied to human generation as freely and successfully as it is to that of other animals," Noyes indicated.[4]

More than anything else, *Bible Argument* (**Figure 21**) was meant to justify a communitarian venture duplicating life in heaven—a place of group matrimony—in order to bring that kingdom to earth. Noyes's vision in this regard was twofold. On the one hand, complex marriage would hasten Christ's return, bringing it to earthly fruition through the practice of righteous, unrestrictive love. On the other, collective marriage would transform society and correct its ills. Noyes's essay, as it pertained to the latter point, was a prospectus for social reform through associative action, a plan recasting Fourierism around the practice of free love. Accordingly, two lines of argument were advanced in support of complex marriage. The first, concerned with the advent of Christ and the coming of heaven, was religious.

Figure 21: *Bible Argument*
Photo by Jim Demarest

This exposition began with the assertion that group or "complex" marriage is both the way of heaven and the earthly means for bringing heaven about. The Bible tells us there is no marriage in heaven, Noyes conceded, but that does not mean, as Shakers suppose, that there is no sex. The true meaning is that there is no monogamous or exclusive marriage. In the kingdom of God, there is a state of unrestrictive love for several reasons.

First, sex is a natural act because God created human maleness and femaleness as fitted to each other to achieve perfect union physically and spiritually.

Heterosexual bonding is a holy act because God is a bisexual duality in whose image men and women were created," and of whose nature the whole creation is a reflection."[5] In coitus, the conjoined partners selflessly recreate and draw nearer to the Godhead as the spirit of God passes between them.

Second, it is illogical to suppose God excluded from heaven a sacrament so important and good. "It was manifestly the design of God, in creating the sexes, to give love more intense expression than is possible between persons of the same sex;" Noyes explained. "And it is foolish to imagine that he will ever abandon that design by unsexing his children, or impede it by legal restrictions on sexual intercourse, in the heavenly state."[6] Noyes found it inconceivable that God would not feature sex in heaven.

Third, any restrictions or exclusiveness in marriage are incompatible with the biblical emphasis on common ownership and, inferentially, complete communism. In the heavenly state, all property is communally owned as was the case among the first Christians at the time of Pentecost. This condition would be called "Bible communism" in the future although that term is not used here. That sexual exclusiveness is incommensurate with communism is demonstrated by "the love-relation required between all believers by the express injunction of Christ and the apostles, and by the whole tenor of the New Testament. 'The new commandment is, that we love one another,' and that not by pairs, as in the world, but *en masse*." In heaven, Noyes insisted, "the intimate union of life and interests, which in the world is limited to pairs, extends through the whole body of believers."[7] Logic tells us, Noyes reasoned, that complex marriage exists in heaven.

The relevance of complex marriage to earthly existence is that the heavenly kingdom is coming and Christ is returning. Christ must have control over the marriage system "and arrange sexual conditions according to the genius of his own kingdom, before he can push his conquests to victory over death." Establishing the heavenly conditions of marriage is "the very means by which the resurrection power is to be let in upon the world."[8] This theological purpose is stated more clearly in a summary of Noyes's religion appearing in a preface to the text of *Bible Argument*.

> [We believe] that the second advent of Christ took place at the period of the destruction of Jerusalem; that at that time there was a primary resurrection and judgment in the spiritual world; that the final kingdom of God then began in the heavens; that the manifestation of that kingdom in the visible world is now approaching; that its approach is ushering in the second and final resurrection and judgment; that a church on earth is now rising to meet the approaching kingdom in the heavens, and to become its duplicate and representative; that inspiration, or open communication with God and the heavens, involving perfect holiness, is the element of connection between the church on earth and the church in the

heavens, and the power by which the kingdom of God is to be established and reign in the world.[9]

Noyes and his disciples regarded themselves as the earthly duplicate and representative of the kingdom of heaven. It is they, through the practice of perfect holiness, who will serve as the medium for establishing God's kingdom here. And perfect holiness, the means by which resurrection power is to be let into the world, is defined and equated with complex marriage. What the Oneida Community intended to do to expedite the earthly appearance of heaven was to duplicate the heavenly state by engaging in heavenly sex.

In celebrating free love and sexual intercourse with startling candor, *Bible Argument* must have shocked many at the time. But there was nothing surreptitious in Noyes's action of writing and distributing it. Published in the Oneida Community's "First Annual Report" of early 1849, it was also printed as a pamphlet mailed out to prominent public figures throughout the state to inform them what was occurring at Oneida.

The wonder of it all is that Noyes's ideas about sex in heaven and on earth transcended abstraction--this was a philosophy that became living experience. Sex, at Oneida—let it be said again—hastened Christ's return by duplicating heavenly practice and uniting one with God.[10] A couple conjoined in coitus was recreating the godhead and drawing closer to it. Noyes's aim, according to historian Robert Parker,

> was to integrate sexual love with the life of the spirit, to make a sacrament of physical love, the outward and active sign of inward, spiritual grace. Love should be a science as well as an art--the deepest and most engrossing of all sciences. Only through this function, so long abused and misunderstood, could men ever truly experience unity with God and Humanity. Its value was not merely in a rite sacredly fulfilled, but in its power to awaken complete realization of divine unity--the knowledge that all love is one and indivisible. Sexual love, transcending individual consciousness, Noyes explained, provided the experience through which we, as members of the human race, are enabled to experience the ecstasy of true communion, to break through the dark isolation of egotism and self-hood.[11]

As one Community member put it, the Perfectionists considered their sexual organs to be "the highest instruments of praise and worship in the Heavenly world." That person added that the Oneidans claimed liberty "for the free use of our sexual organs as a means of social enjoyment."[12] What he meant was that, in addition to its spiritual value, sex at Oneida was celebrated as pleasurable. In the bigger picture, Noyes insisted that life was meant to be enjoyed. People should be happy and, if necessary, work hard to be happy because human joy pleases God. Oneida Perfectionism "was a happy religion, never a gloomy one," remarked one who grew up in it. "The grown folks seemed almost as bent on being happy as they did on being good." God, in Noyes' opinion, was "not on the side of asceticism...God made our bodies to rejoice and be happy in his creation." As a part of life, sex was something given by God and intended by God for people to enjoy to please him.[13]

Oneida sex was said to increase the satisfaction of both lovers who, thanks to male continence, "may enjoy the highest bliss of sexual fellowship for any length of time, and from day to day, without satiety or exhaustion," as Noyes thought.[14] The male was supposed to experience elevated spiritual pleasure, the result—apparently—of suppressing ejaculation, thereby subordinating his interest to that of his lover. The female's amative nature was "developed to its fullest extent" in the estimation of Perfectionist George E. Cragin who also reported that women experienced orgasms. Medical doctor and Community child Hilda Herrick said some women welcomed the variety of lovers made possible by complex marriage. That diversity, in one known instance, amounted to having four sexual partners in the course of a month. A popular woman, according to a popular woman, might have intercourse two to three times a week.[15]

Having longer and more enjoyable sex experiences meant that married life in the Oneida Community was, as Noyes enthused, "permanently sweeter than courtship, or even the honey-moon"—the high points of romantic excitement in matrimony of the outside world. "A state of continuous courtship," Community member Abel Easton agreed, was an accurate characterization of the communal experience. One child of the Community fondly recalled the romantic atmosphere that seemed to emanate from the adults. The sexual dimension of Community existence rendered life more colorful there than elsewhere, in the memory of that individual, and enlivened the elderly with "a vivid, youthful interest in life that looked from their eyes and spoke in their voices and manners."[16]

Text 23: Excerpts from "Bible Argument" by John Humphrey Noyes[17]

"Bible Argument" was written as a series of numbered propositions, some of which included "Notes" written by Noyes.

. . . .

Proposition XIII.

The law of marriage "worketh wrath." 1. It provokes to secret adultery, actual or of the heart. 2. It ties together unmatched natures. 3. It sunders matched natures. 4. It gives to sexual appetite only a scanty and monotonous allowance, and so produces the natural vices of poverty, contraction of taste, and stinginess or jealousy. 5. It makes no provision for the sexual appetite at the very time when that appetite is strongest. By the custom of the world, marriage, in the average of cases, takes place at about the age of twenty-four. Whereas puberty commences at the age of fourteen. For ten years, therefore, and that in the very flush of life, the sexual appetite is starved.

This law of society bears hardest on females, because they have less opportunity of choosing their time of marriage than men. This discrepancy between the marriage system and nature, is one of the principal sources of the peculiar diseases of women, of prostitution, masturbation, and licentiousness in general.

. . . .

Proposition XVII.

Dividing the sexual relation into two branches, the amative and propagative, the amative or love-relation is first in importance, as it is in the order of nature. God made woman because "he saw it was *not good for man to be alone*;" (Gen. 2:18;) i.e. for social, not primarily for propagative purposes. Eve was called Adam's "help-meet." In the whole of the specific account of the creation of woman, she is regarded as his companion, and her maternal office is not brought into view. Gen. 2:18-25. Amativeness was necessarily the first social affection developed in the garden of Eden. The second commandment of the eternal law of love—"thou shalt love thy neighbor as thyself"—had amativeness for its first channel; for Eve was at first Adam's only neighbor. Propagation, and the affections connected with it, did not commence their operation during the period of innocence. After the fall, God said to the woman—"I will greatly multiply thy sorrow and thy conception;" from which it is to be inferred that in the original state, conception would have been comparatively infrequent.

. . . .

Proposition XIX.

The propagative part of the sexual relation is in its nature the expensive department. 1. While amativeness keeps the capital stock of life circulating between two, propagation introduces a third partner. 2. The propagative act, i.e. the emission of the seed, is a drain on the life of the man, and when habitual, produces disease. 3. The infirmities and vital expenses of woman during the long period of pregnancy, waste her constitution. 4. The awful agonies of child-birth heavily tax the life of woman. 5. The cares of the nursing period bear heavily on woman. 6. The cares of both parents, through the period of the childhood of their offspring, are many and burdensome. 7. The labor of man is greatly increased by the necessity of providing for children. A portion of these expenses would undoubtedly have been curtailed if human nature had remained in its original integrity, and will be, when it is restored. But it is still self-evident that the birth of children, viewed either as a vital or a mechanical operation, is in its nature expensive; and the fact that multiplied conception was imposed as a curse, indicates that it was so regarded by the Creator.

. . . .

Proposition XX.

The amative and propagative functions of the sexual organs are distinct from each other, and may be separated practically. They are confounded in the world, both in the theories of physiologists and in universal practice. The amative function is regarded merely as a bait to the propagative, and is merged in it. The sexual organs are called "organs of reproduction," or "organs of generation," but not organs of love or organs of union. But if amativeness is, as we have seen, the first and noblest of the social affections, and if the propagative part of the sexual relation was originally secondary, and became paramount by the subversion of order in the fall, we are bound to raise the amative office of the sexual organs into a distinct and paramount function. It is held in the world, that the sexual organs have two distinct functions, viz., the urinary, and the propagative. We affirm that they have three-- the urinary, the propagative, and the amative; i.e., they are conductors, first of the urine, secondly of the seed, and thirdly of the vital and social magnetism. And the amative is as distinct from the propagative, as the propagative is from the urinary. In fact, strictly speaking, the organs of propagation are physiologically distinct from the organs of union in both sexes. The testicles are the organs of reproduction in the male, and the uterus in the female. These are distinct from the organs of union. The sexual conjunction of male and female no more necessarily involves the discharge of the testicles than of the bladder. The discharge of the seed, instead of being the main act of sexual intercourse properly so called, is really the sequel and termination of it.

Sexual intercourse, pure and simple, is the conjunction of the organs of union, and the interchange of magnetic influences, or conversation of spirits, through the medium of that conjunction. The communication from the testicles to the uterus, which constitutes the propagative act, is distinct from, subsequent to, and not necessarily connected with, this intercourse. On the one hand the seminal discharge can be voluntarily withheld in sexual connection; and on the other it can be produced without sexual connection, as it is in masturbation. This latter fact demonstrates that the discharge of the seed and the pleasure connected with it, is not essentially social, since it can be produced in solitude; it is a personal and not a dual affair. In fact this is evident from a physiological analysis of it. The pleasure of the act is not produced by contact and interchange of life with the female, but by the action of the seminal fluid on certain internal nerves of the male organ. The appetite and that which satisfies it, are both within the man, and of course the pleasure is personal and may be obtained without sexual intercourse. We insist then that the amative function--that which consists in a simple union of persons, making "of twain one flesh" and giving a medium of magnetic and spiritual interchange,--is a distinct and independent function, as superior to the reproductive as we have shown amativeness to be to propagation.

. . . .

Note 3.---Ordinary sexual intercourse, i.e. the performance of the propagative act, without the intention of procreation, is properly to be classed with masturbation. The habit in the former case is less liable to become besotted and ruinous, than in the latter, simply because a woman is less convenient that the ordinary means of masturbation. It must be admitted also that the amative affection favorably modifies the sensual act to a greater extent in sexual commerce than in masturbation. But this is perhaps counterbalanced by the cruelty of forcing or risking undesired conception, which attends sexual commerce and does not attend masturbation.

Note 4.---Our theory, which separates the amative from the propagative, not only relieves us of involuntary and undesirable procreation, but opens the way for scientific propagation. We are not opposed after the Shaker fashion, or even after Owen's fashion, to the increase of population. We believe that the order to "multiply" attached to the race in its original integrity, and that propagation, rightly conducted and kept within such limits as life can fairly afford, is the next blessing to sexual love. But we are opposed to involuntary procreation. A very large proportion of all children born under the present system, are begotten contrary to the wishes of both parents, and lie nine months in their mother's womb under their mother's curse, or a feeling little better than a curse. Such children cannot be well organized. We are opposed to excessive, and of course oppressive procreation, which is almost universal. We are opposed to random procreation, which is unavoidable in the marriage system. But we are in favor of intelligent, well-ordered procreation. The physiologists say that the race cannot be raised from ruin, till propagation is made a matter of science; but they point out no way of making it so. True, propagation is controlled and reduced to a science in the case of valuable domestic brutes; but marriage and fashion forbid any such system among human beings. We believe the time will come when involuntary and random propagation will cease, and when scientific combination will be applied to human generation as freely and successfully as it is to that of other animals. The way will be open for this, when amativeness can have its proper gratification without drawing after it procreation, as a necessary sequence. And at all events we believe that good sense and benevolence will very soon sanction and enforce the rule that women shall bear children only when they choose. They have the principal burdens of breeding to bear, and they, rather than men, should have their choice of time and circumstances, at least till science takes charge of the business...

Note 6.---The separation of the amative from the propagative, places amative sexual intercourse on the same footing with other ordinary forms of intercourse, such as conversation, kissing, shaking hands, embracing, &c.--So long as the amative and propagative are confounded, sexual intercourse carries with it physical consequences which necessarily take it out of the category of mere social acts. If a gentleman under the cover of a mere social call upon a lady, should leave in her apartments a child for her to breed and provide for, he would do a mean wrong. The call might be made without previous negotiation or agreement, but the sequel of the call--the leaving of the child--is a matter so serious that it is to be treated as a business affair, and not be done without good reason and agreement of the parties. But the man who under the cover of social sexual intercourse, commits the propagative act, leaves his child with the woman in a meaner and more oppressive way, than he would if he should leave it full-born in her apartments; for he imposes on her not only the task of breeding and providing for it, but the sorrows and pains of pregnancy and child-birth. It is right that law, or at least public opinion, should frown on such proceedings even more than it does; and it is not to be wondered at, that women, to a considerable extent, look upon ordinary sexual intercourse with more dread than pleasure, regarding it as a stab at their life, rather than a joyful act of fellowship.

But separate the amative from the propagative--let the act of fellowship stand by itself--and sexual intercourse becomes a purely social affair, the same in kind with other modes of kindly interchange, differing only by its superior intensity and beauty. Thus the most popular, if not the most serious objection to free love and sexual intercourse is removed. The difficulty so often urged, of knowing to whom children belong in complex marriage, will have no place in a community trained to keep the amative distinct from the propagative. Thus also the only plausible objection to amative intercourse between near relatives, founded on the supposed law of nature that "breeding in and in" deteriorates offspring, (which law however was not recognized in Adam's family,) is removed; since science may dictate in this case as in all others, in regard to propagation, and yet amativeness may be free.

Note 7.---In society trained in these principles, as propagation will become a science, so amative intercourse will become one of the "fine arts." Indeed it will take rank above music, painting, sculpture, &c.; for it combines the charms and benefits of them all. There is as much room for cultivation of taste and skill in this department as in any.

Note 8.---The reformed practice which we propose, will advance civilization and refinement at railroad speed. The self-control, retention of life, and ascent out of sensualism which must result from making freedom of love a bounty on the chastening of physical indulgence, will at once raise the race to new vigor and beauty, moral and physical. And the refining effects of sexual love (which are recognized more or less in the world) will be increased a thousand-fold, when sexual intercourse becomes a method of ordinary conversation, and each is married to all...

Part Two: Complex Marriage

Lawyer, Civil War veteran, and member of the Berlin Heights (Ohio) free-love commune, James Towner (1823-1913) joined the Oneida Community

Figure 22: James W. Towner (1823-1913)

in 1874[18] (**Figure 22**). One Oneida Community member remembered Towner as being endowed with "a singular dignity of soul," but also shrewd and inclined to political scheming.[19] Late in the 1870s, he became identified with a party opposed to John Noyes and Noyes's policies. The position of these disloyalists—they were called "Townerites"--called for representative government lodged in a president freely chosen by all Community members. They asked, further, that social life be returned to the "old principles of the Community," a situation in which "every member is to be absolutely free from the undesired sexual familiarity, approach, and control of every other person."[20]

A vote taken when the Community broke up established a leadership board of six directors for the new company (Oneida Community Ltd.) loyal to Noyes, as opposed to only two belonging to the Townerite faction. Feeling frozen out of power, Towner emigrated with about forty of his adherents to Santa Ana, California, in 1882. There they did well. Towner chaired the committee that organized Orange County, then served as that county's first superior court judge.[21]

Prior to disaffection, however, Towner was an effective spokesperson for Oneida and an enthusiastic promoter of Noyes's religious tenets. In this two-part series on marriage for the Oneida Circular, Towner characterizes Noyes as a visionary who, in troubled times, offered the world the panacea of Bible communism. Noyes's manner of love, the author asserts, promotes "the intercourse of the sexes, delicacy, modesty, chastity and self-denial rather than indulgence." In doing so, it brings forth "social blessings of the best quality and in the greatest quantity."

Towner elaborates the historical context of public sexual concerns by referring in the first article to Biblical and current social contexts and in the second, to the writings of well-known radicals Fanny Wright and Robert Dale Owen, advocates of open discussion of sexual matters.[22] He also mentions the socialistic expositions of Robert Owen, a wealthy Welsh reformer best known for starting up the utopian experiment of New Harmony in Indiana in the late 1820s. A staunch believer in environmental determinism, Owen held that human character is formed by the individual's background and upbringing. Give a person a good environment, and that individual will do the right thing. Owen tried to provide his community with basic necessities of life and with the opportunity to enjoy cultural activities. In exchange, each resident was to contribute labor. Having no entrance requirements, however, Owen ended up with a crowd of argumentative freeloaders. New Harmony collapsed within two years.[23]

Further, Towner refers to the mystic doctrines of Emanuel Swedenborg who preached "spiritual affinity," a mystical bond between a man and a woman justifying sex regardless of whether or not they are married to others.[24] Swedenborg's ideas about what came to be called "special affinity" and "spiritual wifery" influenced the spiritualist craze which had just swept the country with galvanic force. The movement was grounded in the assumption that the soul lives on after death and retains earthly ties directly accessible to the living. Requiring no church or body of dogma, spiritualism was an immensely appealing and wonderfully democratic faith. By the early 1850s, there were an estimated 1.5 to 4 million believers in spiritualism, compared to about 2.8 million Protestants (Baptists, Congregationalists, Methodists, Presbyterians) in a population of some 23 million. America, at that point, seemed to be on the verge of becoming a land of spiritualists.[25]

Text 24: "Decadence of Marriage I," *Oneida Circular* **13, No. 4, January 27, 1876, p. 28. Signed J.W.T. (James W. Towner)**

The opinion is held to some extent, that what is called complex marriage, is really nothing but a combination of polygamy and polyandry. This arises from misconceiving and confusing things which are in no wise akin to each other. The terms "polygamous polyandry," which have been applied to us, express no idea belonging to our social theory, save perhaps the single one of plurality in the relations of the sexes. And, surely, no Bible believer will venture to assert that such plurality is impure and sinful *per se*. The American Board of Commissioners of Foreign Missions decided, years ago, that converts in polygamous countries should not be required to abandon polygamy as a sin.

We reject polygamy because it multiplies the radical evil of monogamy, *viz.*, property in woman. Webster defines polygamy as, "having more than one wife." Polyandry, also, is having more than one husband. And the word "having," so used, has its primary meaning, that is, "*owning*, having in possession." The fundamental idea of marriage, polygamous, or monogamous, is that of ownership and exclusive possession as of property. Take that away, and marriage, considered as the ground of the existing social order, is gone.

That was what the Sadducees wanted to know about, when in the case they supposed, they asked the question," *whose* wife shall she be, for the seven *had* her?" The seven had owned her in this life, who should own her in the next, or the resurrection? And Christ's answer simply negatived the idea of ownership. He did not say there should be no relations or love between the sexes in the resurrection, but simply, "they neither marry, nor are given in marriage." That expression, "*given* in marriage," implied in primitive speech, a transfer of property as much as giving or selling a servant or slave did. The essential idea of marriage and slavery was the same. The forms of both institutions have varied at different times and among different peoples, but not the essence. Marriage by capture was the first form. The lowest savage went out with club in hand, knocked down the woman he fancied, dragged her to his hut and made her his wife. The Benjamites lay in wait in the vineyards, and when the daughters of Shiloh came out to dance, they rushed out and caught, every man his wife. Marriage, or obtaining wives by purchase, succeeded marriage by capture. In later times, under the English common law, the getting of wives by contract came into fashion; but when obtained, the status of the wife was that of a chattel. For most civil purposes, she had no legal existence; that being merged in her husband, who had a right to imprison or whip her if he chose, so he did it moderately! He owned her person, her service, her property, her society, and could sue and recover damages for her abduction, and for sexual intercourse with her, as for injury to any other article of property. Upon this ground, the famous action of *crim. con.* of Tilton v. Beecher, which set public curiosity all agog, was based. The wife never had such right to damages, simply because she never had any property in the husband.

Now this property in persons we utterly disown and repudiate on religious grounds. We look upon marriage as slavery. We regard them both as institutions adapted to a state of bondage to selfishness and sin, and not to a state of holiness and liberty. We find them treated in the New Testament substantially alike. We find marriage there tolerated under circumstances of necessity for good reasons, distinctly placed on the ground of a choice of evils, and spoken of as belonging to the "fashion of this world," which was destined to pass away. And we hold and declare the belief that to avoid worse evils there is place for it, and need of it still among those who cleave to selfish possession and private property; and we would not do anything to further weaken it with such persons, but are only seeking to put something better in its place; and would not destroy it, but would restore it rather where such substitution is impracticable. In our system there is no sexual ownership or slavery, on the one hand; nor, on the other hand, is there with us any liberty but the liberty which is to be found in earnestly seeking the Spirit of the Lord; "where that is, there is liberty." If those who denounce us cannot understand what we mean by that, we will be patient with being misunderstood. We would assure them if we could, that it is not what they conceive it to be. And we sincerely believe that if they would devote themselves, as we have done, to finding out the meaning of such injunctions as this, "Whether ye eat or drink, or *whatsoever ye do*, do all to the glory of God," there would be a much better appreciation of our position than now.

The case seems to us to stand thus: certain very zealous, probably conscientious, but plainly narrowminded people have views of us which fill them with holy horror of us. If their views of us were correct, it might follow that we deserve all their denunciations; but we think they have not yet calmly studied the nature and objects of the social changes which we propose. We think, and would say it modestly, that they do not see the real origin of their difficulty. They probably see and feel that society is upturning, that something is wrong and should be righted; but they proceed upon the mistaken assumption that marriage is a permanent institution, when the fact is, it is, in the Divine order, to be superseded, and really became, long ago, seriously affected with decay; and they are worshipping a falling idol. They seem to have studied its history during the last half-century to little purpose. But we reserve some hints on this point, as we view it, for another article.

[Signed] J.W.T.

Text 25: "Decadence of Marriage II," *Oneida Circular* **13, No. 5 February 3, 1876, p. 36. Signed J.W.T (James W. Towner).**

The following seem to us to be facts bearing on the point with which we closed the article under the above head in last week's paper: The religious revival which swept with such power over the country, beginning some fifty years ago bred extensive social irregularities and inaugurated a revolution in marriage. Anti-Revivalists aided that revolution in various ways. Fanny Wright and Robert Dale Owen greatly aided it by their attacks on religion, property, and society, in 1828, which shook New-York city and even the nation and indoctrinated its politics in various ways. Then came the elder Owen and Fourier with their writings upon Socialism largely contributing to the same end. Then came the writings of Swedenborg with his doctrines of mistress-keeping, concubinage, spiritual affinities and free and easy divorce; the last two of which doctrines obtaining a large acceptance and inoculating literature, have helped swell the tide against marriage. And lastly, those connected in one way or other with "Modern Spiritualism," now a host in this country, have rolled on the tide of marriage revolution, till, among the masses of the people, the decadence of marriage as a sacred and binding ordinance, has for some time been an established fact. Very many among the married discovered that they were mismatched; a general hunt for affinities supervened; and to aid in getting them, great liberality and even laxity of divorce legislation has taken place; the courts have been crowded with a constantly increasing number of applicants, who, in a great majority of cases, are asking liberation only to unite with some already discovered affinity. Little but the form of marriage remains, the soul having long since well-nigh departed.

The founder of our Community saw these things as they were transpiring, and realized the evils incident thereto. He saw a tendency to social anarchy in that revolution; that in the roaming about from mate to mate which took place, multitudes of people fell into hopeless licentiousness; that the blessings of the sexual relation and of the family were threatened with destruction; that, especially, was the natural desire for children dying out in general society; that the inconvenience of the burden of children in the race for affinities, and the natural dread of involuntary child-bearing in an age of growing intelligence, combined with other causes, had introduced the frightful practice of abortion, which forty years ago was of rare and secret occurrence but now became frequent and bold, and more common even in the older States and among people of respectability and high social standing than elsewhere. Seeing these things and many other evils which might be named, attending the natural revolt against the sexual bondage and affectional proverty of marriage, he set about devising some remedy for them, and saving what is valuable in the family, something to take the place of the "fashion of the world" that was passing away. An unwavering believer in the Bible and in Jesus Christ as a Savior from all sin, he naturally turned in that direction for such remedy and substitute. He found in Christianity the germs of a social as well as a religious system; that it was to introduce a reign of the heavens superseding all other kingdoms; and in the manifestation of the outpouring of the Holy Spirit on the days of Pentecost and in the Communism which followed, he found the key to understand Christianity as a social force and organization. Faithfully studying that and following its logical development through years of persecution and social outlawry, with great labor and unspeakable trial he brought forward our system of Christian Communism as a truly conservative method of averting social anarchy and the various evils mentioned. And in this view is to be found its merit. It is not offered to the world in the interest of lawlessness and disorder. Our position may be one of non-conformity to lower laws in some respects, but we claim it to be in conformity to the higher law which should govern the truly humane, God-fearing and conscientious, the man who would love his neighbor as himself. We claim that in the social sphere our system is the natural complement of the improvements making in other departments of human knowledge and effort, whereby it is constantly demonstrated that any good can be better attained by cooperation and association, than by single persons or small partnerships. We have believed that candid, thinking people would study us in this aspect, and still believe they will do so. We are on trial, and we expect to be able to prove on the trial that we are in favor of good order, peace, industry, and improvement. We expect, too, if we shall be allowed a fair trial, to prove that, as a practical fact, our system tends to promote the intercourse of the sexes, delicacy, modesty, chastity, and self-denial rather than indulgence; and that in fact there is less of the latter under our system than in any other society, except the Shakers or others who practice celibacy. We also expect to prove that we are able to produce in all the relations of the family, in the exercise of all the kindly charities of our nature—when regenerated—social blessings of the best quality and in the greatest quantity. If we cannot, we expect to fail. We only ask lovers of truth and of our race to give us that trial, and we cannot doubt that they will.

Part Three: Education

From the beginning of the Community, John Humphrey Noyes was committed to education for both men and women. Children were taught by Community members who had previous experience as teachers or who were considered to be expert in a particular subject. Young children attended several hours of schooling in dedicated spaces within the Mansion House and followed a basic curriculum of reading, writing, arithmetic, and geography each day. Adults in the Community frequently formed classes in a variety of subjects. As just one example, when *Uncle Tom's Cabin* was published as a novel in 1852 and reviewed in the *Circular* on May 30, 1852, several Community members read the book and had a series of discussions about it. In 1855, articles in the *Circular* report that adults attended a variety of evening classes in Greek, French, mathematics, and grammar, as well as writing bees. Over time, more systematic courses were arranged for astronomy, mathematics, geography, Latin, French, as well as music, which the members of the Community enjoyed a great deal.[26] The Community valued higher education and several of the young men of the Community were admitted to college and graduated with degrees in engineering, medicine, and law. When the new Mansion House was built in 1862, the library was a source of great pride. Ultimately the wide-ranging collection of books would include some 3500 titles and over one hundred current periodicals. Community members visited the library throughout the day.

Text 26: "Home-Talk—No. 131, Reported July 28, 1850. "Education," [**John Humphrey Noyes**], *Circular*, October 10, 1852, p. 195.

As we understand God's plan, his attention, from the beginning, has been steadily fixed on Education—education combing intellectual with religious culture. He has not been diverted from the single object of preparing a people to receive and propagate his gospel.—It took ages to education the Jewish nation till they had faith enough to receive the gospel, and so it has been with the Gentiles. In looking back at the Reformation, and following on the work then begun, we see that God's great purpose has been to *education the world*.—He has stimulated and prospered education, and constantly sought to develop a spirit that values it. The Reformation commenced in Germany, and there education has reached its greatest height, in schools, colleges, and universities. The spirit of education then invaded England, where it was stimulated by the invention of printing. Then followed the settlement of this country, by men who feared God, and valued education—men who built meeting-houses, school-houses, academies and colleges, and reared their children to fear God, and value education.

The kingdom of god is a *kingdom of education*, not a kingdom of laws: it is a kingdom in which education takes the place of laws.—The political institutions of this country, both before the Revolution and since, have been only provisional governments. God has allowed them to rise to protect the system of education, till it can be *welded* on to the kingdom of heaven. To effect this junction, is the grand business of the church that God is building up, and to which we profess to belong. So, let us regard the educational spirit as our best friend, wherever it is. That is the spirit which will receive us. The real enemy of progress is the *institutional spirit*—the spirit that clings to institutions when they are no longer needed, and are in the way. But the spirit inside of them, the spirit that appreciates education is our friend, and the friend of all improvement. The iniquity of the system of slavery does not consist so much as in the positive oppression of the blacks, as in its depriving them of education. All systems which are opposed to education are false, and must sooner or later decay.

We will take up education where New England has left it. They insist on having meeting-houses, academies, schools, and colleges. We will insist on having a printing-press in every household, so that every branch of education can be cultivated. Instead of having a school part of the time, we will have it constantly and a meeting every day. Every house shall be a college; and instead of an education covering the first few years of a person's life, we will have it go right on eternally. Let us set our helm by this observation, and go for the educational spirit, against the *institutional*. We will not put them together, and cast them both off.—The *educational spirit*, God loves; and he has set up the various institutions of the time to protect it. The institutional spirit is the *shell*, and the educational spirit is the *bird* that is to be hatched; and when the bird is strong enough to break the shell, it must crumble to pieces. The educational and the institutional spirits will at last come into collision. The kingdom of God is in the one, and the kingdom of the devil is in the other; and where the educational spirit is the strongest, the institutional spirit is the weakest; and vice versa. New England is more full of reforms and radicalisms, than all the rest of the country. Notwithstanding the fixedness of character of the New Englander, which makes their institutions very strong, no where else are institutions handled with so much freedom and scrutiny. While in contrast, at the South, where the educational spirit is the weakest, the institutional spirit is the strongest.

Education is the only way out of *law*. A thoroughly educated man may safely do as he pleases. He requires no legal influence to make him do right. Salvation is perfect education—the moulding of character till it is so perfectly harmonized, that it is safe to make a man free. A man once said at Tammany Hall, that he 'would be a tyrant in one thing: he would compel every body to have an education.' I will be a tyrant in the same way: *I will compel all, young and old, to be perfectly education.* Then they may do as they please. That is the tyranny that is exercised in the Association, and the tyranny that some of our good-natured friends complain so much of.—The only way for a man to reach the spot where he has a right to do as he pleases, is to take a thorough education under God. If people were not restrained by law, or external interference, and yet were without education, their own passions would bring them in to the worst kind of bondage. They could not be free if they were alone in the universe. Discordant passions are at war with one another, and restrain one another as to freedom. We have said that *love of the truth is king of our passions*; and we may add, education is the nourisher of love of the truth: so wherever there is the most education, there our king has the largest constituency. Education and love of the truth are to each other, as male and female—truth being the male, and education the female.

The educational spirit is, properly speaking, *the New Jerusalem spirit.* It is the spirit of light opposed to the spirit of darkness. It is the spirit that is friendly to love—that love can rest in. You can love an apple for the time being, but it is soon eaten up; there is no progress of love in it. So a man may love a woman for her natural beauty, comeliness, and pleasant spirit, for a short time. But if she has not a spirit that loves improvement, and is always increasing her beauty, we can only love her as an apple. She must have a spirit of progression, a spirit that is ever producing beauty, or else love toward her will be a temporary thing. That is why beauty in the world is such a perishable article; but introduce the principle of progression, and love is an eternal principle. A woman who knows her own interest, will first of all cultivate the progressive, reproductive spirit in herself; and then she will be able to renew her beauty, and vary its forms, and become more and more attractive eternally.

Part Four: Mutual Criticism

As important as complex marriage was to the Oneida Community, the doctrine of "mutual criticism" was a significant part of the daily lives of the Community members. The origins of mutual criticism can be traced to the Puritan reform of the Church of England. Puritans, who eventually came to America to establish a colony for their independent ideas, believed that it was the responsibility of everyone to share in the responsibility for sin and to expose it where it was found. Puritan clergyman often spent long parts of their sermons in the examination of the sins of the congregation. John Humphrey Noyes was originally a minister of the Congregationalist Church, a direct descendant of the Puritan theology. He was trained in these ideas about the necessity for identifying and rectifying sin. Further Noyes was a citizen of the mid-nineteenth century U.S., which was preoccupied with societal reforms of many kinds: abolition, temperance, prison reform, women's rights, and a host of others. For Ralph Waldo Emerson, a thinker whom Noyes greatly admired, self-criticism was a part of self-cultivation, the idea that the cultivation of the self was the first step toward the cultivation of society as a whole. Noyes developed the idea that mutual criticism was a more communal effort toward the reform of society. Individuals needed to learn both their strengths and weaknesses from their family members. Noyes later published a pamphlet, *Mutual Criticism* (1876) in which he formalized the guidelines that he had developed through the years of the Community. In the first text, [H], the author of an article for the *Circular*, traces the beginnings of mutual criticism in the Oneida Community. The second text provides mutual criticism reports of individuals, which were frequently printed in the pages of the *Circular*.

Text 27: From "Criticism," H. *Circular*, March 21, 1852, p. 74.

Paul praises the brethren at Rome, as 'full of all goodness, filled with all knowledge, *able also to admonish one another*.' We have learned to appreciate this commendation in the progress of our experience as a church. We have found out that the fact of their being able to admonish one another, or as we should say, *criticize* one another, was evidence of the maturity of their spiritual growth. The little school at Putney went through a long discipleship before their system of mutual criticism was originated. The process was perfectly scientific. Love for the truth, and love for each other, had been nurtured and strengthened till it could bear any strain—we could receive criticism kindly, and give it without fear of offending, in the element of tried affection. Association had ripened acquaintance. We had been fed for many years on the truths presented in the Berean—on systematic Bible studies— and had been trained like Timothy, to 'meditate on these things and give ourselves wholly to them.' The Berean was in course of print at the time our first series of criticisms commenced, in the fall of 1846. Our doctrinal basis was finished, and we were studying the true expression of our principles in external forms, and working out salvation from selfishness by the test of circumstances. . . .

Figure 23: The *Circular*
Photo by Jim Demarest

It is a year in our history known among us as the *year of revival*. There was a spring-like awakening of the affections, and a baptism of the spirit of unity which was new and supernatural. It was the precursor, as it proved, of the *spirit of judgment*, another supernatural effusion. This spirit was invited by our new ordinance of

Criticism. And that originated something on this wise: In one of our evening meetings, Mr. Noyes talked about the rending of the veil, which was in prospect, between us and the invisible world, and our expectations of open intercourse with the Primitive Church. But how were we prepared to make music with this glorious company? Our hearts might be in tune, but in beauty of expression we must be for the present extremely awkward and unpractised. We were, in our external characters, comparatively uncivilized—rude and uncultivated in taste and manners—barbarians to the refined society of heaven. But, he said, there was one chord of sympathy between us, one spirit in which we could flow together now, and make music, and that was the *spirit of improvement*. That spirit animates all heaven, and no matter how green we are, it will put us in musical sympathy with every good being in the universe. With this for a beginning, we wanted to increase our points of harmony, and make ourselves attractive to them by all the refinement and civilization of which we were capable; and as one measure, he proposed the plan of mutual criticism, which is now such a pillar in our system. The plan was received with enthusiasm, and one of our most earnest members offered himself immediately as the subject of the first experiment. The others engaged to study his character, get their impressions clear, and bring to the next meeting the verdict of their sincerest scrutiny. We were to tell our whole mind, 'without partiality, and without hypocrisy' 'I nought extenuate, nor set down aught in malice,' but hold up to him as perfect a mirror of his faults as possible. When the affair transpired, we were not prepared for its solemnity. If some of us were sportively disposed in the beginning, we were serious enough before the surgery was over. There was a spirit in our midst, which was like the word of God, 'quick and powerful, and a discerner of the thoughts and intents of the heart.' All that winter we felt that we were in the day of judgment. Criticism had free course, and it was like fire on the tender life. Each in turn submitted to the operation we have described. It was painful in its first application, but agreeable in its results. One brother who has a vivid memory of his sensations, says, that while he was undergoing the process he felt like death, as though he was dissected with a knife; but when it was over, he felt as if he had been *washed*. He said to himself, 'these things are all true, but they are gone, they are washed away.' Criticism is our interpretation of Christ's saying to his disciples, 'If I then your Lord and Master have washed your feet, *ye also out to wash one another's feet*. H.

Text 28: From "A Community Journal: Criticism," *Circular*, March 26, 1863, p. 14.

As before mentioned, this winter has witnessed a revival of criticism in the Community. It is attended with much power and inspiration, and deep, searching discrimination of character. There is also a spirit of kindness and love present, which, while it disarms hardness or evil thinking, gives to the sincere expression of truth that irresistible power which carries conviction to the heart. Old and young alike submit to the ordeal voluntarily.

Criticism in the Community this winter has for the most part taken this form: The person desiring to be criticized selects a committee of four to six persons, who meet and consider the case.— A report is then made out and presented to the general meeting. The case is then open for general expression, by the family. As illustrations we give below two examples of committee reports:

Criticism of Mrs. R.-- Mrs. R. is a kind-hearted, friendly woman. There is much natural dignity, and self-possession in her character. Has a good mind and is quite clear in her intellectual perceptions of truth. But her perceptions of truth are more intellectual than spiritual; more through her mind than through her heart as the result of inspiration. It was though that she placed a higher appreciation on the intellect and intellectual attainments, than on spirituality, and that the same was true in regard to social fellowship. It occupied her attention more than spiritual growth and improvement.

It was thought she was affected somewhat by a complaining spirit in regard to love. She sometimes makes the remark that she hoped the time would come when every one would have all the love they wanted. She seems very desirous that others should love her—thinks it very desirable to be loved—which is all true enough—but she does not sufficiently appreciate the profound blessedness of simply *loving*, whether she is loved in return or not—of being so swallowed up in the element of love—in God—that we can be happy and full of joy and contentment, whether we realize any outward returns or not. It is a good thing to be loved; it is better to *dwell* in love, and love for love's sake only. She has never had her heart thoroughly mellowed by abandonment to the love of Christ. In heart-fellowhip with her, one does not meet that openness of heart into the heavens and God which is the highest and final bliss of love.

It was thought that there was a good deal of pride in her character, and that it had never been thoroughly humbled and subdued. She is self-complacent and whole in her spirit, and it is not easy to bring her into the judgment. Her influence on her children is not of a character to make them humble and receptive. It was mentioned in connection with this, that the faults in the characters of the children, the wholeness and self-complacency which shield them more or less from the judgment, and prevent spiritual growth and mellowness, have their source perhaps more in Mrs. R than in Mr. R; that Mr. R has more of the Puritanic element of sincerity and openness to the judgment—lives more in the sense of the presence of eternal things, than Mrs. R. Her spirit is one which would shield itself and her children under a kid of intellectual self-complacency. She needs to examine her heart in regard to her influence upon her children, and see if she does not lack in righteous earnestness and sincerity.

There were some complaints about her in regard to her work—that though she did well in places of responsibility, yet when she worked with others and under others she was apt to shirk a little; hardly does her share, sometimes, and is not quite conscientious and public-spirited enough.

She needs more of the spirit of charity.—Though a woman of fine mind, and a good critic, she needs the softening influences of love, heart development and spiritual culture, to give her true influence and perceptions, and make her a full Community woman. There is much simplicity about her, which makes her a pleasant companion. Is an improving woman.

Criticism of H.—The committee all agreed in saying H—is a kind-hearted girl, obliging and sisterly and made herself useful to those about her in a great many ways; that she is loyal to the truth and frank—takes criticism well and improves by it. They all said she had improved much within a few years; and that her ill health had been beneficial to her spirit; she is soft-hearted and cheerful under her bodily difficulties. One member thought her late illness, and particularly her fasting from talking, had improved her general state—chastened her life. Leting her life run out in talking, was considered one of her greatest faults. Her flow of life is turned the wrong way; she is then superficial and unedifying. Her apparent effort to make herself agreeable in this superficial way, rather than by good works and meekness, is unedifying; she would be appreciated more, if she was demonstrative. Her conversation is not enough seasoned with serious thought. The chief point for her to improve upon is to be more silent and deep. She should keep herself more reserved, except toward Christ and those who approach her in the name of Christ, and not be open to any little attention that comes along.

The committee liked her new position about dress—heretofore she has had a weakness in that direction; has bestowed too much thought and life upon her dress. She satisfied her conscience by wearing her dresses a long time—fixing over things that some people would throw away—thinking she was economical, and not showy; but there was evidently something in her dress that attracted attention and set a fashion. Her way of dressing her hair had the same effect. It was thought that she could lay out her strength in a more edifying way. She had too high an estimate of outward adorning, and should seek the inward adorning recommended by Paul. She is fond of poetry—gets excited sometimes in praise of something she likes, and over-does the matter. In short, she is too demonstrative in everything—should keep the edge of modest on all expression.

Part Five: Community Property and Legal Obligations

In 1864, the attention of the Oneida Community was fixed on a series of unpleasant incidents John Noyes called the "Mills War." William Mills, about the same age as Noyes, had joined in 1857. Seceding shortly after, he demanded the return of his money with interest and the Community complied. Somehow he obtained re-admission on a probationary basis about 1859. Over the succeeding five years, he made "a nuisance and a stench" of himself endlessly importuning the females for sex (unsuccessfully, they said) "by boring, goading and forcing." Noyes detested Mills as "the meanest human parasite we have ever encountered."[27]

Figure 24: Jessie Kinsley (1858-1938)

Eventually, Mills "was carefully set out of doors." "I heard sudden angry shouts and a struggle," young Jessie Kinsley (**Figure 24**) remembered years later. "Then from the window came into view the sight of a man thrown by other men into a snow drift--violently thrown, without excuses. I saw the man emerge, pick up the things that had been thrown out with him, and walk away sending back loud, angry words and burning glances, shaking his fist as he shouted. That was the last act, I believe, of 'The Mills War.'" Mills was the only person forcibly expelled from the Community and even this ejection could only be effected with a substantial cash settlement for the miscreant.[28]

The Mills War caused the Community to tighten admission policies and to rethink the nature of legal protection for the organization. Since the beginning, it had been understood that all members ceded all property to the associative whole. If the individual seceded, his or her property would be returned. "This practice, however," it was explained in the Community's first annual report, "stands on the ground, not of obligation but of expediency and liberality; and the time and manner of refunding must be trusted to the discretion of the Association. While a person remains a member, his subsistence and education in the Association are held to be just equivalents for his labor; and no accounts are kept between him and the Association, and no claim of wage accrues to him in case of subsequent withdrawal."[29]

That arrangement, it was now clear, did not accord adequate protection from suits for back wages. Nor did it discourage the efforts of former members more inclined toward blackmail and extortion. To better protect the organization, the Bible Communists now chartered the Oneida Community as a legal entity owned by four individuals: John Noyes, Erastus Hamilton, William Woolworth, and Otis Kellogg. "It was understood at all times that this arrangement was merely one of convenience," according to Holton Noyes. "Really every member had equal ownership in the property under communism."[30]

Nevertheless, there must have been general suspicion that there was still inadequate protection against legal attack. One of the first things lawyer Towner did on joining the Community was to look into this problem. The measure he suggested was to have everyone promise not to seek enrichment by lodging a court suit against the Oneida Community. Accordingly, he drew up this document stating that no one would ever "bring any action, either at law or in equity, or other process or proceeding whatsoever against said Community...nor make any claim or demand... of any kind or nature whatsoever." Towner then solicited the signature of every adult

Figure 25: The Oneida Community's Agreement Not to Sue Handwritten Scroll. Photo by Jim Demarest

to this statement, then continued to update and collect signatures through 1880. Altogether, there are about 250 signed names affixed to this document beginning with that of John Noyes.

Whether the agreement had any actual effect is unknown of course. It should be remembered in this connection that during the bitterly divisive period of the breakup, Oneida Community members found—remarkably--the good will to reach peaceful agreement on profound and complicated issues. Perhaps some of that amity in division is attributable to the influence of this pledge.

This document, in the form of a handwritten scroll (**Figure 25**) signed by Noyes and dozens of community members, is not mentioned in Community writings. Whatever the force of law in such an agreement, it was regarded by former Bible Communists and their offspring as important enough to be deposited for safekeeping in the fireproof vault of Oneida Ltd.'s administrative building sometime after 1926. It lay there for years—presumably forgotten—until rediscovered by Community descendant Rhoda Vanderwall in 2014. [31]

Text 29: The Oneida Community's Agreement Not to Sue by [James W. Towner]

Whereas, the society called the Oneida Community, having its headquarters at or near the village of Oneida, County of Madison, and State of New York, and branches at Wallingford, State of Connecticut, and other places, was founded by John H. Noyes and others for the purpose of religious fellowship and discipline; and

Whereas, it has been and is the agreement of the members of the said Oneida Community, and of all its branches, by and with each other, that on the admission of any member all property belonging to him or her becomes the joint property of the Community, and of all its members, and the education, subsistence, clothing, and other necessaries of life furnished to members and their children in the Community are agreed and held to be just equivalents for all labor performed, and services rendered, and property contributed, no accounts being kept between any member and the Community, or between individual members, and no claim for wages accruing to him or her in case of subsequent withdrawal; and

Whereas, it has heretofore been the practice of the Community to keep a record of the estimated amount or value of the property put in by every member joining the Community, and to refund the same or an equivalent amount or value, without interest, use, or increase, in case of the subsequent voluntary withdrawal of the member

Yet, as this practice stands, and has always stood on the ground, not of obligation, but of good-will and liberality, the time and manner of refunding such property or its value resting entirely in the discretion of the Community through the voice of its members, who may also discontinue this custom of refunding at any time they see fit, or refuse in any case to refund all or any part of such property contributed by any member, upon or after his or her withdrawal, at their pleasure; and

Whereas, it is also agreed that on the death of a member, or his or her expulsion for just cause, the Community, its trustees, officers, or other representatives are not bound to refund all or any part of the property contributed by such member, to his heirs, executors, administrators, or assigns;

Therefore, we, the undersigned, acknowledge the above as the terms of our connection with and membership in the Oneida Community and all its branches now existing or that may hereafter exist and we severally for ourselves, our heirs, executors, administrators, and assigns do agree and covenant with it, and with its members, and with each other, and with the present property holders thereof, and their successors in office, that neither we nor our heirs, executors, administrators or assigns, will ever bring any action, either at law or in equity, or other process or proceeding whatsoever against said Community or its branches, or against the agents or property-holders thereof, or any person or corporation, for wages or other compensation for service, nor for the recovery of any property by us or either of us contributed to the funds or property of said Community or its branches, on or before our entering the same, or at any subsequent time, nor make any claim or demand there—for, of any kind or nature whatsoever.

In witness whereof, we have hereunto set our hands and seals this Eighteenth day of August 1875.

Signed and sealed in presence of J. W. Towner

Notes

1. The publication history of this treatise is as follows: *First Annual Report of the Oneida Association: Exhibiting Its History, Principles, and Transactions to Jan. 1, 1849* (Oneida Reserve, N.Y." Oneida Association, 1849), 18-42; *Bible Communism: A Compilation from the Annual Reports and Other Publications of the Oneida Association and Its Branches* (Brooklyn, N.Y.: Office of Circular, 1853), 24-64. *The First Annual Report* (including *Bible Argument*) was reprinted as the Appendix (295-361 in Lawrence Foster, Ed., *Free Love in Utopia: John Humphrey Noyes and the Origin of the Oneida Community, Compiled by George Wallingford Noyes* (Urbana: University of Illinois Press, 2001), 295-361. The latest reprint is in Anthony Wonderley, ed. *John Humphrey Noyes on Sexual Relations in the Oneida Community: Four Essential Texts* (Hamilton College Library, Clinton, NY: Richard S. Couper Press, 2012), 53-91.
2. See Wonderley, *John Humphrey Noyes on Sexual Relations in the Oneida Community: Four Essential Texts* (Hamilton College Library, Clinton, NY: Richard S. Couper Press, 2012), 73-78.
3. Wonderley, *John Humphrey Noyes on Sexual Relations*, 79.
4. Wonderley, *John Humphrey Noyes on Sexual Relations*, 80.
5. Wonderley, *John Humphrey Noyes on Sexual Relations*, 68.
6. Wonderley, *John Humphrey Noyes on Sexual Relations*, 65. This, incidentally, may be the only passage in which Noyes apparently makes reference to the existence of homosexuality. The documentary record of Oneida is essentially silent in this regard.
7. Wonderley, *John Humphrey Noyes on Sexual Relations*, 61 ("the intimate union") and 63 ("the love-relation").
8. Wonderley, *John Humphrey Noyes on Sexual Relations*, 70.
9. Oneida Community, *First Annual Report of the Oneida Association: Exhibiting Its History, Principles, and Transactions to Jan. 1, 1849* (Oneida Reserve, NY: Oneida Association, 1849), 11-12, and *Bible Communism: A Compilation from the Annual Reports of the Oneida Association and Its Branches* (Brooklyn, NY: Office of the Circular, 1853), 7.
10. Richard DeMaria, *Communal Love at Oneida: A Perfectionist Vision of Authority, Property, and Sexual Order* (New York: Mellen Press, 1978), 104.
11. Robert Allerton Parker, *A Yankee Saint: John Humphrey Noyes and the Oneida Community* (New York: G. P. Putnam's Sons, 1935), 184.
12. *Daily Journal,* September 5, 1866.
13. "A happy religion" according to Pierrepont Burt Noyes, *My Father's House: An Oneida Boyhood* (New York: Farrar and Rinehart, 1937),

138; "not on the side of asceticism" quoted from *Circular*, April 4, 1852, 273-275 and *Circular*, August 21, 1862, 113-114; Wonderley, *John Humphrey Noyes on Sexual Relations*, 64-65.

14. Wonderley, *John Humphrey Noyes on Sexual Relations*, 79.
15. William T. La Moy, "Two Documents Detailing the Oneida Community's Practice of Complex Marriage," *New England Quarterly* 135 (no. 1, 2012), 125, 132; Herrick quoted from Carl Carmer, *Listen for a Lonesome Drum: York State Chronicle* (Syracuse: Syracuse University Press, 1995 [or. 1936]), 197; Stephen R. Leonard, Jr., "Recollections," photocopy of unpublished manuscript (Oneida Community Mansion House Archives, ca. 1951), 1. The popular woman was Tirzah Miller as cited in Spencer Klaw, *Without Sin: The Life and Death of the Oneida Community* (New York: Allen Lane, Penguin Press, 1993), 176.
16. Wonderley, *John Humphrey Noyes on Sexual Relations*, 79; Allan Estlake (pseudonym of Abel Easton), *The Oneida Community: A Record of an Attempt to Carry Out the Principles of Christian Unselfishness and Scientific Improvement* (London: George Redway, 1900), 90; P. B. Noyes, My Father's House, 131.
17. Wonderley, *John Humphrey Noyes on Sexual Relations*, 68-69, 72, 75, 77-78, 80-82.
18. John B. Teeple, *The Oneida Family Genealogy of a 19th Century Perfectionist Commune* (Oneida, NY: Oneida Community Historical Committee, Mansion House, 1985), 128; Taylor Stoehr, *Free Love in America: A Documentary History* (New York: AMS, 1979), 35.
19. P. B. Noyes, *My Father's House*, 215.
20. Constance Noyes Robertson, *Oneida Community: The Breakup, 1876-1881* (Syracuse, NY: Syracuse University Press, 1972), 126.
21. Anthony Wonderley, *Oneida Utopia: A Community Searching for Human Happiness and Prosperity* (Ithaca: Cornell University Press, 2017), 164 nt7; Corinna Ackley Noyes, *The Days of My Youth* (Hamilton College Library, Clinton, NY: Richard W. Cooper Press, 2011; originally published 1960), 151-52; Holton V. Noyes, "A History of the Oneida Community Limited," unpublished typescript, ca. 1930, Oneida Community Mansion House Archives, 44; Spencer C. Olin, Jr. "Bible Communism and the Origins of Orange County, California." *California History* 58 (Fall 1979), 220-32.
22. Helen Lefkowitz Horowitz, *Rereading Sex: Battles over Sexual Knowledge and Repression in Nineteenth-Century America* (New York: Alfred A. Knopf, 2002), 6, 49-52.
23. Arthur Bestor, *Backwoods Utopias: The Sectarian Origins and the Owenite Phase of Communitarian Socialism in America, 1663-1829*, 2nd enlarged ed. (Philadelphia: University of Pennsylvania Press, 1970;

originally published 1950.), 160-201; Edward K. Spann, *Brotherly Tomorrows: Movements for a Cooperative Society in America, 1820-1920* (New York: Columbia University Press, 1989), 29-49; Chris Jennings, *Paradise Now: The Story of American Utopianism* (New York: Random House, 2016), 79-148; Wonderley, Oneida Utopia, 43, 66.

24. Mark Holloway, *Heavens on Earth: Utopian Communities in America, 1680-1880*, 2nd ed. (1951; New York: Dover, 1966), 53; Louis J. Kern, "Breaching the 'Wall of Partition between the Male and the Female': John Humphrey Noyes and Free Love," *Syracuse University Library Associates Courier* 28 (Fall 1993), 89n9; Emanuel Swedenborg, *A Compendium of the Theological and Spiritual Writings of Emanuel Swedenborg: Being a Systematic and Orderly Epitome of All His Religious Works* (Boston: Crosby, Nichols, and Otis Clapp, 1854), 300; Jocelyn Godwin, *Upstate Cauldron: Eccentric Spiritual Movements in Early New York State* (Albany: SUNY Press, Excelsior Editions, 2015), 127-28.

25. Whitney R. Cross, *The Burned-Over District: The Social and Intellectual History of Enthusiastic Religion in Western New York, 1800-1850* (Cornell University Press, 1950), 345-49; Hubbard Eastman, Noyesism Unveiled: *A History of the Sect Self-Styled Perfectionists* (Brattleboro, VT: the author, 1849), 254; Hal D. Sears, *The Sex Radicals: Free Love in High Victorian America* (Lawrence: Regents Press of Kansas, 1977), 7-8.

26. See Spencer Klaw, *Without Sin: The Life and Death of the Oneida Community* (New York, Penguin, 1993), p. 92-99 for a discussion of the various activities of the Community, including educational practices.

27. *Circular,* November 14, 1864, 273-275; December 26, 1864, 323-324; and February 6, 1865, 396-370.

28. *Circular*, December 19, 1864, 313-314 ("set out of doors"); Rich, *A Lasting Spring*, 18 ("I heard sudden angry shouts"); Circular, February 27, 1865 (the only person forcibly expelled).

29. Oneida Community, *First Annual Report*, 16.

30. H. V. Noyes, "*A History of the Oneida Community, Limited*," 7-8.

31. This untitled document in the form of a handwritten scroll is filed (accession number 2014.004.008) in the archives of the Oneida Community Mansion House.

Chapter 4. Business

While most of the utopian communities established in the nineteenth century were based on agriculture, John Humphrey Noyes was shrewdly aware that farming could not be the sole basis for the economic success of the Community. He and the members of the Community developed what would today be called a business plan and modified it as conditions and circumstances changed. Ultimately, the Community had a saw mill, a grist mill, a foundry, a silk mill, a trap factory, and workshops for a number of home industries. For many years, the economic engine of the Community was the animal trap business, but the members developed a variety of other business ventures including the manufacturing of travel bags, farm implements and tools, household tools such as mops and brooms, silk thread, small wooden boxes for storage, and a variety of canned fruits and vegetables. In the late 1870s, they began to experiment with manufacturing flatware, which would eventually become the basis for Oneida Ltd. the company that was formed after the breakup of the Community. Their location, originally close to the Erie Canal and then to the railroad made it possible to transport goods easily, and they employed large numbers of people in the surrounding areas. The texts in this section are evidence of the variety of ways in which the Community developed ways to finance their home and lifestyle.

Part One: Trap Manufacturing

For decades, trap manufacturing was the central economic support of the Community. In the text below, the history of the trap business is recounted in the series, "One of the Four: "A Memoir of Charlotte A. Miller." Beginning with the traps made by Sewall Newhouse and culminating with the large manufacturing facility built to produce the traps, the business boomed during the thirty years the Community operated as a communitarian society. Initially, the traps were hand-forged but soon the Community developed a method for automating the production. By 1857, the Community was producing some twenty-six thousand traps a year; later the figure would rise to two hundred thousand units a year. The successful trap business brought economic stability to the Community and made it possible to build the large Mansion House in 1862 and the subsequent buildings the formed the house in later years. Further, the trap business provided opportunities for many people in the surrounding area as many non-Community members were employed in the business.

Text 30: [Sewall Newhouse and the Trap Business] "A Community Transplanted. From Putney to Oneida, VI," *American Socialist*, September 18, 1879, p. 301.

Mr. Burt, as we have said, owned a small saw-mill, and this forlorn hope of infant Associations was a great treasure to us at the start. We had our nest to build,

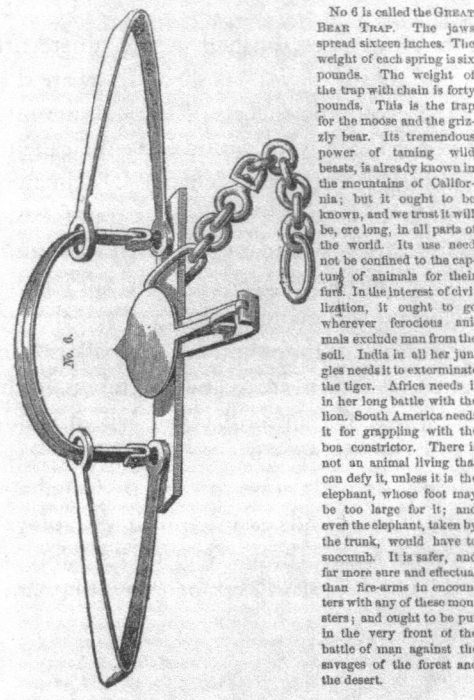

THE GREAT BEAR TAMER!

No 6 is called the GREAT BEAR TRAP. The jaws spread sixteen inches. The weight of each spring is six pounds. The weight of the trap with chain is forty pounds. This is the trap for the moose and the grizzly bear. Its tremendous power of taming wild beasts, is already known in the mountains of California; but it ought to be known, and we trust it will be, ere long, in all parts of the world. Its use need not be confined to the capture of animals for their furs. In the interest of civilization, it ought to go wherever ferocious animals exclude man from the soil. India in all her jungles needs it to exterminate the tiger. Africa needs it in her long battle with the lion. South America needs it for grappling with the boa constrictor. There is not an animal living that can defy it, unless it is the elephant, whose foot may be too large for it; and even the elephant, taken by the trunk, would have to succumb. It is safer, and far more sure and effectual than fire-arms in encounters with any of these monsters; and ought to be put in the very front of the battle of man against the savages of the forest and the desert.

Fig; 26: Newhouse's "Great Bear Tamer" trap

and the saw-mill furnished sticks and straws. Then it helped build a great industrial edifice (we thought it great till it was dwarfed by later buildings for the same purpose), in which it got new quarters for itself, and which contained a grist-mill and carpenters' shop, a printing-office, and indefinite space for thick-coming fancies in the eye mechanical of the young Community. There the manufacture of the Newhouse trap (**Figure 26**) was developed and grew, till monopolizing room and power, it pushed out the grist-mill, and the old faithful saw-mill itself was finally displaced.

Dixon says that Mr. Newhouse was "the founder of our fortunes." That would be a great deal to admit, but it certainly was a part of our good luck in coming here to get into connection with him. His name had been on the subscription-book of our Putney periodicals for eight or ten years, and such an odd name it was—"Sewell Newhouse"—we could not easily forget it. But that was all we knew about him till we came to Oneida. The first summer we lived here we occupied three different houses, and had no room in either of them large enough for a full gathering; so our immemorial evening meeting had a temporary suspension of several months at that time. The little Indian hut, in which Mr. Noyes lived, frequently witnessed a kind of levee at the usual hour, so many of us calling that bed and windowsills, doorsteps and floor, added to the chairs, could not furnish us seats, and one person after sitting awhile would go out and give place to another. But every Sunday afternoon we had a meeting in full, on a barn floor cleanly swept and furnished extemporized benches from the ever-handy saw-mill. Here strangers from the neighborhood occasionally stepped in. One day a well dressed, pleasant appearing couple alighted from a carriage, and the horse being hitched they came up to the door. Mr. Burt knew them by name, and introduced them as Mr. and Mrs. Newhouse from Oneida Castle. Not many months after they joined the Community.

Mr. Newhouse had made a moderate living outside by the manufacture of steel-traps. His family came to this state from Massachusetts when he was about

14 years old. The country was new, and the woods and steams abounded in game. He was a boy for the place, full of the hunter's instincts, very fond of the gun and trap. The trap then in vogue did not suit him, and he set himself to make a better, and succeeded so well that a local demand for his traps soon sprung up, and he found he had a trade. His tools were a blacksmith's forge and anvil, a hand-punch, a swaging mold, a hammer and file. The extent of his manufacture was from one to two thousand traps a year. We find in the "Trapper's Guide," published by the Community some years ago,[1] a sketch of Mr. Newhouse from which we make a short quotation:

> "The characteristics which Mr. Newhouse possesses as a mechanic are, a critical eye, sound judgment of material relations, nicety of hand, and a conscientious attention to the minutiae of any mechanism on which so often its working depends. As a trap-maker his original idea was to make faultless traps, and nothing could swerve him from this point. His solicitude has been that they should catch game, whether they caught custom or not. The reputation which has come to him on this basis has made it seem desirable to other manufacturers in some instances to pirate his name for the sake of giving currency to their imitations of the 'Newhouse Traps.' But this quality of particularity, so valuable in the pursuit of excellence, if not combined with other talents does not always lead to great business success; and the Oneida trap-maker would perhaps have scarcely risen above a local celebrity but for the introduction of him and his business to a new element of energy and enterprise in the Oneida Community."

In receiving Mr. Newhouse as a member, the Community had no thought of adopting his business; and his tools and his genius lay idle for the most part for the ensuing five or six years, he finding employment in the gardens and nurseries which was somewhat congenial to his taste. Meanwhile a dozen of our young men had been getting an education in the machine-shops of Newark, New Jersey, and in 1855 the manufacturing destiny of the Community began to make a "humming in the tissues" of our dreams. Mr. Noyes had come on from a three-years' publishing campaign in Brooklyn, and was hungry for some diversion in the way of physical labor. About the same time came inquiries for Mr. Newhouse's trap from New York City and Chicago. Mr. Noyes, with that instinctive sagacity which makes him trusted in the Community as well nigh infallible in business counsel, directed attention to this opening, and the manufacture of traps was started. It were a long story to tell from beginning to end the growth of the trap business, from the time when it occupied a shop twenty-five by fifteen and was carried on by three men (J. H. N. being one), without water or steam or mechanical appliances only such as a good blacksmith has, till when it filled a great brick factory and the invention of machinery had reduced hand-labor in it to a minimum. Suffice it to say, that the average number of traps made now by the O. C. *daily* is equal to what Mr. Newhouse made in a year.

The trade was a lucky thing for us, but Mr. Newhouse himself would have been a treasure without the trade. To the sanguine eye of the Community there is a providence in the character of every particular member. Each individuality contributes to the perfection of the body. Each member is a "medium;" and Mr. Newhouse is our medium with Nature. We would keep in rapport with modern civilization the most elevated and *recherché*; but we would not lose our connection with the wild and primitive, or the barbaric if you please. We would know how to enjoy palatial luxury, everything good and beautiful that art has achieved—we would be at home in the precincts of a college—and yet we would not lose the woodman's tastes and pleasures. Mr. Newhouse is not a Hoosier, nor typical trapper in speech and manners; but love of the woods is ever green in his breast, and he keeps it green in the Community, inoculating every generation of boys with a taste for woodcraft. We should scarcely have had a Joppa (our cottage on the lake) but for Mr. Newhouse. From a boy he had haunted the lakeshore, and when we felt the need of rough refreshment, he knew the place for our cabin; he knew where there were friendly people, and where wood and lake and river combined to make it delightful.

Part Two: Farming, Fruit, and Canning

Many of the utopian communities of the nineteenth century began their ventures dependent on agriculture—specifically farming—for subsistence and income. But few of the adherents of those communities had the expertise to develop long term strategies for survival, especially those established in the northeast where weather was often problematic. For the Oneida Community, farming on their hundreds of acres was always going to be just one means of economic survival in their plan for an income from diversified ventures. In an article for the *Circular* on January 8, 1857, a community member made a distinction between "agriculture" and "horticulture." They grew as many fruits and vegetables as they could but limited the number of animals

Fig; 27: Strawberries Label

they held. Since the Community members consumed almost no meat, this plan suited them very well and provided a concentrated effort on their main crops. The Community was successful, this member explained, because they concentrated their efforts on plants and not animals. In addition to growing much of their own food, they also developed means to can and preserve vegetables and fruit for regional markets. Eventually, they also bought fruits and vegetables and canned them in their own facilities where they employed dozens of people from the surrounding areas. By the 1860s, the Community was well known for its quality fruits, especially strawberries, which they celebrated each year with a festival, to which neighbors in the surrounding areas were invited, including members of the Oneida Nation. In the following articles from the *Oneida Circular,* James Towner describes a lawsuit brought against the Oneida Community for patent infringement in their production of canned corn. The suit, eventually settled in their favor by the Supreme Court of the United States, shows the sophisticated legal, technological, and food production expertise of the members of the Community.

Text 31: "Corn Packing: Patent Litigation [1]," J.W.T. [James W. Towner], *Oneida Circular,* **November 23, 1874, p. 380.**

The policy of the Community ever has been and is to avoid litigation. We seldom resort to it for the collection of debts, and when threatened with the prosecution of apparently unjust claims, we prefer to yield somewhat for the sake of procuring a compromise, or to find some equitable ground of settlement, rather than be involved in the uncertainty and strife of legal proceedings. Yet to manifestly unjust and groundless claims we do not feel called upon to tamely submit. If by resisting them we see that we are vindicating the truth we are ready to do so at any sacrifice.

In July last, without previous warning, process was served upon us from the Circuit Court of the United States for the Northern District of New York, summoning us to answer the bill of complaint in equity in that court of one John W. Jones and others of Portland, Me., for infringement of two patents for preserving Indian corn in its green state in hermetically sealed cans. The complainants claimed the exclusive right under these patents to thus preserve green corn, and claimed it as the invention of one Isaac Winslow, dating his invention in the year 1842. We had been engaged in the business of preserving corn in sealed cans for domestic use and for market for many years without molestation, or objection even, from any one; and had carried it on in connection with, and as a part of, our general business of packing and preserving fruits and vegetables. We began in that business as early as 1854, and almost wholly through the investigations and experiments of our own members, learned the art of such preservation and established a successful business in that line, and as is well known, our canned goods have achieved a high reputation in market for superior quality, and reliability for keeping a long time. For years we knew nothing of the so-called Winslow invention, and successfully preserved green corn before we ever heard of it.

As readers of the CIRCULAR may know, we made no secret of the art, but on the contrary published in the columns of our paper from time to time, especially during the last ten years, all the information we had obtained, for the benefit of the public. Least of all, did we suspect we were violating any one's rights or infringing any patent. In 1864, we learned that a man in Portland, Me., named Jones, claimed a patent right on canning corn, and that he had sued in New York city, parties who were engaged in packing and selling that article, for infringement of that right. But soon afterward we learned that he dismissed and abandoned his suit, and hearing more from it, supposed his pretended claim was abandoned also. We continued in the business as before. In 1866, two of our members having invented a machine for cutting corn from the cob for canning, and obtained a patent for it, knowing as we did, that a large business of corn-canning was carried on in Portland and vicinity, we sent one of them in September of that year to that place with the machine for the purpose of introducing it into use with corn-packers. He went for that purpose to the factories of the present complainants, Jones having sold shares in the patents to others, and had interviews with them on the subject, and though they were advised that we too were canning corn, no one made any objection to it, nor claimed any patent, nor even mentioned a patent, except that one said that Jones claimed to have something of that sort, but he (the speaker) did not believe it was good for any thing. Two years later, this same man came to our factory to see us about buying a right to the corn-cutting machine, and went through it and saw what we were doing (we were then engaged in putting up corn), and made no objection, not even intimating any intention of setting up any claim to the exclusive right to do that business.

It has since transpired that at that time a suit on these patents was pending in the U.S. Circuit Court for Maine, and that this man had become a party to it. This suit was commenced in November 1867, but lingered along and was not tried till 1872, nor decided till 1873, in May. We first heard of this suit early in 1873, and in April of that year sent one of our members to Portland to ascertain what Jones and others claimed, being desirous of avoiding all difficulty, if any were possible. He saw and had an interview with one of the complainants on the subject and from all the information he could get he and we came to the conclusion that the methods we used in canning corn was no infringement of their patents, even if they should prove to be valid. The case referred to was decided in favor of the patents by Judge Clifford who presides on that Circuit, but no question as to infringement was tried or raised in that case. We continued in the business that year without notice of any objection to our process, and made extensive preparations to prosecute it this year, and had no notice or knowledge of any objection to it until legal process was served upon us as before stated. Then, but a few weeks before the time of canning corn, when we had fifty acres of corn or thereabouts on our hands, suit was commenced against us by these parties who had slept upon their pretended rights for years with a full knowledge of our doings in the premises, and an injunction was asked, restraining us from further working in that business and from dealing in the article.

In their complaint and in the affidavits filed in support of their motion for an injunction, they charged us with knowing of their exclusive right to preserve green corn, with belonging to a combination of persons who were infringing their patents, organized to resist any steps which they might take to enforce their rights, with offering to undersell their corn in the Market, and with injuring their trade by offering inferior corn, with many other things of like character, all and every one of which were untrue. They also charged us with manufacturing an article substantially like their and by the same process. We could not but resist their summary application for an injunction, with such evidence as we were able to obtain to rebut their charges. A hearing was had and a decision has just been rendered by Judge Wallace of Syracuse, in our favor, denying an injunction on two grounds; first, because the complainants have not shown an infringement on our part, and secondly, because of their own conduct in neglecting so long to prosecute their claims, knowing as they did what we were doing. The case is yet to be tried, if further prosecuted by the complainants, upon its merits, with what probably result we will not now undertake to say. Numerous suits have been commenced by them against packers and dealers throughout the country. In many cases they have been allowed injunctions without contest, the parties sued not being directly interested to an extent sufficient to warrant it. In other cases, where resistance has been made, the complainants have failed as in ours. Much interest is felt, and an appeal has been taken to the Supreme Court of the United States from the decision of Judge Clifford in Maine, and that appeal will probably be heard during the coming winter. We give these facts as a contribution to current knowledge upon a subject in which many people feel a deep and abiding interest. It is difficult to avoid the feeling that these complainants, whose patents were issued in 1862, and who have not sought to enforce them till this late day, except as above stated, but have waited till green corn, like other canned goods, through the independent efforts of numerous persons in different parts of the country who have invested large amounts of capital in the business, with little or no objection, has become an article of common consumption and a staple in market, are setting up a stale and unfounded claim, and one that in equity ought not to be supported.

J.W.T.

Text 32: "Corn Packing: Patent Litigation [2]," J.W.T. [James W. Towner], *Oneida Circular***, December 27, 1875, p. 412.**

In our paper of Nov. 23, 1874, may be found an article under the above heading, giving a detailed account of a suit in equity commenced against us, seeking an injunction to restrain us from carrying on the preserving of green corn in cans, which is one of the principal branches of our fruit and vegetable-preserving business. Reference was there made to a case which had been decided in Maine, sustaining certain patents granted covering an alleged invention of such preserved corn, and of the process of preserving the same, claimed to have been made by one Isaac Winslow. That case was appealed to the Supreme Court of the United States and has but lately been heard and decided. The Supreme Court reverses the decision of the Circuit Court for the District of Maine and holds that the Winslow patents are void for want of novelty of invention. To make a patent granted to a person valid, he must be not only a true or actual inventor, but an *original* inventor as well.

The Supreme Court holds in this case, that the invention claimed by Winslow for preserving corn in hermetically sealed cans, was anticipated substantially in England, in 1810, by a patent granted there to one Durand, and also in France by the discovery of M. Appert, an account of which was published in 1814 in No. 45 of the Edinburgh Review, and also in Rees's Cyclopedia in Philadelphia, Pa., published in Nos., from 1810 to 1824. Winslow was in France about the year 1842, the time of his pretended invention, and it was alleged that he learned the process there; which allegation the Supreme Court considers probably true.

Mr. Justice Hunt pronounced the decision, and all the Judges concurred, except Justice Clifford, who dissented. He rendered the decision below and could hardly be expected to do otherwise. Thus ends what at one time threatened to be a long and vexatious litigation, injurious to an important interest.

We can not, refrain, in conclusion, from noticing what seems a radical fault in the Patent Office. Winslow claimed to have made his discovery in 1842. In 1853 he applied for a patent, and his application was rejected for want of novelty. He assigned his interest in the invention to J. Winslow Jones, a relative, who was engaged with him in the manufacture of canned corn; and in 1863, Jones made another application and succeeded somehow in getting four patents; one for the product, viz., Indian corn preserved green, and three for different features of the process. Jones rested till 1867 with his patents, except in one instance, in New York, where he sought to set them up, but finally abandoned his suit. Then he commenced his suit in Maine which dragged along in court for five or six years. In the mean time he assigned shares in the patents to three others and finally in Nov., 1872, the four assigned the whole interest in trust to their attorney in the case, Wm. Henry Clifford, son of Justice Clifford who held the Circuit Court in Maine; and in the following spring the case was brought to a hearing and a decree rendered sustaining two of the patents, one for the product, and the other for the process. Armed with this decision, Jones, Clifford, et al. began, as stated in our former article, to prosecute all over the country, those engaged in the canning business. Some who could not afford to resist them allowed injunctions to go against them and paid royalty on the business. Those who resisted have been subject to large expense in money and time, and all to defend themselves against a claim with the highest court of the land now, with the exception of Justice Clifford, pronounces baseless and void, and which the Patent Office should never have countenanced at all. Our readers will, we believe, rejoice with us that the right has triumphed at last.

J.W.T.

Part Three: The Silk Thread Business

While the manufacturing of traps was the central business venture of the Oneida Community, John Humphrey Noyes felt that diversifying the Community's business was important for its longevity. Early efforts to develop a sewing machine date back to the 18th century, but in the 19th century, significant developments served to transform the clothing industry. The invention of the sewing machine by Elias Howe in 1846 and then the refinements made by Isaac Singer in 1851 set the stage for a new approach to making clothes and home goods. Noyes saw an opportunity; sewing machines would need spools of thread, and he began the process of researching a new business for the Community in 1865. Some members of the Community served as apprentices in silk twist manufacturers and brought their new skills back to the Mansion House. By 1866, the Oneida Community was producing its own, high quality silk thread. Another successful business was supporting the members of the Community.

Text 33: "Silk-Manufacturing in the O.C.: Its Conception," by C.A.C. [Charles A. Cragin], *Circular***, December 3, 1866, p. 299.**

[Editor's Note: Our people at Oneida have long been engaged in selling silk; but have only just commenced manufacturing it. Some very beautiful specimens of their work having reached this office, we asked for the story of the enterprise. Those engaged in it have built their machinery and learned the trade within nine months; and must have exploits to tell, as worthy of being sung as those of Homer's heroes. Here is the first book of the Silkiad. We regret that it is not put up in verse; but our poet has only got so far as 'base-ball." (See p. 301). That is better sport than war, to be sure, but not half so good as wide-awake work:]

The month of December 1865 was spent by J.H Noyes at Oneida. It was a season of severe but victorious struggles with the powers of darkness, which "the whole Community moved as one man." Near the middle of this period, Dec. 19th, the project of Silk-manufacturing had its conception. On that day J.H.N., accompanied by E.H Hamilton, went over to the Willow-Place Factory. Half a dozen of the leading business men were called into the office to hear a new business proposition.

Fig. 28: Silk Twist Logo

J.H.N. spoke as follows: "I have a new project to present to you. Thinking of our financial situation, I see we need some business to fill the place of the Trap-trade when that is dull. Trap-making cannot be relied upon as a steady business. Sometimes the trade is good, and at others there is scarcely any. We want something that will bring us an income when the Trap business does not. We have a splendid building here, and more room than is needed for Trap-making; a first-rate water-power, and a well-manned machine-shop. Now I propose that we go into the manufacture of silk. We shall meet competition in whatever business we take up, and probably as little in this as in any. Our agents say that it would be a great advantage in selling silk to manufacture it ourselves. This will accord, too, with our principle of doing away with the services of middle men as fast as possible, so that the producer and consumer may come together. And making the requisite machinery will be a fine job for the machine-shop, and foundry. Our head machinist, Mr.Inslee, was brought up among such machinery; were you not, Mr. Inslee?"

Mr. Inslee,--"Yes, sir. I was put to work in a cotton factory when I was eight years old; at fourteen, I went into a machine-shop where that kind of machinery was made and repaired, and worked there till I was past thirty."

J.H.N.—"Then this job would be just in your line. I understand that there is some talk among our men of taking a contract for manufacturing a lot of horse pitch-forks. From some things I have heard about it, I am not very favorably impressed by the proposal. I am told that it is a recent invention, and the patentee wishes you to make two or three thousand of them and have you wait for your pay till he sells them—probably some time next summer, if something better is not got up meantime to supersede it. And then, too, in this kind of jobbing you do not control your work; you are, in a sense hired out."

After some further talk the session closed.

In the evening meeting of the same day, J.H.N. delivered a discourse on manufactures, in which he proved that the machine-shop is really the foundation of our business prosperity and success. Then he spoke of the languishing condition of that department, and sought out the hidden, spiritual cause. He thus concluded:

"Now I wish to seek the truth on this subject with a view to our future course; and my vote is given for invigorating the machine-shop, as the mother of all our past manufactures, and to be the mother of new enterprises in the future.

"I have been talking with John Lord about what he and others connected with the silk business have long desired, i.e., the starting of a silk manufactory. They think it would greatly improve their trade if they could be certain of the quality of the article they sell. There is a numerous class who will not buy when they find you are only dealing in an article at secondhand; as they act upon the principle, which seems to be a good one, of going to the manufacture for their goods. It is evidently desirable that we should manufacture our own silk in order to make the most of the business. Mr. Lord was going to Boston; so I asked him to find out what had become of the old Morrisville Silk Manufacturing Co., and in the meantime I got some acquaintance with the business by visiting the manufactories in Paterson, N.J., and I made such inquiries as I wished concerning the suction. I have since received a letter from Mr. Lord giving much information about the manufacture of silk machinery, saying that most machine-shops are far behind their orders, and suggesting that we might make our own machinery. And that letter turned my attention to the question whether we could not make machinery for the manufacture of silk, for other parties. It appears to be a growing business, and the machinery seems to be in good demand. We learn from Mr. Inslee that he has the repairing of silk and cotton machinery, and was brought up in a cotton factory; and he seems perfectly at home in this sort of work. We want something to do in our large shop, and it seems to me we might commence this business with a view to becoming users of the machinery as soon as we see the way to it, and thus be sure of at least one good customer. We have a foundry where all the casting could be done; and it would not be a difficult business, nor one requiring a great capital, to start the manufacture of these silk machines. We have plenty of space in the shop at Willow Place in one of the upper rooms which could be used for a silk factory. There is also plenty of power there. And furthermore we are in the habit of hiring just such help as would be required in this business. The machines are tended by young women, children, and a few men.

"I don't wish to rush into this scheme rashly, but only to lay it before the Community that they may see which way our past history seems to be drawing us. My impression is that now, if properly invigorated, our machine-shop may help us to a great silk factory that possibly will lead us to a great future. I would recommend that we look to God for help and providential guiding, that he may make us secure from the fluctuations of commerce, and place us where we shall not be liable to be thrown "on our beam-ends" every little while, as we have been by the failure of the trap business. I recommend that we do not rush into anything, but pray to God and look to him to help us take hold of it in the right way. I expect he will find us men and capital in the right tie. I expect the machine-shop will fertilize us and be to our minds a school of education, so that we shall perhaps invent and improve machinery. I feel eager for another campaign, and for a revival of the inventive spirit we had in making traps and the necessary machinery. A glorious time we had of it in those days; it was not work, it was not toil, it was glorious sport, and we made it true pleasure. The same God is over us now as then, and he has not lost any of his power or will to help us."

This proposal was received with enthusiasm by the family. But amount of capital supposed to be necessary to start actual silk-manufacturing, together with our somewhat depressed financial condition, made the fruition of the project seem far in the future.

Text 34: From "Community Gossip: The Silk Maker's Bulletin" by H [Harriet Worden], *Circular*, **August 6, 1866, p. 164.**

The Silk Maker's Bulletin

The opening year projected a new feature in the business of Willow Place. The order came—"Prepare for silk making—Forward march!" On the 20th of January Mr. Inslee went east to make investigations in regard to the construction of the requisite machinery. By the 15th of February, three students, one young

Figure 29: George E. Cragin (1840-1915)

man and two young women, had been established in the factory of C.L. Bottum, at Willimantic, whose Machine Twist stands highest in market, and by 10th of June they had all graduated. July 17th Messrs. Hadden & Co. sold to the Oneida Community one bale of raw silk, weighing 103 lbs., Saturday, the 18th inst., found the first lot of machinery in running order, and a part of the fine room devoted to silk-making fitted up. Monday, the 30th of July came, and with it the beginning of silk-manufacturing by the OC. The acorn has sprouted. A vigorous young seedling from the Communistic oak, watered by the rain of special Providence, and warmed by the sunshine of loving hearts. All day a changing group of admiring spectators hovered around the Winder, watching the slender threads as they were slowly reeled off.

"Is it horse hair?" soberly questioned a six-year-old urchin.
"Not much," we replied.

Part Four: Silverware

As a young boy, George Cragin (1840-1915) (**Figure 29**) had been present at the founding of the Oneida Association. As a young man, he was one of the first Oneidans to be sent into the outside world to acquire professional training. He obtained, as a result, a medical degree from Yale's Sheffield Scientific School in 1867. John Noyes once declared him fit for the "School of Prophets," evidently meaning that Cragin was regarded as suitable for Community leadership. Cragin supervised a short-lived experiment in employee relations (1867-1868, the "Boarding House Commune") and, over the years, contributed numerous writings to Community publications. In post-Community days, he became a spiritualist in which capacity he supervised the hardware department of the Oneida Community Ltd. during the 1890s. As Cragin neared the end of his days, he wrote a number of reminiscences about long-ago Community life including the one given here.[2] In this selection, George E. Cragin introduces the Community's beloved Wallingford Community in Connecticut as well as Oneida's closing years. The end time of the commune, we learn, witnessed the beginning of silverware production which long sustained the Community's successor organization, Oneida Ltd.

Text 35: "1877—The Iron Spoon" by [George E. Cragin] *Quadrangle*, September 1913, p. 15-17.

For ten years we had fought the malaria fever at Wallingford. We were loath to give up and abandon the great scheme of founding a great Religio-Educational Publishing College on the sunny slope of Mt. Tom. We had sent our young men to Yale College. We had invested a hundred thousand dollars in creating the largest and finest water power in the valley of the Quinnipiac. The "Circular" had indeed gone back to Oneida, but only that we might have more room for developing the book publishing business. We had printed the "American Socialist," a magnificent specimen of the printers' art; we were starting a bindery; we were doing high-class catalogue work; and we were looking forward with bright hopes to the realization of J. H. N.'s life purpose of founding a Publishing House devoted to spreading the truths of Bible Communism and establishing the Kingdom of Heaven on Earth. But it was not to be.

The "Dweller of the Threshold," the malaria monster was implacable. One after

Figure 30: *The Quadrangle*
Photo by Jim Demarest

another of our strongest workers had felt the blight of this pitiless invader and had left this beautiful home for a clime that knew no malaria. Our brilliant editor and father of the Wallingford family, George W. Noyes, had fallen before this disease. His sister, Charlotte A. Miller--Mother Miller of both Wallingford and Oneida, had also left us, a victim of this insidious foe; and finally J. H. Noyes himself was attacked.

To meet this invisible enemy we had started a Turkish Bath sometime before, and with a strong faith in its efficacy, it did seem for a while to check the rush of new cases, and to help those afflicted with the endless chills and fever. But it did not cure, and we finally realized that we were steadily losing ground. In this emergency J. H. N. with his usual practical good sense said: "We have tried both faith and the Turkish Bath and if they do not win the fight, we will now try Quinine." This new departure did, indeed, check the ravages of the disease, but it kept everybody dosing with quinine and kindred things that left us but little better off while we remained on the ground.

In the fall of '75 Mr. Noyes at last gave up the fight and brought on to Oneida a bus-load of what he called "a refuse lot." A lot indeed! Pale, anaemic, shivering with daily chills, half dead with quinine, but glad enough to escape anywhere away from that pest infected region, fair to the eye but deadly to the health.

In 1876, J. H. Noyes announced the appointment of his son, Dr. T. R. Noyes, his successor, as leader and head of the Oneida Community. Dr. Noyes had escaped the fever and ague epidemic at Wallingford and, undismayed by the dismal tales of the returning victims, proceeded to build a new dwelling at Wallingford in place of the old Allen House that had sheltered the Wallingford family for twenty-five years. In planning this work he had a devoted assistant in Charles A. Cragin who had but recently graduated from the Sheffield Scientific School at New Haven as a mechanical engineer.

The house was built, and a very attractive one both inside and outside it proved to be, and then in the minds of the leaders the question kept intruding itself "What shall we do to earn our living?" Lectures, classes and educational work generally was all right, but they cost something and gave us no income. The Job Printing business had disappeared. It never had paid a profit anyway, and our one hundred fifty horse power plant was practically idle, to say nothing of five thousand dollars annual loss in interest.

One morning, it must have been in the early summer of 1877, brother Charles was sitting on the bridge abutment looking at the rush of water through the waste gate that he had just raised to supply the Wallace tableware factory a quarter of a mile below with water until the flow of the river from the ponds above reached our Community Lake; he could hear the noisy crescendo of the factory as it started into its daily toil: the muffled crash of the "drops" mingled with the steady hum of the polishing wheels, all indicating that R. Wallace & Sons were making tableware at a great rate. Suddenly the thought came to him, "Why couldn't we make spoons as well as Wallace?" Here was the power and the empty factory only waiting for someone to start a busy hum of our own.

Full of this new idea he hastened up the hill and laid the matter before Dr. Noyes who listened quietly to Charles' eloquent plea and he replied: "Go ahead and find out what it will cost to get the machinery and skilled help, but keep mum about the matter." This order was enough for Charles and off he went to get the necessary information.

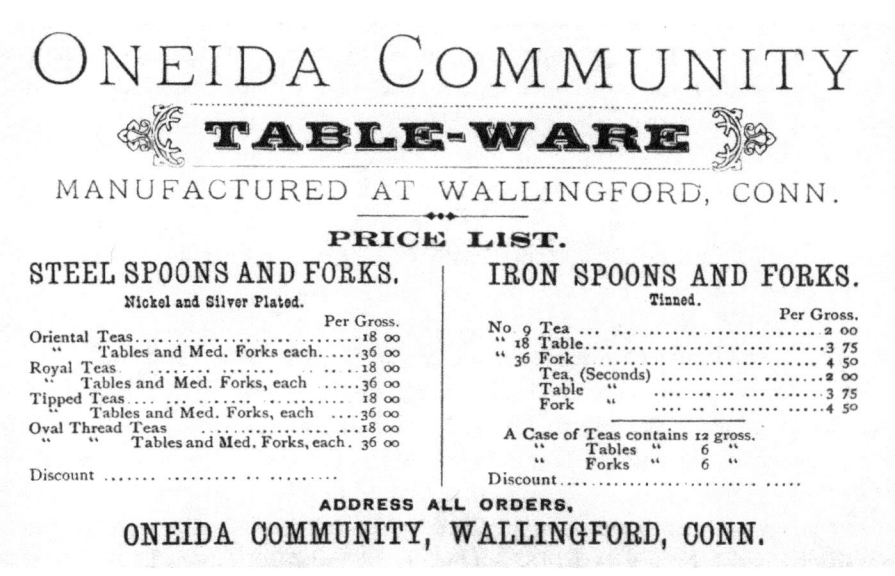

Fig. 31: Oneida Community silverware advertisement

The first thing was to find a man who knew spoons and could tell what was needed in the line of machinery. In this emergency he asked our friend Edmonds, station agent in Wallingford, to recommend a good foreman. Mr. Edmonds told him that all the best men were under long contracts but he thought that Henry Bassett, formerly of Hall, Elton & Company, would help us to start manufacturing. Mr. Bassett, who was then out of a job, a significant fact that we remembered later, readily agreed to help plan the new spoon plant with the understanding that he would be hired as factory foreman. To this Charles promptly agreed without any special inquiry as to Bassett's antecedents. We also remembered this later on, and the two pitched at once into the details of getting the cost of a plant equal to one thousand gross per week of ungraded tinned iron spoons.

Early in June the approximate cost of the new venture was laid. Before Dr. Noyes who promptly gave the order to "Go ahead."

On June 18th we mutually signed a 3 year's contract with H.W. Bassett beginning July 1st, 1877 as factory foreman on a yearly salary of $1,500. We should have known better, but we found that out later. We were a little crazy to start making spoons. By mid-July or thereabouts the first spoon was cut out of the "Oval Thread" pattern. This humble forerunner of our "N. F." and "Community Silver" was given to one of our young women by Charles who made a hurried visit to the Oneida Community Home in September, '77 and can be seen in our show case. Other patterns were made and the business started off with a pretty rosy outlook. Our first salesman in this line was W. R. Bristol who was hired October 15th, 1877.

We now come to the sad event of Charles' death just at the onset of what proved to be our greatest venture in the manufacturing world.

Of an ardent temperament in whatever he undertook, Charles was reckless of his own health if the business emergencies seemed to demand it, and with him it was emergencies pretty much all the time. Early in 1877 he was attacked by the fever and ague [malaria] then so prevalent in Wallingford, but he refused to either give way to the disease or to take any rest from his day and night devotion to the new business. Only by saturating his system with quinine could he manage to keep the pace he had set for himself. At Christmas, '77, he finally took to his bed with what soon proved to be brain fever and died on Jan. 2nd, 1878.

For a few weeks after Charles' death things were in a sad way with the infant industry. He had carried most of his contracts for material in his head and for a time more or less confusion and uncertainty prevailed. The position of Superintendent went begging for nearly a month. Finally M. H. Kinsley was appointed January 25th, 1878. Under his vigorous personality the business grew with great rapidity. One of Myron's first moves was to buy out and get rid of H. W. Bassett who had proved a failure as a shop manager. It took just three weeks to come to an agreement and he was discharged February 15th, 1878. During '78 and '79 we made large quantities of these iron spoons of various patterns for the Meriden Britannia Company. But the fever and ague still crippled us and in 1880 we accepted an invitation from the Niagara Falls Hydraulic Power Company to locate on their premises at Niagara Falls, N. Y.

An agreement was made and signed September 9th, 1880, for leasing power, land and buildings, and one year more saw the Tableware business of Oneida Community at Wallingford, Conn., under the new name of Oneida Community, Limited, moved into a new factory on the banks of the great Niagara Gorge a short distance below the upper Suspension Bridge. Here we will leave the history of the "Iron Spoon" and its successors to those who took an active part in the long struggle through the "Carbon" Spoon; the rush into brass goods; the Wanzer lamp; the advent of the "N. F. 1877" line; the timid start into 18 per cent goods, and the final growth into Community Silver and the exhibition of a few patterns at the Pan American Exhibition in Buffalo in 1901, the beginning of a new Era in the Tableware business. The Iron Spoon had served its end.

Notes:
1. "The Trappers Guide" was a pamphlet issued by the Community in 1865 with authorship attributed to Sewell Newhouse. See Wonderley, *Oneida Uto*pia, pp. 118-23.
2. *Community Journal,* October 3, 1863 ("School of Prophets"); John B. Teeple, *The Oneida Family Genealogy of a 19th Century Perfectionist Commune* (Oneida, NY: Oneida Community Historical Committee, Mansion House, 1985), 156; Anthony Wonderley, "The Oneida Community's Forgotten Commune," *New Circular* 9 (December 2017a): 1-4; and *Oneida Utopia*, 8, 136, 166-68; and George E. Cragin, "1877: The Iron Spoon," this chapter, originally *Quadrangle* 6, no. 9 (September 1913), 15-17.

Chapter 5. Practices

This section deals with a variety of specific social and religious practices of the Community, as explained by Community members in a series of primary sources. These texts concern numerous daily activities within the Community—from governance to dress reform to childcare to women's lives. Three new voices appear in this section. One, William Hinds, was with the Oneida Community during its entire existence. The other two, Harriet Worden and Tirzah Miller, were of the generation that grew up in it. The section concludes with an account of the Community's important social practice of welcoming visitors to the Mansion House.

Part One: Governance

One of John Noyes's earliest recruits in Putney, Vermont, William Hinds (1833-1910) (**Figure 32**) was a fifteen-year-old boy at the time the Oneida

Figure 32: William A. Hinds (1833-1910)

Community started up in New York. He enthusiastically endorsed the Community's commitment to universal education which, as he put it in 1850, "comprises knowledge of all trades, as well as mere book-knowledge. No one here thinks of making some one or two things the business of his life. By rotation of employment, persons learn to do a great many things. This system has also entirely displaced the feeling that one kind of business is more honorable than another, and tends to cultivate unity and love between the different departments." "Improvement is the motive power here," he enthused, and he saw it present everywhere.[1]

Like John Noyes, Hinds became an acknowledged scholar of socialism and communalism. He edited the Community's latter-day magazine newspaper, the *American Socialist*. Like Noyes, he wrote a book on the subject, *American Communities and Co-operative Colonies* (**Figure 33**). That work is still an important source for the study of nineteenth-century communitarianism. In later years, Hinds became a prominent Townerite in opposition to John Noyes's leadership. When the Community disbanded, he served conscientiously on the board of directors of the successor organization, the Oneida Community Ltd., from 1881 to his death in 1910. He continued to revise *American Communities* even while serving as the company's president (1903-1910).

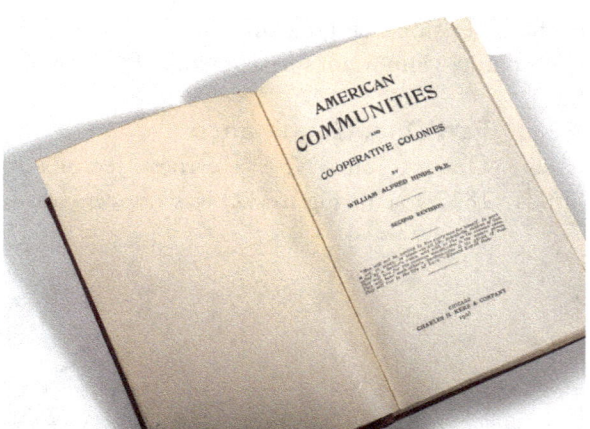

Figure 33: *The American Communities and Co-operative Colonies*
Photo by Jim Demarest

The Oneida Community often was and is portrayed as a totalitarian enterprise under the direction of one man. What it really was—or at least, how it actually seemed to work—is described by one who was present throughout its duration.

Text 36: "Internal Governance" from William Alfred Hinds, *American Communities and Co-operative Colonies*, 2nd rev., 3rd ed. (Chicago: Charles H. Kerr, 1908, originally published 1878), p. 97-202.

For securing good order and the improvement of the members, the Community placed much reliance upon a very peculiar system of plain speaking they termed Mutual Criticism, which originated...in a secret society of missionary brethren with which Mr. Noyes was connected while pursuing his theological studies at Andover Seminary and whose members submitted themselves in turn to the sincerest comment of one another as a means of personal improvement. Under Mr. Noyes' supervision it became in the Oneida Community a principal means of discipline and government. There was a standing committee of criticism, selected by the Community, and changed from time to time, thus giving all an opportunity to serve both as critics and subjects, and justifying the term "mutual" which they gave to the system. The subject was free to have others besides the committee present, or to have critics only of his own choice, or to invite an expression from the whole Community. The Communists had this to say of the practical application of the system:

> "It is not easy to overestimate the usefulness of criticism in its relation to Community life. There is hardly a phase of that life in which it does not play an important part. It is the regulator of industry and amusement—the incentive to all improvement—the corrector of all excesses. It governs and guides all Criticism, in short, bears nearly the same relation to Communism which the system of judicature bears to ordinary society. As society cannot exist without government and especially without a system of courts and police, so Communism requires for its best development Free Mutual Criticism.
>
> "Our object being self-improvement, we have found by much experience that free criticism—faithful, honest, sharp truth-telling—is one of the best exercises for the attainment of that object. We have tried it thoroughly; and the entire body of the Community have both approved and honestly submitted themselves to it.
>
> "In the great majority of cases criticism is desired and solicited by individuals, because they are certain from their own past experience, or from observation of the experience of others, that they will be benefited by it; but in some instances, where it is noticed that persons are suffering from faults or influences that might be corrected or removed by criticism, they are advised to submit themselves to it. In extreme cases of disobedience to the Community regulations, or obsession by influences adverse to the general harmony, criticism is administered by the Community or its leaders without solicitation on the part of the subject. In general, all are trained to criticize freely and to be criticized without offense. Evil in character or conduct is thus sure to meet with effectual rebuke from individuals, from platoons, or from the whole Community.
>
> "We only claim for our system of criticism that it is a new and improved application of old principles. Common society is not exempt from criticism. Thought is free, and faults draw censure

wherever they exist. Every person is more or less transparent to those around him, and passes in the surrounding sphere of thought for pretty much what he is worth. Speech is free, too, in a certain way, and industriously supplies the demand for criticism with an article commonly called backbiting. If you have faults you may be sure they are the measure of the evil-thinking and evil-speaking there is going on about you. Supply meets demand, but not in a way to tell to your account under the common system of distribution. Criticism is not more free with us, but it is distributed more profitably. We have a systematic plan of distribution, by which criticism is delivered in the right time and place, and in a way to produce the best results. Criticism as it goes in society is without method; there is no 'science' in it; it acts every-where like the electric fluid, but is not applied to any useful purpose. It distributes itself, and sometimes injuriously. In the Community we draw it off from the mischievous channels of evil-thinking and scandal, and apply it directly to the improvement of character."[2]

The Community had another ordinance which they regarded as of great importance to their harmony and general progress, viz., *Daily Evening Meetings.* These were of an hour's duration, and conducted with little formality. Matters of business, of Community order and government, the news of the day, scientific discussion, home lectures, religious testimony and discourse, music, and every thing of common interest, here came in for their share of attention. There was of course a moderator, but every member was free to take part in both the presentation and discussion of subjects. There were short-hand reporters, who noted down for permanent record or transmission to the sister Community matters of special importance.

The Community had no definite regulations respecting hours of rising and of labor, leaving such matters for the most part to the judgment and inclination of the individual members; and they had little trouble from the lazy and shiftless. Where reproof or counsel was needed it was given through their system of criticism, already described.

Several of the Communities have fallen upon similar customs respecting labor; one of which is to work *en masse*, or muster together in "bees" for the performance of certain definite enterprises. The Oneidians from the first made great account of this custom, as a means of increasing both the attractiveness and the productiveness of labor. In the earlier days they had "bees" for cutting and husking corn, working in the hay-field, harvesting peas, beans, etc., in which men and women and children took part with great enthusiasm, sometimes marching to the field with music. Later these occasions of gregarious industry were mostly restricted to indoor labor, taking volunteers by scores to the kitchen, laundry and fruit-packing room,

Figure 34: Harriet M. Worden (1840-1891)

with an occasional outdoor "bee" especially for the harvesting of fruit.

In common with the Shakers and Harmonists the Oneida Communists had some peculiarities of dress. They were, however, confined to the women, who wore a costume which originated in the Community, consisting of short dress and pantalets. They were enthuiastic in praise of its convenience, but had less to say of its beauty. The women also adopted the practice of wearing short hair, which saved time and vanity.

The Oneida Communists, like the Shakers, Harmonists and other Communists, were long-lived. Many lived to be over four score years, and 22 died between 85 and 96. They gave much attention to hygienic conditions, living on simple food and following after temperance in all things. Among other health-maintaining and health-restoring agencies their Turkish baths deserve mention. Perhaps credit is due also to the facilities which such a Community has for taking care of the sick. A large Community naturally accumulates the conveniences which belong to a hospital, and in addition has at command cheerful and experienced nurses, such as few hospitals can supply.

Though the Community claimed that their system was founded on religion, and they had little faith in the success of any system of Communism which had not a religious basis, yet they were practical rather than theoretical religionists, and were far from being mere formalists. Their reverence even for the Bible was reverence for its spirit rather than its letter. They paid little attention to the ordinances deemed so important for many sects. They were not afraid that religion would suffer from any truth which science might discover; and the works of Huxley, Tyndall, Darwin and Spencer, were well represented in their library. Neither did they believe that religion necessarily expresses itself in ascetic forms. Hence their freedom to encourage education, art, music, amusements, and every thing which tends to human culture and happiness.

Part Two: Dress Reform

These three writings by Harriet Skinner (attributed), Harriet Worden (**Figure 34**), and Tirzah Herrick (née Miller), describe how the distinctive female garb of the Community came about. The life of Harriet Skinner is described in Section 2, Histories.

Harriet Worden (1840-1891) taught music in the Oneida Community and served what was probably the longest term of editorship (total of eleven years) of the Community's periodical. As a young woman growing up in the Community, Worden would have experienced "ascending fellowship" with John Noyes in the ascendancy. Noyes was the one who usually initiated the young women at puberty, an arrangement his son Theodore (**Figure 35**) regarded as the keystone of the social fabric. "In our society," as Theodore explained it, "the consequences of the first sexual experience were to lead the women on to an honorable position, in every respect as desirable, from our point of view, as in hers in a monogamic marriage...It eliminated the whole mass of sentiment and passion which, in the world, revolves around the question of virginity." In performing the office of "first husband,"[3] John Noyes came to enjoy the trust and love of many young girls as exemplified in this letter almost certainly from Harriet Worden to the older man.

Figure 35: Theodore R. Noyes (1841-1903)

> Last evening there was a call for volunteers to give a little extra help in the trap-shop, at putting together traps; and as I used to work at that, I thought I would volunteer...My work--the noises and the odors of the shop,--everything around me--reminded me of old times; and when not looking up, I could almost imagine that you were standing at the bench with me. And so my thoughts went gliding down the gulf of time, and I saw myself at your side, heating springs for you to hammer out, a girl of fifteen just waking up to the idea that this world contained many things not dreamed of at the children's house. Then I found myself weighing steel for you, and could see your every attention to detail, and myself grown a little older, having just launched out in the great ship of experience, and met one or two icebergs; confiding in you for guidance, yet wayward and thoughtless.
>
> Again, the trap-shop was enlarged, and you and I were putting together traps with the greatest zest. I could see you screwing the posts so carefully, and inventing little improvements until we reached the maximum of speed. With every little improvement and incident in the trap-shop, my own life seemed intertwined; for thinking of one brought up the other; and at this stage, I could see myself wild with youthful excitement--having seen the end of several flirtations, but under new fascinations, and still clinging to you as my guide and refuge. And with this reminiscence, I was truly astonished at your patience with me. I cannot imagine what encouraged you to hold on to me, for I was indeed very wayward, but God alone put it into your heart.[4]

From a series of articles by Worden, called "Old Mansion House Memories," come some of the best descriptions of Community life in the 1850s. Here, for example, is how she described the satisfaction Perfectionists derived from working together:

> The [washing-room] is brightly lighted, the tubs filled with water, and every preparation made for the morning's event. An odor of soap-suds, emanating from two large caldrons of boiling clothes, fills the atmosphere. One by one the washers come in, some looking rather sleepy, others wide-awake for the work. Finally, the wash-boxes are surrounded, the partners standing vis-a-vis. In a few moments all are busily washing—a pleasant hum of voices can be heard, despite the thumping of the one washing-machine in the corner.
>
> A few of the men are discussing the latest political news; another group are absorbed in topics nearer home; others are

rehearsing, with comments of their own, the play enacted the previous Saturday evening. Anon, the whole group are formed into a grand musical chorus; now singing snatches of an old anthem, and now divided into sections, the air is soon resonant with such rounds as, "Scotland's Burning," "Merrily, Merrily Greet the Morn," "Glide along my Bonny Boat," etc.....Before another song can be produced the breakfast bell sounds, announcing to the astonished company that they have washed an hour and a half.[5]

The Oneida Community put an end to the practice of complex marriage on August 28, 1879. Many who had been lovers bid a fond sexual farewell to one another for the term of their remaining earthly lives. Soon after, most of the younger people bonded monogamously in the world's fashion of husband and wife. Thirty-seven marriages were performed. Men, in general, married the mothers of their Community children. That, of course, was not always possible, and about a dozen women with children remained single. For single mothers, it was a time "of heartache and pain that came like a bitter wind," Jessie Kinsley reflected. "I do not understand how the misery was borne."[6]

Worden, with three children, fell into the unmarried category. Her post-Community life, in consequence, could not have been an easy one. One of her children recalled how she "met the problems forced upon her by the breakup with a practical optimism...She often said, 'We have a good home, we have each other, and what is most important, we all have good health. God is good to us.'"[7]

Daughter of John and Charlotte (Noyes) Miller, Tirzah Miller (1843-1902) (**Figure 36**) was a piano player, music teacher, and sometime editor of the Community's newspaper-like publication. Community men regarded her as extremely desirable and, as one of the most sought-after sexual partners, she was very active in that department. For example, there is only one documented instance of the Community intervening in sexual affairs during the years 1863-1864—and it involved Miller. She and Frank Wayland-Smith were criticized for continuing their affair after having been "pointedly censured" for their special love. Miller "was aware," Robert Fogarty remarked, "both of her own attractiveness and the passion she aroused in others." "I should be insincere,' she modestly conceded, "if I did not admit that I know that I have been one of the most attractive women in the Oneida Community."[8]

Covering the years 1867-1874, her private diary furnishes details about Oneida's sex life not available from any other source. We learn from it, for example, how a belief in personal magnetic power was linked to sex in Community thinking. Coitus supposedly involved the transmission of magnetic energy—having nothing to do with semen—between the partners. In *Bible Argument*, Noyes had explained that "sexual intercourse, pure and simple, is the conjunction of the organs of union, and the interchange of magnetic influences, or conversation of spirits, through the

Figure 36: Tirzah C. Miller (1843-1902)

medium of that conjunction."⁹ A passage by Miller illustrates how that worked:

> Slept with J.H.N. [John Noyes] I dreaded to go, because he must discover my unmagnetic condition. He did fast enough. In the night he said: "Would you like some criticism?" "Yes, I should very much." "Well, there is no disguising the fact that you don't attract me. You impress me with the feeling that your sexual nature has been abused by your entering into sexual intercourse without appetite. Spirits of men which are indigestible to you have come between you and me.¹⁰

Miller's diary also provides perspective on how Noyes viewed the eugenics or stirpicultural program instituted in 1869. Noyes's study of animal breeding had convinced him that males are more important than females in a program of selective breeding. Males, he reasoned, contribute more offspring. Some males, furthermore, are more important contributors than others. After reading Galton's *Hereditary Genius* in early 1870, Noyes was confirmed in the suspicion that eminent men throughout history have been the result of superior "strains of blood." Noyes's interest in Galton's "great man" concept gave rise to Noyes's emphasis on the male's contribution and to the especial importance of males with "good blood."

It gave rise, as well, to the conviction that his own eminence owed much to the superiority of his own stock. The Noyes blood line, it followed, was deserving of special encouragement by selectively breeding carriers of Noyes blood. That, in turn, led Noyes to propose to Tirzah Miller—his niece—that he should have a child with her. "I told him," Miller related,

> I should like that. He said he believed it to be his duty, and he had considerable curiosity to see what kind of a child we should produce. He said to combine with me would be intensifying the Noyes blood more than anything he could do. He was just waking up to a full sense of his duty, which is to pursue stirpiculture in the consanguineous line.[11]

At this point, therefore, Noyes's Perfectionism had become genetic, a state of sanctification carried in the blood. And the highest sanctification, as Miller discovered, would result from incestuous relationships. Noyes, as it turned out, did not have a child by Miller although his brother (George Washington Noyes) did in 1870.

The real work of stirpiculture, of course, fell on the women as mothers. Being counted on as breeders, however, ran counter to the Community ideal of voluntary assent to sexual intercourse. Now that Noyes's "science" had taken precedence, women may have perceived stirpicultural coitus as an exacting and perhaps distasteful duty. At the same time, Noyes's desire to reproduce his bloodline and his increasing age must have lessened his attractiveness in the eyes of younger women. The latter now began to question the rightness of these relations. Alice Ackley reported that, when Noyes engaged in sex with her, he "quite disregarded the rules," presumably meaning he ejaculated. Ackley, according to Miller, became "very much disaffected" with him. Even the ever-loyal Miller dared to entertain this disturbing thought: "Oh! Is he a crazy enthusiast, who is just experimenting on human beings?"[12]

Glimmers of doubt concerning the future of the commune shine through Tirzah Miller's writing. Following his dismissal as Community leader in early 1878, for example, Theodore Noyes exited the commune leaving behind three children by three different women. Theodore "claims that it is not his fault, but the fault of the system," Miller recorded. "The outlook for the future looks very dark for the women, if men can desert their children with so little compunction."[13] Miller's private journal brings us closer to Oneida's sexual intimacies than any other primary source. Yet, her references to the sex act are not detailed. Neither are they graphic or even particularly numerous. That is typical of Oneida Community writings. In general. allusions to sex are few and discretely phrased.[14]

The three writings below by Skinner, Worden, and Miller describe how the commune's distinctive female garb—"short dress and pantalet"—came about. Responding to John Noyes's recommendation that women adopt practical clothing, three individuals invented the new apparel. While they were at it, they also created a new look by cutting their hair short. Hence, women of the Oneida Community struck mighty blows for mobility and against vanity from the outset.

These texts refute two misconceptions about the authorship of feminine reform clothing. The first, current in their day, pertained to the circumstances under which the famous women's costume called the "Bloomer suit" came about. *That* look apparently originated with Elizabeth Smith Miller, daughter of abolitionist Peter Smith, then (1851) living in Peterboro near the Oneida Community. At that time, it was asserted that Miller's new feminine costume (featuring trouser-like pants) inspired the Oneida Community garb. All three Oneida writers here point out that this is backwards as regards chronology and fact. The Community mode of dressing clearly was known to Miller and clearly preceded Miller's design. Insofar as Miller took credit for the invention, one would have to conclude (as the Oneida Community women politely indicate) that she, Miller, forgot to mention she had been looking at similar clothing being worn by her Community neighbors for some time.

The second misconception refuted by these writings is contemporary. I have frequently been told that the Oneida Community's short dress was inspired by the apparel of Oneida Indians. This assertion apparently originated with historian Sally Roesch Wagner who remarked that Elizabeth Smith Miller's reform costume "bore an uncanny resemblance" to the "loose-fitting tunic and leggings" worn by her Oneida Indian friends. The Bloomer costume as well as the Oneida Community's short dress and pantalets, in Wagner's view[15] were imitations of apparel worn by Iroquois (Haudenosaunee) women. It is clear from these descriptions that no one, at the time, thought anything of the sort.

Text 37: "Origin of the Short Dress Costume" by Harriet Skinner, *Circular*, **August 28, 1856, p. 126.**

In a letter recently published in the *Home Journal*, Mrs. Bloomer disclaims the credit of being the originator of the short-dress costume, and transfers it to Mrs. E. S. Miller. She writes:

> "The appearance of Mrs. E. S. Miller (daughter of Gerrit Smith of Peterboro, N. Y.) in our streets, attired in short dress and

trousers, induced myself and others to adopt that style of dress. Mrs. Miller had been wearing the dress some two or three months, and was the first, so far as I know, to appear thus attired in public. (This was in 1851.) A similar dress had for years been worn by ladies at water-cures, and for calisthenic exercises in schools; yet to Mrs. Miller belongs the credit of being the originator of the reform dress for general wear. I never claimed to be the originator of the dress, or of the movement, but, on the contrary, did all I could to disclaim it, and to place the credit to Mrs. Miller, to whom I felt it properly belonged....My having been first to bring the matter before the public I suppose was the cause of my name being given the dress, and of my being made the mark for writers to shoot at."

We are interested in the above statement, but have the advantage of Mrs. B., in being able to date the origin of the short-dress movement still further back. *The Annual Report of the Oneida Association*, Jan., 1849; contains a notice of the adoption of short dresses by the women of the Association, which we copy:

"In consequence of some speculations on the subject of women's dress, some of the leading women in the Association took the liberty to dress themselves in short gowns or frocks, with pantaloons, (the fashion of dress common among children,) and the advantages of the change soon became so manifest that others followed the example, till frocks and pantaloons became the prevailing fashion in the Association."

It required not a little heroism to make this innovation, as will be seen from the following paragraph written by a sister and published in *The Free Church Circular* of 1851. This extract may be also gratifying to those who are interested to know how, when and where this movement originated. She writes:

"It was in the upper room of an Indian log house, which we think of now as the cradle of the community, rich in memories, that the writer assisted in the clandestine preparation of two short dresses for Mrs. C---- and Mrs. N----, who proposed to experiment on the fashion described in the Annual Report. This was in June,1848. In the present mellow state of public sentiment, it is impossible to appreciate the heroism that was then required, to appear in the semi-masculine attire, now so much applauded. There seemed to be but one opinion in the world, that it was unfeminine and immodest; and the whole atmosphere was charged with this accusation. The principality of shame was the power that was met and broken by this movement.

We were accustomed to defy fashion, and felt freedom and toleration in disputing its sway; but the despotism of shame was absolute. All our spiritual sensations convinced us that this principality suffered irrecoverable injury at that time.

"The style adopted by Mrs. C---- and N----was the plain, loose pantaloon; and though some of us have tried at different times the Turkish fashion it has never suited; we have always returned with decided preference to the first pattern, originated in the Indian cabin, as the most simple and convenient, if not the most elegant."

It is interesting to look back and see the victory that has been gained over the public sentiment and fashion of the world, in this matter of dress. We distinctly felt at the time that a principality was broken which had held us in bondage; and the effect produced on our spirits was that of simplicity, freedom and youthfulness. This innovation was not made from a sport of fancy, but was entered into as simple followers of the truth. We care little about the name of being the originators of the short dress; we are much more interested in the general truth, that all popular reforms begin with some individual victory over a spirit, and hence that their real history does not lie on the surface.

Text 38: [On the Short Dress and Short Hair], Harriet M. Worden, *Oneida Circular,* **February 6, 1871, p. 46**[16]

In the midst of the hurry and confusion incident to the early days of the O. C., the women quietly achieved a great reform. During the summer some new ideas had been broached on the subject of woman's dress; Mr. Noyes in his Bible Argument, then in manuscript, had made the following remark:

"The present dress of women, besides being peculiarly inappropriate to the sex, is immodest. Woman's dress is a standing lie. It proclaims that she is not a two-legged animal, but something like a churn standing on castors! When the distinction of the sexes is reduced to the bounds of nature and decency, by the removal of the shame partition, and woman becomes, what she ought to be a female-man (like the Son in the Godhead), a dress will be adopted, that will be at the same time the most simple and the most beautiful, and it will be the same, or nearly the same, for both sexes. The dress of children—frock and pantaloons—is in good taste. This, or something like it, will be the uniform of vital society."

This suggestion was taken seriously by some of the more thoughtful women, who resolved to use their influence in favor of simplicity in dress. Not long after, three women might have been seen in the garret of the Log House (then one of the temporary dwellings of the O. C.) contemplating their wardrobe with eager, earnest countenances. They were Mrs. M. E. Cragin, Mrs. H. A. Noyes, and Mrs. H. H. Skinner; and they had met in this secluded place to devise a fashion adapted to the every-day life of a Community—dress, at once simple, modest and attractive. After various experiments and many "contrivings," they finally made short dresses of their long ones, and of the part cut off made pantalets to correspond. They tried them on, and were almost frightened at themselves. Had they courage to wear them? This innovation upon worldly fashions was entirely original with them (Bloomerism had not been heard of then), and in adopting it they might be considered bold and unfeminine. But conscious of a right motive, they resolved to don the new suit and take the consequences. Their first appearance took the family by surprise, and, as they had apprehended, produced a sensation. To some they looked exceedingly comical; a number of the women were very much shocked; others declared the new costume ridiculous and absurd; and a few were greatly distressed. But the voice of the majority commended their trim appearance, and after the first surprise most of the family were delighted with the change. The advantages to be derived from its adoption were very apparent to the more candid, and it was not many weeks before the fashion became universal. This was in June, 1848. After more than twenty years' trial, the short dress and pantalets are still worn by the women of the O. C., and it is needless to say, greatly preferred to any other costume now in vogue.

Nearly a year after the dress reform was started another innovation was made. As a matter of taste, it was discovered that short dresses and long hair looked incongruous. Then the usual practice of letting the hair grow indefinitely, often taking an hour to comb and arrange it properly, is incompatible with true simplicity in dress. Several of the women declared it was becoming distasteful and burdensome. The idea of wearing the hair short often occurred, but Paul's theory of the natural propriety of long hair for women seemed to stand in the way. But after a careful examination of the subject, it was found that Paul's language expressly points out the object for which women should wear long hair; and that was not for ornament, but "for a covering." The popular fashion of combing and coiling the hair upward on the top of the head made it anything but a covering. The simple style of little girls, with short hair, falling round the neck, answered to Paul's advice a great deal better. The argument was conclusive. Some of the braver women set the example of cutting their "shining locks;" and in a short time a wonderful change had taken place. Short hair altered the looks of the women still more than the short dress. These reforms not only had the effect to make the women appear younger, but proved very beneficial to their health. I doubt if there are any among us who could be persuaded to go back to the old style of long hair, especially in these days of chignon and folly. For the reason that the short dress and short hair make a woman appear youthful, visitors often mistake our middle-aged women for girls, and our young women for children.

Text 39: On the Short Dress (1895) Tirzah Herrick (née Miller), *The Quadrangle*, September-November 1912, 13-14.

To the Editor of the Sunday World,

In your Sunday issue of January 20th is an interesting article about the bloomer, or short dress. The writer attributes its invention to Gerrit Smith's daughter, Mrs. Elizabeth Miller, and says that the Oneida Community adopted the costume after Mrs. Bloomer had gained for it considerable notoriety. This seemed to me an error, as I had always understood from my mother, who was among the earliest members of that institution, that the idea of the short dress originated with Mr. John H. Noyes, the founder of the Oneida Community. As his widow is still living at Niagara Falls, Ontario, I mailed to her the World article and asked for reminiscences of the short dress.

She replied that the idea first occurred to Mr. Noyes in 1838. They were climbing Mt. Holyoke together, and she was so much impeded by her long skirts that he suggested the plan of having a short dress for such excursions. About ten years later the Oneida Community began its existence in an old log hut on Oneida Creek. Among the many innovations of that unique coterie was the interchange of labor between the sexes--the men helping the women with their washing, sweeping and cooking, and the women helping the men with their corn planting, hoeing and haying. It can readily be seen how inconvenient the ordinary mode of dress would be to women essaying to wield the rake and hoe, and, as "necessity is the mother of invention" they were driven by the exigency of the occasion to the discovery of the peculiar costume worn by the Community women for thirty years.

Mr. Noyes suggested the idea, and Mrs. Noyes and Mrs. Cragin, secreting themselves in the garret of that historical log hut, made and put on the first short dress in June 1849. [sic. 1848] It was entirely original with the O. C. and was adopted by the Community women a year and a half before the first whisper of it got abroad from any other source.

Gerrit Smith's estate at Peterboro, N. Y., is only about 9 miles from the Community and as his family often made friendly calls at the O. C., his daughter may have adopted the dress after seeing it worn there. In those early days many a house-wife throughout Oneida Valley lightened her morning labors by wearing the short dress of the Oneida Community.

T. C. Herrick
78 West 103rd St.
New York City
Jan. 25, 1895

Part Three: Childcare

Child-raising, carried on as a cooperative activity separate from the adult world, was one of the most distinctive features of Oneida Community life. Its purpose, as Jessie Kinsley put it, "was to assure the children that their parents were the entire Community; and, as to the older people, the feeling was ingrained in them that they were mothers, fathers, grandparents, aunts, and uncles to all of us children"[17].

Figure 37: Pierrepont B. Noyes (1870-1959)

Because the children seem to have slept with Community adults at night, it was really a system of extensive daycare. It meant, however, that youngsters would be raised and educated together by a few care-providers. It also meant that children would be apart from parents most of the time and parents would have to accept the arrangement. Oneidans, as is affirmed in these writings, loved their children dearly. However, parental love was institutionally discouraged if it became "sticky," that is exclusionary in its focus. When that happened, it became a sin called "philoprogenitiveness." Originally a phrenological term, the Perfectionists used the word to mean loving one's own progeny more than those of another.

"The Community system was harder on mothers than on their children," Pierrepont Noyes (**Figure 37**) learned from first-hand experience. "Whenever I was permitted to visit my mother in her mansard room [a section of the Mansion House]—once a week or twice (I have forgotten which)—she always seemed trying to make up for lost opportunity, lavishing affection on me until, much as I loved her, I half grudged the time taken from play with those toys which she had—I think somewhat surreptitiously—collected for my visits."[18] Pierrepont's mother was Harriet Worden, author of the second piece on childcare given here.

The pain this system could instill and the discipline required to conceal that pain were remembered vividly by another of the children:

> Poor Mother, so loving, so unselfish, so truly good, how I can now sympathize with her "trials and temptations" in her struggle against "idolatry" towards her first baby. All this, of course, was long before my own memory begins. She must have slept with me at night during my first year, as that was the Community custom, but I was too young to have kept in mind more than an instinct of deep attachment which persisted through later years, when she was being disciplined for the "mother-spirit" and we were often kept apart for a week or two at a time.
>
> What she felt during these periods I can only guess, but I can remember well my own feelings when, during one two-week

Figure 38: Corinna Ackley (1872-1968)

period of separation, I caught a glimpse of her passing through a hallway near the Children's House and rushed after her, screaming. She knew--what I was too young to know--that if she stopped to talk with me another week might be added to our sentence. There was no time to explain. Hoping, I suppose, to escape, she stepped quickly into a nearby room. But I was as quick as she. I rushed after her, flung myself upon her, clutching her around the knees, crying and begging her not to leave me, until some Children's House mother, hearing the commotion, came and carried me away.[19]

This writer was Corinna Ackley (**Figure 38**); her mother was Alice Ackley (**Figure 39**). Both appear in the first article on childcare given here.

The established system of childcare, we learn from Skinner's article, was that babies were left in the mother's care for fifteen to twenty months. After that, the youngsters were delivered into a daycare situation supervised by other adults.

Figure 39: Alice Ackley (1847-1922)

At night, a child customarily slept with an adult who was not the child's biological parent. These arrangements, in Skinner's view, promoted the happiness and health of both mothers and children. It was good for the young because a child's natural propensity was to enslave the mother, to demand as much of the mother's attention as possible. Learning unselfishness and sociability made for a better child. It was good for mothers because women were made for God, for themselves, and to be companions and lovers to men. They should not have to forfeit their lives to their children. The Community way of raising children freed women from the child-raising burden and got them out into the social stream of Community life.

But as of Skinner's article in 1873, the Community is trying something new with younger children. Four babies (seven to eleven months) spend the day together in the drawing room of the Children's

Department supervised by two care-providers. Both of the latter provide statements about this arrangement (one is identifiable as Emily Otis – "E. E. O."). The supervisors "are relieved by other motherly women at meal times and fixed hours and with the fathers to take the babies to ride and little girls to amuse them and kind hands on every side." At the end of the day, the mothers pick up their little ones, keep them at night and, in the morning, dress and feed them, then take them back to the drawing room.

The four mothers responding to Skinner in this article dutifully endorse the experiment. They say they are happy to be able to join in public work (Alice Ackley—"A. M. A."), that that gives them "time and opportunity for other occupation" (Ann Hobart—"A. S. H."). They state further that they are grateful to be freed from the sin of philoprogenitiveness--"the degradation of so many women" (Charlotte Leonard—"C. M. L."). They affirm that their children are learning to be less selfish in this system (Martha Hawley—"M. J. H.").

The second article, "The Crushing System," announces that the experiment of putting the infants into the children's department at an earlier age has apparently been discontinued. The Community has returned to the idea of admitting them when older. Author Worden emphasizes that Oneida Community mothers love their children and, of course, being separated from them is a hardship. However, Community mothers exercise real will-power and unselfishness in this regard on behalf of their offspring. Experience has shown that children turn out better when raised in this collectivized fashion.

This article reacts to the charge that Perfectionist women now receive a yearly allowance for "pin-money." "The system that has managed to crush so thoroughly a mother's love for her own child," an unnamed outsider sarcastically noted, "cannot, it seems, crush a woman's love for her own finery." Worden, strangely enough, seems to agree with much of this. She concedes that love of dress really is a great feminine weakness. It is true, furthermore, that money is doled out individually. And incidentally, Worden adds, the clothing of Oneida women is individually, not communally, owned.

Text 40: "Our Youngest" by [Harriet Skinner] *Oneida Circular,* **June 23, 1873, p. 205-6.**

There are certain hearsays about the Community which are as inexpugnable as the Canada thistle. You may root them out year by year, but they reappear with the visiting season as persistently as the white daisies in the meadow. One of these is that we take the babies away from their mothers at a frightfully early age, and after that the poor little things never know their mothers from the rest of womankind. Heretofore we have been able to repel this odious impeachment in toto. We could say that our babies were left in the entire care of their mothers till their fifteenth or twentieth month, according to their comparative development. But the era of scientific propagation is leading us into new courses, and now we shall have to own up to the first half of that immemorial hearsay. We have four babies under a year—from seven to eleven months—and we are trying the experiment of putting them together through the day. Instead of each mother taking care of her own child in her own room, we put the four into one room, and under the care of two women not their mothers. Perhaps if we tell more about it, and the mothers themselves are heard on the subject, this will not appear such an "awful disclosure."

Of course our reasons for this move connect with our Community principles and our Community circumstances. First as to our circumstances: if mothers are to have the chief care of their own babies, the Community is not so good a place on some accounts as the isolated family. The mother in a private household has a round of cares and duties which force her to turn off her child and make it learn to take care of itself. She is compelled to be wife and housekeeper as well as mother. Then her second child soon crowds out the first, and she cannot stop to dote. But the young mother in the Community is under no such necessities. Her housekeeping is all done for her. She has no cooking nor washing nor ironing to do—no imperious calls of any kind. These are circumstances of temptation. A baby soon finds out how much care it can have, and exacts more and more. Let a fond mother have no compelling cares, and there is great danger that her child will enslave her and get spoiled itself for want of wholesome neglect.

Then on the other hand Community circumstances are always teaching us new economies and better ways of doing things. We have found that children a year and a half old can be brought up together to a great advantage. They can have the best kind of care at a vast reduction of cost—better, far better care than a weak and over-burdened mother could give them; better care than a mother under any conditions could give them. A child that has been in the way of teasing its mother half to death and making itself sick with its innocent restlessness, will go into our nursery and soon become well and happy. Here is philosophy, as every one knows that has studied the habits of children. In a department on purpose they can have selected guardians—the most gifted infant-culturists we can find among us—and so the best kind of training is insured. Well, why not begin earlier—as soon as the baby is weaned, at least? (By the way the nursing period is somewhat shortened with us, not often exceeding nine months. We have no occasion to protect it to avoid undesired increase, and the health of mother and child, moral and physical, is conserved according to our experience, and we believe according to the best science of the day, by this practice.) We resolved to have the benefits of the gregarious system as soon as possible.

Our Community principles in regard to "Woman's Sphere" have governed in this movement. We do not believe with Rev. Dr. Todd that motherhood is the chief end of woman's life; that she was made for the children she can bear. She was made for God and herself. She has a spiritual nature which lifts her up to God, and there is her highest sphere, where there is "neither male nor female." Then in association with man she was not made first of all to be the mother of his children, but to be his companion and lover—to be what she is in courtship rather than what she is in marriage. Set aside sentimentalism and exceptional cases, and woman's sphere under marriage is well characterized by Mr. Noyes in his Bible Argument, as that of a "propagative drudge." She is not that in the Community. She has children only by choice, and her drudgery as a mother is to be reduced to the minimum. And here we will introduce a paper we have received from a sister on this subject:

> "We have only modified and adapted to Community principles a custom that has from time out of mind prevailed in the very highest and most enlightened circles. Queens and princesses by universal consent are considered of too much value in themselves, too necessary as leaders and ornaments of society, to be allowed to surrender their time and attention day and night for months to the care of their infants. Women of rank and wealth are accorded the same privilege everywhere. Especially is it claimed by women of genius and women devoted to art or literature. The mother herself, her health, her faculties, her own wellbeing as a member of society receives the first consideration, and her function as nurse is subordinate. This is undoubtedly the law of nature and justice, which, as the world becomes enlightened and women rise to their true place, will be more and more observed. As this law is observed in worldly society and even in the highest, it has many drawbacks. The Princess of Wales to purchase her own personal freedom must resign her new-born child to the bosom of a hireling and an inferior. This is true of all women who do not nurse their children. This state is indeed unnatural, and must give a true mother many a pang. We have said we modify this custom here, and most assuredly we do in a way that relieves it of all that mothers dread. The mother nurses and cares for her baby with undivided attention for the first few months of its novitiate in this strange world, and then when it is nicely weaned, no stranger or alien comes between her and her child."

Now as to the details of the change: The babies are all weaned—the last within a week, its mother choosing to wean it at seven months rather than wait as she would have to do till cold weather. They continue to sleep with their mothers, who dress them and give them their breakfast and keep them till half-past seven. At that hour they are carried into the drawing room, where their foster mothers are waiting to receive them. The "drawing room" is in the children's wing, and was used through the winter to take our next youngest into for a change, but their play-yard serves a much better purpose at present. It is a large, airy room, twenty-eight by twelve, four windows to the east; is carpeted and furnished with cribs, a low bed, etc. The two in charge are relieved by other motherly women at meal times and fixed hours, and with the fathers to take the babies to ride and little girls to amuse them and kind hands on every side, they are not over-taxed. The mothers take their babies at six again.

Further particulars will be gleaned from the following papers which were solicited for this story, and which will make it long enough. We think we have shown the art of a true story-teller in keeping them for the close. The first is from one of the foster mothers, and shows how the movement was precipitated, though it has long been remotely considered, and had been the subject of conversation in Mr. Noyes's room the day before the incident she mentions:

> "The way I happened to offer to take care of little Theodore for a few weeks was by my rooming next door to his mother. He had not been very well for a number of nights, and she had been broken of her rest so much that I knew she must be nearly worn out. One night about one o'clock I was awakened by her trying to sing him to sleep. I suppose it was owing to my being aroused out of a sound slumber, and that her voice was subdued for fear of disturbing the occupants of the adjoining rooms; but it sounded so plaintive to me that I thought I never could go to sleep while I knew she was there so much in need of rest; so I left the three little boys who sleep in my room and went and told her to go away and I would be glad to take care of little T. He soon became quiet, and as I watched his precious face I felt such a warm love for him that I thought I would willingly do anything for him. I could hardly wait till morning to tell his mother how glad I should be to take care of him until she could recruit. When I proposed it to her she said that she should be glad to have me take him awhile, and presumed that he would do better with some one who felt strong and well. In the evening I was in Father Noyes's room and I told him I was going to take care of little Theodore; he said, 'Why don't you take four? Such a strong woman as you ought to be able to manage as many as that.' I replied that I would take all he gave me. I did not know but he was jesting at first, but as I had often thought of the subject of simplifying the rearing of small children, when I found he thought seriously of the plan and others were enthusiastic in making arrangements for securing helpers and putting it into execution, I did not feel like retreating. My only hope of success from the first was in the revival spirit. I knew that would give us enthusiasm and loving hearts for our work, and insure good results. And now after two weeks' trial, I can truly say that I never enjoyed any business as I have my work in the nursery. It is very plain to me that the move has the approval of the heavens. -E. E. O."

[The writer of the foregoing has had one child born in the Community in circumstances of comparative luxury. She is an enthusiast in all progress—has great strength of character—is strong in tenderness and strong in common sense. The writer of the following, Mrs. B., had five children in marriage outside, in somewhat straightened circumstances, which gives her some very desirable qualifications. She knows how to make the babies take care of themselves all they should. She has displayed in our other infant departments a remarkable faculty for making the little ones happy by making them good.]

"When the new way was proposed by Mr. Noyes I felt very enthusiastic in regard to it, not dreaming, however, that I should have anything to do with it except to look on. It was with some fear and trembling that I began to help in this work. The first morning I went down to the drawing-room expecting only Theodore and Allan would be there, when the door opened and Alice came in bringing Corinna, and placed her in my arms saying to her, "Here is your mamma B-----." I do not know how she felt, but my own heart was full and I had hard work to keep back the tears. It seemed to me that the spirit and presence of Christ came in with that baby and her mother, and it has stayed with us. I said to myself, If God has given Alice grace and strength to give up her babe into our care he will give us grace and strength to do the right thing by it, and I had a new baptism of faith and love. The feeling that the mothers are in full sympathy with us gives us good heart, and the babies do not suffer from the separation as they would if their mother's hearts were bleeding. I have never felt so interested and given up to any work that I have ever been in as this, and it was never so easy for me to ask God for help in any work as this. Little Allan who cried for his mother and would hardly be comforted for the first two days, is now very happy and lets her come in and go out without any perturbation. The babies are all well. We spread an old quilt on the carpet and they sit on it with their playthings a good share of the time, and seem to think it is the nicest place in the house. Their fathers come in often and give them a tossing, and baby-lovers all through the Community find a new source of enjoyment. The four are getting into the habit of taking their naps at about the same time, which gives us a chance to rest. -M. B."

The four letters that follow are from the four "bereaved" mothers.
Sunday, June 15, 1873
"DEAR AUNT H.:----You asked me to tell you my feelings and experience since giving up the care of my baby, and I am glad to

do so, as you know so well my trials and temptations when the move was first proposed. My troubles were of short duration, and I gave her up at last with the others, heartily, feeling that she would have every want supplied, and that I should be a better and happier woman for doing so. Corinna has now been in the nursery two weeks, and as my room is near by I have had a chance to observe the working of the new plan, and am convinced that she is happier, and has as good if not better care than when I had entire charge of her myself; and when I go every evening at six to get her she is always delighted to see me, and I, feeling rested and fresh instead of tired and often impatient, take more real comfort than before. The love I have had for my baby has never given me the happiness that I expected to realize, for with it has been a feeling of anxiety and worry lest she should be sick, and perhaps taken from me, or that some accident or other might come to her; but since I gave her up that trouble has been taken from me, and in its place I have a feeling of rest and thankfulness. I now realize as I did not before, that the old way of each mother caring exclusively for her own child, begets selfishness and idolatry, and in many ways tends to degrade woman. The new system works well in every respect, but particularly do I appreciate the opportunity it affords me of not only joining in public work but of self-improvement and "going home" to God every day.

"Yours for giving up every thing that stands in the way of improvement and the revival, A. M. A."

"The proposition to have the babies cared for together during the day, by others than their respective mothers, seemed to me, after the first flutter of motherly feeling had subsided a little, a really wise and beneficial one—good for both mothers and children. I was better prepared to accept it perhaps because I had not been strong enough to take the entire care of my child myself, and had previously become accustomed to leave him with others. But the advantages of this new method are much greater than I anticipated. The love between me and my boy is not lessoned but rather enhanced by standing a little aloof from him. I do not suffer about him but truly enjoy my liberty; he never cries when I leave him. When I take him in the evening instead of being tired and worn, and he sympathetically nervous, I feel strong and fresh, and he is full of glee and baby joy. He is happier during the day to be with his mates than when alone with me. Before putting him in with the others he was a difficult child to manage about his naps—often tiring me completely out before going to sleep. I might rock him, walk with him, swing him, or draw him in his basket, it was all the same—always a struggle. Now I have only to lay him on the bed and in a few moments he is sound asleep, with seldom any resistance. The benefit to me is very great: it relieves me of a care that was too great for my strength; it gives me time and opportunity for other occupation; it chastens my affections and frees me from absorbing distractions. –A. S. H."

"DEAR AUNT H.:----I am glad to respond to your invitation to tell you some of my experience about putting little Stephen into the nursery department. When the plan was first proposed it took me somewhat by surprise, and I hardly need tell you that I had some conflicts with my motherly nature for a few days; but I resolved that my feelings should not govern me; that I would be obedient to the Community inspiration and trust God to take care of my feelings. And sure enough he has. After two weeks' trial of the new plan I can assure you that I like it. I like if for my own sake and I like it for my baby's sake. It commends itself to me as a wise move, and as a blessing to both mothers and children. I am perfectly sure that it is better for both of us in many ways. It relieves me from a long confinement and puts me again into the family current and public service, where I am always happy, while I know that my babe is just as well cared for and is happier even than when I had him all to myself. His necessary wants are all supplied, but he does not have that special exclusive attention which so often spoils a child. I enjoy my work during the day and enjoy my baby at six o'clock. He is always tickled to see me, and when I take him back the next morning he is glad to see his mothers there and the other babies again. I am not afraid that the love between me and my child will be diminished at all, but it will be chastened by a higher love—a love for serving God and the Community—and that is just what I want. I am thankful for anything that will save me from idolatrous philoprogenitiveness, which is the degradation of so many women. I attribute my good experience to the revival spirit in the family. I should have been weak by myself, but I am strong in the strength of the whole Community.

"I have weaned my little one the last week and he has scarcely known it—thanks to the new system. I do not believe a baby was ever weaned easier. –C. M. L."

"When the proposal came to us mothers to give up the care of our infants during the day I had many conflicting feelings about it. Although my heart ached at the thought of separation, I had a secret feeling that it would prove a relief in the end. My own experience had taught me that the care and confinement from morning till night entailed on a mother is very wearing. As the child grows older it learns to claim the greatest share of attention and the mother is never free. I could not but feel that a change would be best for both mothers and babies. At the day appointed, I dressed my babe (a boy of eleven months), and gave him his breakfast and carried him into the drawing-room and left him to the care of his new mothers. The first day or two he seemed quite homesick, pining and worrying and watching the door whenever it was opened. I took him every evening at 6 o'clock, gave him his supper, put him to bed and slept with him. I concluded it was best to keep entirely away from him for a week, and invited his Aunt A. to sleep with him. This produced a wonderful change. Before the week was out he was as happy a child as you could wish to see, and when I again saw him I took real comfort with him. Since that time I have left him every morning at half past 7 o'clock with the assurance that he would be as well cared for as any mother could ask, and with a sense of rest, knowing that he would enjoy himself better than when staying with me all day. At night when I take him he is delighted to see me, but the old claiming, sticky spirit (which made us both miserable), is gone, and I have more enjoyment of him than all the time before of his life. As my baby was several months older than any of the others, and took the change so much more to heart, I am convinced that the sooner children learn to love a great many beside their mothers, the surer they are of health and happiness. –M. J. H."

Text 41: "The Crushing System" by R, [Harriet Worden], *Oneida Circular***, February 23, 1874, p. 68.**
The following odious paragraph is going the round of the papers:

> "Communism has received a blow in its stronghold. The Oneida Community has voted to give each of its feminine members a yearly allowance of pin-money. It is evident that having gew-gaws in common is a little beyond the powers of even "Perfectionists." The system that has managed to crush so thoroughly a mother's love for her own child *can not*, it seems, crush a woman's love for her own finery."

This paragraph is not only malicious and false as against Communism, but it is a shameful calumny on woman, and the CIRCULAR, though it is usually content to ignore such lies and let them make their way to Tophet unchallenged, is persuaded to depart from its policy of inertia this once and let a woman protest.

That woman's love of finery is stronger than her love of children is a horrible charge. If women in the world do not cry out against it, I confess it shocks me as a Community mother beyond expression, and I am sure the female friends of the man who make that charge are wretched specimens of their sex. A woman's love for her own child can not be crushed out by any *system*. The extremity of starvation is said to have done this. In pictures of the siege of Jerusalem, the climax of horrors is the tender and delicate woman looking with an evil eye—a hungry eye—on the children she has borne. But starvation produces insanity, and that is what any system must do, before it can crush out a mother's love. That love of dress is a great weakness in woman I cannot deny. The prophet asks "can a maid forget her ornaments or a bride her attire?" But notice, that it is the maid and the bride, not the mother that is so fond of "finery." The mother can forget her ornaments very easily, too easily sometimes.

No, nothing but starvation and insanity can crush out a mother's love. But one mother may have a wise love and another a foolish love for her child. One mother in her foolishness will let her child eat cake till it makes itself sick; another mother more wise will deny her child hurtful dainties. The members of the O. C. have found that their children are healthier and happier and better every way put under the Community care at the age of fifteen or twenty months, and their pure motherly instinct prompts them to give their babies up. It requires self-denial it is true, but where is the mother who is not glad to deny herself for her child's sake, and where is the mother of a good child who has not suffered bitterly in its faithful training? Though we praise the Community mothers in saying so, it is nevertheless true that one of the highest signs of culture in a woman is power to sacrifice her child's present, momentary enjoyment to its future good, to sacrifice in a sense the whole child to the man or woman she wants it to be. An eminent teacher who called here lately, after visiting our children's rooms, made a remark like this: in noticing how many children are spoiled by motherly fondness, motherly weakness and motherly petting, he had often thought it would be an excellent thing if mothers in a neighborhood would change babies after they are weaned, and bring up each other's children to a certain age. However it is not likely he would have hazarded the suggestion any-where but here, and so we suppress his name.

As to any new surrender of principle, any breach in our stronghold lately made, we have to say that the "allowance" made to the women this year is nothing substantially different from what has been done several years past. Five or six years ago our financiers instituted the system of "appropriations," mentioned several times in late CIRCULARS, the object of which is to limit our expenditures to actual income, or rather to keep us from living so close to our income as to lead to financial embarrassment in case of any sudden check to our businesses, or diminution of our usual profits by any accident. In this system of appropriations the item of clothing came in of course. To get at the sum necessary, in past years every person by invitation the first week in January, has handed in a list of what things he or she is expected to want during the year, and the appropriation has been made out on the basis of these papers. Last year the appropriation for the women's clothing was about $3,000, shoes not included. This year, calculating from last year without any specification of wants, the women were allowed $4,000, shoes included; and as they chose for reasons of their own to divide the sum among them equally, nobody interfered. Their principal object was the lesson it would give the young folks in economy. They would find out, for instance, how much their shoes cost and be more careful of them. Some of the girls last year had shoes enough to use up almost their whole allowance this year. They enjoy for a change seeing how far they can make things go.

There is an implication in the odious paragraph, and it is one of the fables often told about the Community, that the women have their ordinary clothes in common. We have our ordinary clothes in common just as much as the mother and daughters of other families do, and no more. Our washer-women will say at least that the articles which go through their hands are marked with all the personality, individuality, and identity possible for indelible ink to express. We have talked of making common stock of handkerchiefs and towels, to save the trouble of distributing them by name, but if we ever make this improvement we protest against its being made the foundation of a thousand new stories.   -R.

Part Four: Outdoor Mingling

Out of the experience of building the Mansion House came a labor pattern that translated Fourieristic work teams ("series") into an American idiom of informal cooperation. "This practice of doing work 'by storm,' or in what is more commonly called a 'bee,' in which the men, women and children engage, has been found very popular and effective," the Community reported in early 1850. "It may be employed in a great variety of occupations, especially of out-door business, and always contributes to enliven and animate the most uninteresting details of work."[20] From the very beginning, then, the Oneida Community hit on "bees" as their preferred method of getting things done.

Proving indispensable to the working together of men and women in real life, the short dress and the bee operationalized mingling. And it was mingling--not Fourier's "passional attraction"--that made communalism work. Of perhaps thirty communities founded on Fourier's principle, hardly any lasted more than two years. "Fourier had a glorious scheme of 'Attractive Industry,'" Harriet Skinner observed more than a quarter century later, "but it was intricate and artificial. In practice the Community have found that the gregarious element, and especially the combination of the sexes, is the main secret." In conceiving mingling as a motive power for communitarian success, Noyes, as historian Carl Guarneri put it, "out-Fourierized the Fourierists."[21]

In the text given here, Charlotte Miller describes an occasion for outdoor mingling as abundant in "mirth and frolic," carried out "with a gush of the free buoyant spirit of childhood," and accomplished "without the weariness of worldly labor."

Text 42: "The Corn-cutting Bee," Charlotte Miller, Circular, November 10, 1852, p. 196.

Oneida, Sept. 18, 1852

You have often heard us speak of our mass-gatherings, or as we call them, Bees, for out-door employment, as one of the most novel and pleasing characteristics of Community life. I will endeavor to describe one of these storming parties to you; though I am aware it requires the powers of a far abler painter than I am, to give you a faithful, life-like picture.

The season for out-door "bees" commences in the latter part of August, and continues till all the autumn work, such as cutting oats, and corn, gathering beans and apples, husking, &c., is finished.

Let us take for our specimen, a bee for cutting corn, the description which is just now in vogue.

The day selected for the occasion, is mild and pleasant; and in the forenoon the chiefs of the farming department are employed in getting together and sharpening tools, and making arrangements. At the dinner table notice is given that a bee will come off in the afternoon at half past two o'clock; and the place of preliminary meeting is under the "butternut tree." This notice quickens the movement of the in-door machinery, at once; and if there is a prospect of some part lagging, a little extempore bee is called, to do up the after-dinner work, such as clearing and setting tables, washing dishes, &c. At the hour specified, the bell rings, and groups of men, women, and children commence gathering under the "butternut tree." A merry sight it is too; mirth and frolic are specially abundant; every one seems inspired by the occasion, with a gush of the free, buoyant spirit of childhood. The dress of the women is sometimes odd, but picturesque, and well adapted for rapid motion, crossing fields and fences, passing between the rows of corn, &c. It consists generally of a frock, pantalets, sun-bonnet and gloves.

When all are assembled, that is, some 70 or 80, men, women, and children, the chief calls off the names as they have been previously drawn, and arranged in groups. A group comprises four men to cut the corn, four women to take it and form it into stooks, and a man for a binder, who follows, with a woman carrying an armful of straw, to bind the stocks. When the groups are all organized, the men take each one a corn-cutter on his shoulder, and with a lady for his companion, the procession marches to the field of operations. Now we are there.—Each group takes a certain number of rows, and the process of cutting, carrying the stalks, and binding, commences with great spirit. In the course of a few moments this army of happy workers are spread over a large field; and the results of their sport are seen in the rapid fall of the luxuriant green stalks before the swift strokes of the cutters—and then, as if by magic, the tall stooks rise on every hand, changing the face of the field as rapidly as an army of locusts are said to do; not however, like them, leaving famine and desolation behind, but bountiful tokens of plenty and fruitfulness. It is an animating spectacle to watch the party as now they plunge into the green depths of the corn, and anon emerge on the other side of the field, with the long rows of stooks behind them as trophies of their march.

In this way, field after field is harvested, without the weariness of worldly labor, and with the keen relish of healthful sport. Old and young—men, women, and children, uniting in these gatherings, each adds to the enthusiasm and enjoyment of the whole.

For women, *the Bee* is an unparalleled opportunity for exercise in the open air—and in companionship with men, too, which is of itself invigorating—and for men it takes off the ruggedness and drudgery of labor, by association with those whose presence naturally calls forth the refinement and chivalry of their nature.

Do you wonder that the *Bee* is one of the great charms of community life—or that Oneida appreciates it as one of her best ordinances?

Part Five: Women Speaking Up

It is "a notorious fact," Miller claims, that women are prone to emptiness, frivolity, and scandal in their talk. But, cultivating fruitful thinking, they can become mediums of truth in their utterances. She herself has learned from speaking up in Community meetings that females should be less bashful and more forcefully vocal. The article closes with a quotation: "They that would be free, themselves must strike the blow." This line is from Byron's poem *Child Herald's Pilgrimage* (Canto 2, Section 76) but, famously and frequently, was repeated by Frederick Douglass. Douglass visited the Mansion House on July 16, 1853 and gave an anti-slavery lecture at a nearby Methodist church.[22]

The subject of women's rights, according to her sister Harriet Skinner, "was ever a live one" with Miller.

> She fully sympathized with the object sought by the advocates of these "Rights"—the enlargement of woman's sphere in respect to labor and education; her influence was always felt on this side of the question in all the discussions of the Community; and practically she did much to bring about the present status of women in the Community, which makes them free to speak and vote on all questions affecting the common interest—to engage in any pursuit for which they have an attraction—to superintend and conduct any business for which they are qualified; and yet there was nothing in her manner, voice or spirit reminding one of the self-asserting masculinity that too often offends in many advocates of Woman's Rights. She neither asked nor sought for herself or others of her sex independence of man. She believed that in the unity of the sexes could be realized the greatest liberty as well as the greatest happiness of woman.[23]

Text 43: "Woman's Rights" (1853) by Charlotte A. Miller. *Circular*, April 27, 1853, p. 196

Where shall the reform begin? At home—is the response of common sense—and in the individual woman. And what is the first right that she ought to secure? I answer, it is the management of her tongue. Let her get that under control, and it will go a great way toward her getting all other rights.

Education and habit, as a general thing, consign woman's tongue to the dominion of emptiness and frivolity, or what is worse, scandal and evil speaking. This is a notorious fact, and a standing matter of ridicule in the world. Here is a species of tyranny that all true women should revolt at. It is not enough to refuse to be tale-bearers, but we must abhor trifling and barren conversation. Let us cease to do evil, and learn to do well.—If the time is coming, as the Reformers demand, when women shall sit in the Legislature and have an equal share with man in guiding public opinion, they must certainly make the government of their tongues a serious matter. As things now are, the great majority of women can carry on any amount of gossip and chitchat in a private way; they find no difficulty in making themselves heard, and no embarrassment, or lack of words. But change the scene, and call upon them to speak to edification of even a small family circle,—and much more if a large one—and immediately there is a shrinking, a confusion of ideas, and a loss of voice. This shows what a tremendous power is concerned in this slavery of the tongue that women submit to. It is a kind of tyranny which gives them unlimited use of speech in a fruitless, frivolous way; but is ready with all the force of bashfulness and nervousness to veto any attempt to speak to public edification. This opposing power must be overcome; and here I think reform properly begins. We need not fear but that women will win all their other rights when they have wrested their tongues from this degrading slavery; and given them up to be mediums of the Spirit of truth.

There are some exceptions to the general habits of women in respect to freedom of utterance. Necessity and attraction induce many women to go on the stage, become actresses, and perform nightly before the largest audiences. They train their voices so as to be distinctly heard all over the house—and laying aside all bashfulness, speak and act the fictitious heroine to the life. The same necessity compels many women to become teachers; and in this profession they are obliged to acquire a full, distinct voice, freedom from bashfulness, and power of thought and language that will edify and instruct their pupils.

Though we do not wish to acquire freedom of utterance in order to become teachers, or actresses, we do all wish to become mediums of truth, and circulators of the true spirit in the largest sphere possible. For that purpose we want, first, liberty of soul to speak the truth to edification, to be fruitful in thought and utterance; and secondly, we want to gain control of the voice, so as to speak loud and distinct, and without bashfulness.

The last year's experience has given me new hope and courage in respect to this reform. I have found myself disposed to abstain from much private conversation, and chiefly inspired in the channel of open, public talk in our family meetings. In following this inspiration, the necessity for a more loud and distinct voice than I had before acquired, made a demand on my faith; but when I determined in my heart that I could control my voice, immediately a sensible obstruction gave way, and I have had very little difficulty since, either from bashfulness, or weakness of voice. I believe that by thus taking one step after another, and keeping the object steadily in view, of breaking up the slavery of habit, and gaining the complete use of our tongues for all edifying purposes, we shall ere long see every fetter broken. "They that would be free, themselves must strike the blow."

Charlotte A. Miller
Oneida, April, 1853

Part Six: Diet

The food of the Oneida Perfectionists was bland, simple, and largely vegetarian. Their diet was dominated by milk, potatoes, bread, baked beans, apple dishes, and—after the first lean years—butter.[24] They agreed with a basic assumption of Sylvester Graham's then-fashionable health regimen, that the state of one's passions is determined by the food one eats. On the one hand, "those who eat swine's flesh will be gross and swine-like." On the other, "certain kinds of vegetable food may have a tendency to reform and purify the life, causing it to repel some forms of grossness."[25] They also agreed with Graham that substances stimulating the passions should be avoided. In accordance with this, they gave up "stimulants" including tobacco, (mostly chewed we will soon learn), medicine (mostly patent concoctions of problematic benefit), and the caffeine-laden drinks of coffee and tea. The most "ardent" stimulant they knew was alcohol. While they avoided drinking it in any quantity, they also tried to avoid zealotry on the subject. A distaste for polemics set them apart from Grahamites as did their religious orientation. What was efficacious about diet was the result, after all, of divine agency. Faith in Christ, they averred, was the surest road to health, happiness, and longevity.[26]

In this letter to her older brother, Harriet Skinner makes two points about Community eating habits. First, the communards have come to consume more vegetables and less meat. Second, the overall amount of the food they eat has declined. These changes were gradual. The Perfectionists simply "slid" into this way of doing things. Skinner emphasizes, as well, the effectiveness of peer pressure: Community "principles and institutions" have the power, she says, "to produce radical changes."

Text 44: "Community Eating" by Harriet Skinner. *Circular*, July 5, 1869, p. 127-128.

O. C. June 22, 1869

Dear John:

I have of late been somewhat interested in the alimentive history of the Community. There appears to be an ill-defined impression among people at large, that they eat too much, and that they eat the wrong things. I don't know how it may be in other countries, but there is a prevailing idea that in America, we eat too much meat. This feeling is doubtless in many cases greatly exaggerated, and wrong. Eating both in respect to quality and quantity has come to be regarded as almost the chief of sins against the body; yet it is doubtless true that a most radical reform is sadly needed in that department, and it is interesting to observe how that reform was initiated and had been carried on among us in the Community. It had more of the nature of a growth than a legislative enactment; a silent growth, which as in the case of vegetation, has been almost unobserved. It is in respect to quality rather than quantity, that we can most easily notice the change. We slid almost unconsciously into the use of a chiefly vegetable diet, and that at a time when fruit was not so abundant as it is now.

I must rely mainly on the cooks for my information in respect to the quantity of food now consumed by the Community, as compared with its consumption in times past. Having been kitchen man for the last eight months, and it being customary for the two mothers (as they are called) to be relieved of their duties every three weeks, I have been in a specially favorable position for collecting testimony; which is invariably to the effect that we do not consume nearly as much as we used to; while our numbers, at this family, are nearly the same. We kitchen folks are in the habit of measuring things by panfuls or dipperfuls, and often hearing the remark, that "we used always to have so many panfuls, and now we don't have but so many," my curiosity became excited some on this point, and I have of late made inquiries of individuals here and there, and the reply has almost invariably been that they eat much less than formerly.

Finally, with a view to approaching still closer to a solution of the question, I undertook the other day to weigh every thing that went to the table, and also weighed every thing that was gathered up afterwards. I found the family consumed of various articles of food, not including the malt coffee, five hundred and twenty-two pounds eight ounces; dividing this between the two hundred and two members, of which the family consists, and adding a small estimate of salt not weighed, and of what was consumed between meals, it amounted to two pounds ten ounces for each person per day. Wishing to ascertain whether this was a large or small quantity as compared with the ordinary standard of living, I hunted up a table in Liebig's Chemistry, which gives an accurate account of the daily amount consumed by the soldiers belonging to one of the German Principalities. All the items added together, not including beer and brandy, amounted to three pounds fifteen ounces, or one ounce short of four pounds daily per man, which is exactly one-third more than the average consumed by each person in the Oneida Community.

I ought, perhaps, to mention that milk is the article that we consume most of; amounting to one hundred and seventy-two pounds, or ninety-seven pounds more than potatoes, the next highest article on the list. Milk is not in the list of articles of food consumed by the soldiers.

I would not, of course, claim that a single experiment like this, would determine the average daily amount consumed by each person in the Community; and moreover, the fact that we have twenty-three children, and about as many women as men, would have an important bearing in the case; as also the fact that people eat least at this time of year. Nevertheless, putting together the few facts which I have obtained, it is easy to see on which side of the question the weight of evidence lies.

Assuming that our manner of living in Community, in connection with our peculiar views, religious, moral and social, have enabled us to change the quality of our living from the ordinary meat diet to one mainly vegetarian; and secondly that it has enabled us to reduce very materially the quantity of food consumed in a given time, the following interesting points naturally suggest themselves. First, the power of our principles and institutions to produce radical changes of the above kind. Secondly, that in a true normal condition of human nature, mankind will consume a great deal less of material food. Without stopping to discuss these points at length in this communication, I will simply suggest for your consideration the words of Christ, where he says, "man shall not live by bread alone, but by every word that proceedeth out of the mouth of God."

Yours truly, H. J. S.

Part Seven: Influence of Women

From early 1849 through late 1854, Brooklyn-based Noyes would suggest various courses of action to his followers in Oneida. In this instance, he proposed that the men should give up tobacco. As always, the Oneidans tried their best to carry out his recommendations. In this case, they threw themselves into eradicating tobacco addiction. The success of the 1853 campaign resulted from pressure applied by the women to the men. "The women of the O. C. seduced the men away from tobacco," Noyes is quoted as saying. "And as their fascinations are growing stronger every day, I consider myself safe out of slavery"—that is, tobacco slavery.

Text 45: "Subjugating the Tobacco Principality" by Harriet Worden, *Oneida Circular*, June 12, 1871, p. 188-189[27]

One of the greatest triumphs ever achieved by the Oneida Community was the complete subjugation of the TOBACCO PRINCIPALITY—the principality to which millions of people are in bondage today.[28] A large majority of the men were addicted to the use of tobacco in one form or other before coming to the Community, and until the year 1853 continued it as freely as formerly. The effect on individuals was often deleterious, causing them from time to time to make strenuous efforts to leave off the use of it in toto: but laws and resolutions were unavailing; their taste for the fascinating "weed" was too strong for them, and they returned to using it as before.

But a short experience in the Community during the existence of this filthy habit was enough to make all wish for a change. It certainly was a great drawback to the attractiveness of home. Even the men were conscious of this fact, but had not the strength to break away from their servility to the tyrannical principality. The women were very much annoyed with the uncleanness of the habit, but were forbearing, remembering that "charity covereth a multitude of sins." Still they could not ignore the fact that at the best, tobacco is a dirty, nasty weed, not only scenting everything with which it comes in contact, but when used in the mouth particularly offensive, as it produces the desire to expectorate often, which is in itself revolting. Spittoons were in requisition, not only in all the public rooms, but in many of the bed-chambers besides; and these nuisances had to be emptied and washed every day by the women—and oh! with such feelings of disgust! Many and many a time was the wish expressed, "that the men would give up tobacco—it would be so much better." Still no one expected such a change would actually be realized during the present generation.

Matters continued in this way for four or five years, when one day, in the month of March, 1853, there came from Brooklyn, a long Home-Talk by J. H. N., entitled "Tobacco Reform." It was a startling title, and produced no little sensation among the tobacco-lovers here at Oneida. However, the Home-Talk was not only received with favor, but after reflection all were ready to carry out the spirit of it. After defining the nature of the tobacco-fascination, and repudiating anything like legality in the matter, Mr. Noyes remarked:

> "I would propose that the Community contemplate as the hope of their calling the entire breaking up of this bondage. I am in no hurry about measures, but let us take this as our 'stint,' so that by faith we can see to the end. If we have a faith that sees to the end, we shall be 'warping up' to it. In one way or another I am confident that the tobacco-devil, instead of leading us captive, is going to be itself led captive.
>
> "To come to something practical, I would recommend that those who are free from tobacco should not contemplate using it, but keep their freedom. And I would recommend to those who can drop the use of it, without quarreling with themselves, to do so at once. While to those who are thoroughly imprisoned in the use of tobacco, I would recommend the experiment of a fast; say, for instance, next Sunday. Let us quit it for one day, and give up our minds to reflection and attention to the Lord's mind about such matters."

The proposal to keep a fast of one day from tobacco was readily acceded to, and Sunday, April 3, 1853, was appointed as the time. Although one day may seem a very limited suspension, it is true that a number of our good brothers underwent a severe struggle in denying themselves their favorite solace for even so short a time. A member writing to Brooklyn about it afterward, said:

"There was one interesting fact connected with our tobacco fast, which I will report. Nearly all the men who had been in the habit of using tobacco were affected with dizziness—making them feel very much as a person who had drunk too much wine. It was also interesting that many, both men and women, who had never used tobacco, were affected in the same way; but had no suspicion of the cause, till they heard the experience of the tobacco-chewers, smokers and snuffers in the evening meeting."

On comparing notes it was found that not only at Oneida, but at our Communities in Newark, Brooklyn, Putney and Wallingford, the experience was much the same while fasting from tobacco. And the event of the fast seemed to loosen the hold of the tyrant, and the Community began to feel an inspiration to conquer the habit such as they never had had before. In a few days Mr. Noyes sent word to Oneida—"Bear it in mind that the purpose which we propose to ourselves is to make an end sooner or later of the bondage we have been in to this tobacco principality. We will set no time and make no resolutions in regard to specific things to be done, for the accomplishment of that end; but we will set it before us as the result for which we are bound in faith. We must be in earnest that legality is not substituted for faith. If we wish to succeed, it will be essential to keep legality out of the matter."

Thus warned, the Community were armed, and the miraculous, magical change was effected almost without an effort. The mood was on for crushing the tyrant forever. Four days after the fast, one reported in Brooklyn, "There is but very little tobacco used here now. Several have left off entirely, and others use it only temperately. We keep the matter open to the light, by telling our experience in the meetings every evening."

There was no condemnation brought upon those who, from time to time, chose to use it, but the prevailing feeling seemed to be, that it was better to abstain from it, as far as possible without legality. In fact, it was a grand, inspired move, entered into by the whole family; and from this very fact destined to succeed. Over thirty of the men left off the use of tobacco simultaneously, and found strength to resist temptation about it afterward. There were others who were weak in temptation, but who finally found strength, in their union with those who were victorious, to abandon it altogether. Gradually tobacco became unpopular, and many who had for years been slaves found themselves free; and before the end of the year tobacco was not used in the Community, and from that time to this (now eighteen years) has found no place among us. We think with thankfulness, what a blessed freedom! What a salvation it has been for the young men growing up in our midst; not one of whom is addicted to this degrading practice. Our house is clean and sweet—no rooms fuming with smoke—no floors discolored with spittle—no spittoons to disgrace our parlors—but home attractive for all to enjoy. Thank God the inspiration, combined with faith, that enabled out brothers to step from bondage to freedom!

A few years since ome of our people wrote their "tobacco experience," from which I will extract a few paragraphs. After relating the story of his tobacco-service, which lasted twelve or fifteen years, Mr. G. W. N. winds up with;

> "Good bye Anderson Lorrillard and Lillienthal. Your companionship, cosy as it is, brings with it a bad smell. Good bye, Mrs. G. B. Miller. Your charming influence does not render a man very acceptable to others of your sex. Thank God, the reign of yellow drizzle, spittoons, stale scents and 'old-soldiers,' is over! Thank God, the most vile, absurd, unclean, slave-driving tyranny that ever cursed humanity is hereabouts broken, and the insurrection is spreading!"

Mr. William H. Woolworth (**Figure 40**) contributes the following:

> "I should no doubt have been in tobacco bonds to this day, but for the combined Community rising and revolt against narcotic tyranny, which carried all irresistibly before it. I did not seem to get free at once, however, from the tobacco principality. But for years after my emancipation from all voluntary bondage, I would be subject to imposition in my sleeping hours, and compelled to imaginary chewing in my dreams. But for the last two years I have rejoiced in complete deliverance from imaginary as well as real narcotic servitude; thanks to the combined movement."

Figure 40: William H. Woolworth (1824-1904)

Mr. J. Burt finishes his story with the following paragraph:

> "My bondage to the habit of chewing tobacco continued without intermission till I was forty-six years old, when Communism finally set me free. It was on this wise: The Community men after due deliberation decided by unanimous vote to expel tobacco from their circle. The rout was complete. More than thirty of us broke from its use simultaneously, and the Community as a body has remained undefiled by it for fifteen years. A few days sufficed to clear me from all hankering for it, and I have been a healthier and happier man in

consequence."

One of the women thus appropriately spoke the mind of her sex:

> "A woman's love must be strong indeed that can surmount tobacco, and her sense of the poetical must suffer when she views the accompaniments necessary for the tobacco-chewer, in the shape of spittoons, etc., or, still worse, when she sees her best beloved, with pursed-up mouth and eager eyes, looking for a suitable place—to spit.
>
> "For myself the antipathy to tobacco grew stronger and stronger, arising partly from disgust and partly from a conviction that its use was injurious to the body and enslaving to the mind. Thus there commenced a series of domestic skirmishes, usually ending in the cheerful surrender of the tobacco-box to my safe-keeping for days together; and as the disbursement of its contents was left entirely to my generosity, it is needless to say that the box was empty at the close of every campaign.
>
> "This state of things continued; dislike on one side, and slavery on the other, until that blessed era in Community history—when the men, with the love of truth for their guide and that stern heroism which goes to battle to conquer—threw aside their tobacco, and declared themselves freemen. That was no less a glorious day for the women. They have no longer a rival in tobacco, but are united with their brothers in abolishing slavery in all its forms. For this and a thousand other deliverances the women of the O.C. have to thank Communism."

Mr. J. H. Noyes, after relating his experience with tobacco quite fully, concludes by giving the women of the O. C. considerable credit for the reform. He says:

> "My final theory was that Communism was to be the liberator from tobacco-slavery. I held Parton's doctrine that tobacco is a rival of woman, and woman is the natural enemy of tobacco; and I had faith that a good time was coming, when Communism would liberate woman from slavery to man, and then she, by her new charms and reactions, would liberate man from slavery to tobacco. In short that genuine Free Love would burn out tobacco from between man and woman. This faith has been realized. Fifteen years ago the women of the O. C. seduced the men away from tobacco; and as their fascinations are growing stronger every day, I consider myself safe out of slavery."

All agreed in saying of tobacco, "Good riddance;" and whether brought about through an influence exerted by the women, or through some deeper influence, we are sure the CURE IS EFFECTUAL.

Part Eight: Visitors to the Mansion House

Almost from the beginning, the Oneida Community welcomed visitors to their house and grounds and are often credited with the development of central New York as a tourist destination. When the first Mansion House was completed in 1849, there was a reception room for visitors near the front door. Members of the community wrote and published guidebooks and even a cookbook. As the house was enlarged and renovated over time, the reception room remained a central feature of the house. In the pages of the *Circular*, visitors were welcomed and letters from thankful visitors were often published. Of all the visitors, the most famous was Frederick Douglass, who visited the Mansion House on July 16, 1853 during an anti-slavery speaking tour of central New York. [29] Douglass was welcomed to the house by J.L. Skinner who showed him some of the rooms as well as the grounds and then accompanied him to the Methodist Church where he gave a speech. Throughout the 1850s, visitors came to the Mansion House where they were given tours of the buildings and grounds. In the 1860s, July 4 celebrations had become annual events, drawing thousands of visitors, who came by canal, stage coach, and increasingly by train. By the end of the decade, some 45,000 visitors had come to the Mansion House. The construction of a depot of the Midland Railroad in 1868 increased the ease with which visitors could come. This article was a part of a special, extra edition of the *Circular*, designed to provide information to visitors to the Mansion House.

Text 46: "Stranger's Guide to the O.C.," *Circular*, March 21, 1870, p. 1

Visitors on arriving at Oneida by New York Central Railroad, may proceed to the Community (distant about four miles) either on foot, or by carriage hired at the livery, or by the cars of the Midland Railroad. The pedestrian follows for most of the distance the straight path of the railway track. The carriage route is through the main street of Oneida, to Oneida Castle, a village of many Indian reminiscences, and thence up the valley of Oneida Creek, a mile and a. half through a well-cultivated district to the Community domain. Time, three quarters of an hour. By the Midland cars, which make two trips a day, the traveler is set down in about seven minutes at the O.C. station, within a stone's throw of the Community dwellings. Fare, fifteen cents. Visitors from the north or south have no change to make, as the Community station is on the new route from Oswego to New York (nearly completed), and is a stopping-place of all the trains.

THE APPROACH

The approach by railroad gives some pleasing views of the Community dwellings, particularly from the south, where at the distance of an eighth of a mile the track is over a high trestle-work. The route which for ten miles descends along the hill-sides bordering the Oneida valley, here opens into the basin of Oneida Lake, which as a broad plain extends for any miles to the north, east, and west. The Community is situated just at the mouth of the valley and at the beginning of the plain.

The railroad passes for a mile diagonally through the Community domain, in the rear of the dwellings. The approach from the station being also in the rear, is through a part of the grounds which has been heretofore the least embellished. Paths, however, have been recently laid out and shade trees planted, which will soon render this an agreeable part of the Community surroundings.

RECEPTION-ROOM

A walk of three minutes from the station brings the visitor to a rear entrance of the mansion, opening into a small summer-court. Passing through it he enters a hall on the right which conducts to a reception-room (**Figure 41**), where he will usually find a gentleman or lady attendant who will answer his inquiries and give him directions for making the tour of the place. If they are absent, a word addressed to any person on the premises will bring the required attention. No pay is taken from those who merely wish to see the institution, but every facility is freely accorded to them.

Directly opposite this reception-room is the visitors' dining-room, where refreshments are served. Persons wishing for dinner should procure their tickets as soon after arrival as convenient, to give the kitchen department suitable time for preparation.

Those who desire to see the public rooms will now be furnished with a guide, or with directions by which they may go alone. Some may be curious to commence at the foundation and visit

THE BASEMENTS

A stairway in the vestibule by which we entered, conducts to them. The visitor on descending finds himself fronted by numerous passages, flanked by stout foundation walls, leading to the store-rooms, the fruit-cellars, etc. The length of these basement- and partition-walls is over one-third of a mile. Most of the apartments and passages formed by them are kept at a summer temperature by steampipes which pass through them, and hence are well adapted to housing exotic plants during the winter months. In the store-rooms are long bins of preserved-fruits and vegetables. Here are also bath-rooms, and play-rooms for the children in stormy weather. The most interesting part of this substructure is the apartment occupied by the steam-heating apparatus. Here is a new Phleger's steam generator of thirty horse-power, which is, materially speaking, the heart of the institution. From it pipes are carried to all the principal rooms of this and the adjoining building, for heating and other purposes. It cooks the food in the kitchen, heats water for all purposes, and drives

Figure 41: Oneida Community members greet visitors in the Reception Room.

a steam-engine for printing and manufacturing. A mile and a half of iron pipe is used for these several purposes. A single man only is required to attend the steam-generator. Yet its genial influence is almost omnipresent, enabling the Community to dispense wholly with stoves in the main building, and furnishing power wherever it is needed.

THE MAIN PILE

Returning to the vestibule on the ground-floor by which we entered, we may now pass out through an eastern door to the lawn in front of the main building. The latter is seen to be of brick, with stone trimmings, and to consist of a center and two wings with a tower at either end. It is 188 feet long by 70 broad and has extensions reaching 100 feet in the rear. The southern wing has been recently built, and with its mansard roof gives three habitable stories. The towers are four stories in height.

PARLOUR AND LIBRARY

The principal entrance, through the portico of the central buildings, leads to various public rooms. On the right, as we enter, is a parlor; on the left a cloak-room and office with toilet conveniences for gentlemen. The parlor contains a stereoscope with views, a few engravings, and a register wherein visitors commonly write their names. Further on, the entrance-hall is crossed by another, leading to the wings on either hand. Next we come to the library on the left of the main staircase. This is a cozy room for the student, containing a collection of 3300 volumes. It is always open for the use of the Community and its guests. The reading-tables are supplied with files of many of the leading newspapers and periodicals of the day.

MUSEUM

Ascending the staircase we enter a vestibule which contains a dozen interesting pictures, and the nucleus of a museum. Among the curiosities are a few animal remains, including the well-preserved tooth of a mastodon, some stalactites, old books, relics from Pompeii and Egypt, medals, Indian weapons, etc. A case of birds prepared by a member of the Community may be examined by persons interested in taxidermy.

THE MEETING HALL

From the vestibule, doors open into the Hall or Chapel, a large room 21 feet high and frescoed. A stage and curtain on the front give conveniences of concerts, lectures and dramatic entertainments. A piano and harmonium, always present, invite to musical practice by the Community members or by visitors. During the summer, music will generally be given here at a certain hour each afternoon, at which visitors may be present. The main use of the Hall is for the social meetings of the Community, which are held in it for an hour every evening. Here, by converse on all topics of interest, the members cultivate the spirit of brotherhood which binds them together.

THE WINGS

The part of the building we have now seen comprise all the public rooms which are ordinarily open to visitors. The north wing of the building contains the living apartments of the family, and the. South wing is occupied by the children, their attendants and others. The quiet of the occupants requires of course, that these portions should be closed from intrusion. To visit them, persons should first obtain permission from an attendant.

THE TOWER

To gain a birds-eye view of the Community grounds and the surrounding country, the visitor may now pass out of the front entrance and ascend the tower. On reaching the top by a winding staircase, a landscape of uncommon beauty lies spread before him. At his feet, the lawn with its neatly trimmed paths, the flower gardens with their brilliant colors, and the rustic seats and arbors, half concealed in shaded nooks, entice the eye with their quiet loveliness. Beyond are the orchards and vineyards, then the emerald meadows and winding stream, and in the distance, the gently rounded hills which bound the sides of the valley. The Community hoe farm extends for half a mile in most directions from this spot, and towards the northeast its breadth is over a mile. Six hundred and sixty-four acres is the whole of the Community domain.

ORCHARDS AND VINEYARDS

If the visitor's curiosity is not satisfied by this general survey, he may walk through the grounds and view more nearly the features of the place. The orchards and vineyards lie mainly towards the west and north. The fruit-products from them in 1869 were:

> Apple .... 400 bbls.
> Pears .... 117 bbls.
> Grapes .... 5000 lbs.

Formerly, large quantities of the smaller fruits were here produced and shipped to the various markets of the country. O.C. strawberries were well-known from Portland to New York. The "strawberry short-cake" here served, gave to thousands of visitors their first idea of the capabilities that delicate compound. A large amount of fruit was also preserved for housekeepers in St. Paul, Chicago, Buffalo, and New York. But the attempt to feed the multitudes abroad on this fare tasked too severely the strength of the Community, and they have recently given up the commerce in small fruits. Berry culture is now nearly restricted to the wants of the family and the supply required for visitors.

KITCHEN

The culinary and dining apartments of the Community are in the Tontine, a large brick building standing a few rods in the rear of the main dwelling. Ordinarily it is reached by passing across the intervening court; but in bad weather persons may enter it through an arched passage leading from the boiler-room without out-door exposure. One half of the basement is occupied by the family kitchen. Much of the cooking is here done by a steam range, and many labor-saving appliances are in use, such as a dish-washing apparatus, mop-wringers, vegetable-washing-machines, etc., in all of which, machinery is made to work in the most effective way for lightening woman's labor. Here also is the bakery, where three or four barrels of flour are weekly made into bread. All the heavier parts of kitchen-work are performed by men. Directly above the kitchen is the Community dining-room, arranged with twelve tables and offering seats to one hundred and twenty-five persons. It communicates with the kitchen by a dumb-waiter.

The building we are in includes, besides the kitchen and dining-room, certain mechanical industries, as we perceive by the hum of business issuing from some of its rooms. Opposite the kitchen in the basement is the

DYE-ROOM

Here all the silk manufactured by the Community receives its many-colored hues, matching almost every tint in nature. This department is under the general supervision of an educated chemist, the practical details being managed by experts of both sexes.

In another part of the basement is an engine, driven by steam from the boiler in the large mansion, and used for driving the machinery of the

SPOOLING-ROOM

This is on the first floor of the building. Here the finished silk which comes from the factory and dye-room is in skeins, is first transferred by a winding machine to "bobbins," and then, by a dozen hands, mostly of young women, seated at spooling machines, is deftly wound on spools, ready for market. Observe the brilliant gloss that the silk takes under their manipulation. The spools are packed ready for shipment in another room. Here you may see in Kelly's Patent Case, the fine prismatic display from which ladies select their colored sewing-silks in many of the leading stores of the country.

PRINTING-OFFICE

Two rooms in the next story are occupied by the printing-office. Here the CIRCULAR, the weekly organ of the Community is printed, folded and mailed. The type-setting is done mostly by young women.

LAUNDRY

Seventy rods from the mansion in a southern direction, is the laundry. This is fitted up with a steam-boiler, washing and wringing-machines, mangle, dry-room, and many conveniences by which the weekly washing, amounting in summer to 4000 pieces, is easily and cheaply executed. The labor in this department is mostly done by hired employees.

SEMINARY

Returning up the road to a point nearly in front of the Community dwellings, we pass the Seminary. This is two stories high, with a tower. Here are the children's schoolroom and recitation-rooms for classes of youths and adults. It is fitted up with a convenient chemical laboratory where regular courses of experimental instruction are given to pupils; and an audience-room where lectures on the physical sciences may be attended by the whole Community.

STORE

To stock-fanciers and others, the barns may next be worth a call. The horse-barn is fitted up for the reception of 25 horses (the usual number of animals belonging to the Community), and can accommodate more. Here the hostler will always be ready to take charge of visitors' teams. The cattle-barn a few rods further on, is a large and rather unique affair, designed with many conveniences to serve the demands of a large farm. Seventy cattle are generally kept here, a fair proportion of which are pure bred Ayrshires. The dairy result is 33,000 galls. of milk per year.

WILLOW-PLACE WORKS

Those who wish to examine still further the Community system of industry, will find the main manufactures at Willow-Place, distant about a mile from the Oneida home. Here, situated on a first-class water-power of the Sconondoa Creek, are the trap-works, the silk-works, the forge and machine-shops, employing in all about 130 hands. The number of traps made annually, for distribution through all parts of the continent where fur-bearing animals are found, is over 300,000. They comprise eight sizes.

SILK FACTORY

In the silk-works is manufactured the machine-twist, which, as a finished article we saw undergoing the final process of spooling at O.C. This manufacture employs about eighty girls, most of them hired from the neighboring villages. A department of ribbon and dress-silk weaving is carried on in one part of the building.

MACHINE SHOP AND FOUNDRY

The machine-shop is constantly busy manufacturing machinery for all the other departments. One quarter of a mile up the creek, situated on another fine water-power, are the Community foundry and saw-mill, whose productions also contribute in many ways to the manufacturing interest.

W.P. COMMUNITY

The Willow-Place Community family, numbering thirty-five, occupy a convenient dwelling separated from the factory by a plot of grass and a few fruit trees. Near them is a pleasant sheet of water for bathing and boating, and beyond is a domain of over two hundred acres of fertile land. The business affairs of Willow-Place are conducted through the home office at O.C. Their interests are wholly in common, and the families make frequent visits and interchanges of members.

Having gone over the principal points of interest we may now return to O.C. in season for music in the Hall. The Community is not a hotel, and does not undertake to lodge visitors over night. It reserves the privilege, however, of treating as non-paying guests those who call with letters of introduction, or who have business with the Society. Good hotels for the accommodation of strangers may be found at Oneida or Oneida Castle.

PUBLICATIONS

All respect inquiries by visitors as to the principles and operation of the institution are freely answered. But to save the great of amount of oral explanation which unlimited curiosity would impose on the attendants, visitors are referred for information to the publications of the Community.

EXCURSIONS

The following places are within excursion distance of the O.C.:

Place	Distance	How Reached
Trenton Falls	44 Ms.	By R.R.
Utica	31 "	" "
Rome	17 "	" "
Syracuse	32 "	" "
Chittenango	15 "	" "
Oneida Lake	13 "	" "
Hamilton	18 "	" " to Eaton
Clinton	13 "	" Carriage
Verona Springs	6 "	" "
Cazenovia Lake	18 "	" "

Almost in sight form the Community tower are two small Indian villages, which represent nearly all that remains in this State of the once powerful Oneida tribe. Clinton, mentioned in the above list, is the seat of Hamilton College, distinguished for its superior observatory. At Hamilton is Madison University, a principal college of the Baptists. Chittenango is noted for its Sulphur Springs and a romantic cascade. Verona Springs is a popular place of summer resort.

Notes

1. Hinds quoted in Lawrence Foster, ed., *Free Love in Utopia: John Humphrey Noyes and the Origin of the Oneida Community, Compiled by George Wallingford Noyes* (Urbana: University of Illinois Press, 2001), 133.
2. Oneida Community. *Mutual Criticism* (Oneida, NY: Office of the American Socialist, 1876). Hinds is apparently quoting freely from p. 79 and, perhaps, elsewhere.
3. Robert S. Fogarty, ed., *Special Love/Special Sex: An Oneida Community Diary* (Syracuse, NY: Syracuse University Press, 1994), 215 ("in our society"). Dating from 1892, Theodore Noyes's description of the Community sex system is quoted extensively in Constance Noyes

Robertson, *Oneida Community: The Breakup, 1876-1881* (Syracuse, NY: Syracuse University Press, 1972), 16-20; in Fogarty, *Special Love / Special Sex*, 214-17; and in Foster, Free Love in Utopia, xxii-xxiii.

4. "Last evening" is from Robert Allerton Parker, *A Yankee Saint: John Humphrey Noyes and the Oneida Community* (New York: G. P. Putnam's Sons, 1935), 258.

5. "Old Mansion House Memories X," *Oneida Circular*, April 10, 1871, p. 115.

6. Maren Lockwood Carden, *Oneida: Utopian Community to Modern Corporation* (Syracuse, NY: Syracuse University Press, 1998; originally published 1969), 119; Robert S. Fogarty, ed., *Desire and Duty at Oneida: Tirzah Miller's Intimate Memoir* (Bloomington, University of Indiana Press, 2000), 178-79; Spencer Klaw, *Without Sin: The Life and Death of the Oneida Community* (New York: Allen Lane, Penguin, 1993), 253-54; Robertson, *Oneida Community: The Breakup*, 160; and Jane K. Rich, ed., *A Lasting Spring: Jessie Catherine Kinsley, Daughter of the Oneida Community* (Syracuse, NY: Syracuse University Press, 1983), 53 ("I do not understand"), 60.

7. Pierrepoint Burt Noyes, *My Father's House: An Oneida Boyhood* (New York: Farrar and Rinehart, 1937), 207.

8. Community Journal, February 17, 1864; Robert S. Fogarty, ed., *Desire and Duty at Oneida*, 36 ("I should be insincere"). See also Taylor Stoehr, *Free Love in America: A Documentary History* (New York: AMS, 1979), 30.

9. Anthony Wonderley, ed., *John Humphrey Noyes on Sexual Relations in the Oneida Community: Four Essential Texts* (Hamilton College Library, Clinton, NY: Richard S. Couper Press, 2012), 77.

10. Fogarty, *Desire and Duty at Oneida*, 60.

11. Fogarty, *Desire and Duty at Oneida*, 72 ("I told him I should like that"). Noyes's 1872 monograph on stirpiculture (Essay on Scientific Propagation) is given in Anthony Wonderley, ed., *John Humphrey Noyes on Sexual Relations in the Oneida Community: Four Essential Texts* (Hamilton College Library, Clinton, NY: Richard S. Couper Press, 2012), 127-62.

12. Spencer C. Olin, Jr., "The Oneida Community and the Instability of Charismatic Authority," *Journal of American History* 67, no. 2 (September 1980), 298; Klaw, *Without Sin*, 242. Ackley's comment is in Stephen R. Leonard, Jr., "Recollections," photocopy of unpublished manuscript (Oneida Community Mansion House Archives, ca. 1951), 1. Fogarty, *Special Love/Special Sex*, 133; and *Desire and Duty at Oneida*, 163-64 ("very much disaffected" and "Oh! Is he a crazy

enthusiast"); Ely Van der Warker, "A Gynecological Study of the Oneida Community," *American Journal of Obstetrics and Diseases of Women and Children* 17, no. 8 (August 1884), 789.
13. Fogarty, *Desire and Duty at Oneida*, 154.
14. One has to read between the lines to detect "the ever-encrypted references to sex in Oneida letters" (Ellen Wayland-Smith, *Oneida: From Free Love to the Well-Set Table* [New York: Picador, 2016], 110).
15. Sally Roesch Wagner, "The Iroquois Influence on Women's Rights," in *Indian Roots of American Democracy*, edited by José Barreiro, 115-34 (Ithaca, NY: Akwe:kon Press, 1992), and "The Untold Story of the Iroquois Influence on Early Feminist," *On the Issues Magazine* (Winter 1996): pagination unknown (Long Island City, NY: Choices Women's Medical Center).
16. Part IV of the series "Old Mansion-House Memories," in *Oneida Circular*, February 6, 1871. Slightly abbreviated and edited, the piece was republished in Harriet M. Worden's *Old Mansion House Memories, by One Brought Up in It* (Oneida, NY: Oneida Ltd., 1950), 10-11.
17. Rich, *A Lasting Spring*, 15.
18. P. B. Noyes, *My Father's House*, 65.
19. Corinna Ackley Noyes, *The Days of My Youth* (Hamilton College Library, Clinton, NY: Richard W. Cooper Press, 2011; originally published 1960), 50.
20. Oneida Community, *Second Annual Report of the Oneida Association: Exhibiting Its Progress to February 20, 1850* (Oneida Reserve, NY: Oneida Association, 1850), 11.
21. *American Socialist*, April 6, 1876, 26 ("Fourier had a glorious scheme"); Carl J. Guarneri, "Reconstructing the Antebellum Communitarian Movement: Oneida and Fourierism," *Journal of the Early Republic* 16, no. 3 (Autumn 1996), 476.
22. *Circular*, July 27, 1853, 291, "The Anti-Slavery Lecture".
23. *Oneida Circular*, May 24, 1875 and (in this volume) "One of the Four," Part XII ("ever a live one").
24. *Circular*, August 30, 1855, 127 and March 10, 1859, 28; Harriet M. Worden, *Old Mansion House Memories, by One Brought Up in It* (Oneida, NY: Oneida Ltd., 1950), 32.
25. *Circular*, March 9, 1853, 181 ("those who eat swine's flesh").
26. *Circular*, January 28, 1854, 94 (what was efficacious); Foster, *Free Love in Utopia*, 249-60.
27. *Oneida Circular*, June 12, 1871, 188-89; Part XIV of the series "Old Mansion-House Memories." Slightly altered, the piece was republished in a 1950 volume (also called *Old Mansion House Memories*) on pp. 40-44.

28. The word "principality" denoted, in the Oneida Community, a bad habit, influence, or state of mind (Klaw, *Without Sin*, 17). A principality seems to have been regarded as a domain ruled by Satan or by one of his minion demons.
29. The visit is described in detail in J.L. Skinner, "An Anti-slavery Lecture," *Circular*, July 22, 1853, p. 291.

Chapter 6. Conclusion

"We made a raid into an unknown country, charted it and returned without the loss of a man, woman or child," Noyes wrote of the Community.¹ This book assembles a number of the dispatches the communards sent from that foreign land. The featured missives convey memories of Community origin and development, musings about principles guiding and inspiring them, and descriptions of activities and habits comprising their daily lives. This testimonial material complements and expands the testimonial legacy of the Oneida Community.

Figure 42: Oneida Community men and women reading, studying, and learning in the Mansion House library.

Histories

Presented first is a selection of rarely consulted, and presumably little known, Community histories. The first two are reminiscences by John Noyes's sister, Harriet Skinner. If members of the Community had been asked who among them was the historian of the collectivity, the answer would have been this individual. She contributed more to Oneida's publications than any other woman or, for that matter, more than any man other than Noyes.²

Originally columns in the Community's newspaper, Skinner's accounts were written to commemorate recently deceased Charlotte Miller and to tell younger members how the Community came about. Together "One of the Four" (1875) and "A Community Transplanted" (1879) paint a portrait of the Noyes parents as unpretentious, approachable, and hospitable. The couple attracted good will. They forged what sounds like a happy marriage and furnished a nurturing environment for their children growing up in Putney, Vermont--a place and time vividly conveyed. During the 1820s, it was home to a brilliant society given over to "music and dancing, jewels and plumes, fine horses and martial parade." But that world was shattered "suddenly and totally" by the financial crash of 1831. As the leading men went bankrupt, their failures set off a "reign of estrangements and separations. Pleasant windows were darkened and every courtesy chilled." These distressing circumstances prepared Putney for the great transformation effected by the Finney revival. "A more powerful control," as Skinner describes that event, "cannot be imagined."

> It made a new society wherever it went. It abolished caste; it raised up the low and humbled the proud; it changed the customs. Vain show of dress and beauty was all forgotten in the solemnity of its presence. The dance gave way to the prayer meeting, and for a time religion was supreme over business. It was the "talk in barrooms and stores as well as in the churches."[3]

Everything, as John Noyes put it, "which does not center on this one object of getting ready to die is vanity and delusion."[4] Such was the fear that swept the countryside and sent Noyes off to study theology. Religion, in fact, was on everyone's mind and the new Perfectionist movement generated considerable enthusiasm. But suddenly turning sour, Perfectionism suffered "discord and dissension."[5] In these circumstances, Noyes returned home to fashion his own organization. Much new information is provided about his Bible study group in Putney—the zealousness of the communicants, their commitment to study and how they became true communists in property and work. They "ceased to say 'mine and thine' respecting houses and lands and goods. The spirit which followed the teachings of their leader and their New Testament studies swept away the claims of selfish ownership as it did with the early Christians, and no man said 'that aught he possessed was his own.'"[6]

After touching on the subject of property, the thoughts of the group turned toward marriage and sexual relations. "The same spirit which swept away property distinctions stayed on in its course till even the selfish claims of marriage were also swept away. These changes were in no sense arbitrary, but the legitimate natural effect of the Pentecostal spirit which had taken possession of the Putney school." While Noyes's ideas about heavenly relations were earnestly considered, however, he and his followers "continued to walk in all the commandments and ordinances of common morality blameless," as Skinner put it. "there was probably never a people where the law of chastity was more respected."[7]

When circumstances dictated removal from Putney, these folk believed God superintended their movement to upstate New York as he did the Old Testament Israelites. God prepared the new setting for them by filling it with such advantageous features as Oneida Creek, Burt's mill, the Indians, and the spiritualistic milieu of the region. God ensured their early development by including the benefits of the Newhouse trap, the railroad, the setting of the Mansion House.

Figure 43: Ellen Nash Wright, Portia Underhill Allen, and Constance Bradley Reeve in the flower garden, once on the northwest end of the North Lawn. Bouquets were sold to the many visitors.

Harriet Skinner's reminiscences are particularly valuable for their information pertaining to the early New York days. There is much here about creating a commune, about inventing the practices of mingling, mutual criticism and bringing a children's department into existence. "The Community was then in its infancy, building houses, clearing land, planting trees, and doing its best "to make a living" from its farm and saw-mill, while disciplining and organizing its members."⁸ They had never been tempted into farming, Skinner affirms, and had always devoted the greatest part of their land to "the gardeners, the vine-dressers and fruit raisers."⁹ From the outset. they worked out a wholly original subsistence economy they called horticulture. They were always aware of how the outside world viewed them—that the doctrines of the OC filled the public with "horror and disgust."[10] This was the context in which the Hubbard affair threatened the fledgling Community's existence: "Our cup of trials seemed full to overflowing; but immediately following these sad events came persecutions from without, and of so bitter and unreasonable a character that the Community considered the question of seeking a new location." But they persevered and won through the crisis. The Oneida Community "died and rose again."[11]

Considerable biographical information is provided especially about Charlotte Miller who, with Harriet Skinner and Noyes, filled the office of "Community Mother."[12] One section of "One of the Four" (Part 18) is of Miller's authorship, a nostalgic account of her youthful friends, most of whom died young. This little cameo conveys how hard and hazardous life could be, especially for young women.

Doctrines

In the early days, Oneida Perfectionists of Oneida were determined to bring heaven to earth by counteracting sin with selfless acts and by duplicating heavenly life. Heaven, they imagined, was a place in which all property is commonly owned and all relations—social and sexual—are equally apportioned. In *Bible Argument*, the theological treatise excerpted here, Noyes focused on the sexual aspect of that belief. God, he reasoned, created men and women to love one another. In heaven, they love each other unstintingly, unselfishly and (he thought) heterosexually. That's what God intended; that's what they should be doing on earth: And loving one another, imitating heaven in this respect, will help to bring the celestial state to this realm.

God, Noyes insisted, created sex to be enjoyable. The way of heaven is to take pleasure in it, in, that is, the "amative" side of sexual intercourse. As in heaven, human lovers should be using their sexual organs as servants of their spiritual natures. In the excerpts given from Bible Argument, Noyes happily trumpets sexual intercourse as "a conversation of spirits," "a medium of magnetic and spiritual interchange," "a joyful act of fellowship," and "a method of ordering conversation."

A result of earthly sex is, admittedly, offspring. Children are a hard burden, especially for women. What we need, therefore, is the means to engage in sex as God intended without fear of pregnancy. The answer, according to Noyes, is that men cease to physically climax in coitus. No ejaculation, he believed, meant no seed to impregnate. In consequence, his Bible Argument set forth the theory of and justification for birth control as practiced by the Oneida Community. The decision to bear a child is, properly, the mother's prerogative. "Good sense and benevolence will very soon sanction and enforce the rule that woman shall bear children only when they choose," Noyes insists. "They have the principal burdens of breeding to bear, and they, rather than men, should have their choice of time and circumstances, at least till science takes charge of the business."[13] Prefigured in this last phrase is the eugenics program ("stirpiculture") which the Oneida Community would institute in the late 1860s.

Included are two pieces by James W. Towner, an individual best known as the leader of the group in opposition to Noyes and responsible for the breakup. Towner's writings remind us that, when he joined, he enthusiastically endorsed Noyes and hailed the Noyes-ian program as the corrective to society's ills.

In the first text, Towner alludes to the public discussion that had occurred over free love and other sexual issues, on the Swedenborgian shadow looming over the topic, and on the spiritualist movement which focused attention on the communicating with the dead. In the second, lawyer Towner sets forth a legal instrument for protecting the Community against court action instituted by disgruntled members, seceders wanting their entrance money refunded and their Community time compensated. With 250 signatures, it looks as though he obtained complete agreement on the promise not to sue the Oneida Community

Business

The production of animal traps—first by hand forge and then by machine—was the economic mainstay of the Oneida Community. At the same time, the Community did not want to depend on one means for their livelihood and developed a series of other businesses, including the canning of fruits and vegetables that they both grew and purchased, the manufacture of farm and household tools, the production of spools of silk threads for the newly invented sewing machine, as well as a number of other smaller ventures, such as making traveling bags. At the end of this session is an article about the beginning of the silverware business, the venture for which the Oneida Community would ultimately be best remembered. George Cragin introduces the Wallingford Community, Oneida's daughter colony staffed by about fifty communards rotating back and forth between New York and Connecticut. The most important and longest lasting of Oneida's satellites, Wallingford was regarded as Oneida's pastoral getaway. It was where Oneida's pastoral dream of a sylvan paradise in which men and women mingled together lasted longest. Additionally, It was the source of malaria that haunted Oneida's closing years. And it was at Wallingford, Cragin reminds us, that tableware was created. Silverware, the last industry developed by the Oneida Community, would support Oneida's successor organization—Oneida Ltd.—through the twentieth century.[14]

Practices

Secondary histories tend to portray the Oneida Community as a totalitarian sex cult run by John Noyes with power derived from doling out the sexual favors of his nubile seraglio.[15] That was not necessarily how the Community functioned in the eyes of those who were there. William Hinds—present at the creation and throughout the tenure of the Community—explains how the place actually worked ("Internal Governance"). The practice of mutual criticism was "the principal means of discipline and government." The forum of the daily meeting was where matters "of Community order and government" were conducted.

Also presented is material about Oneida life by authors of the next generation, those, that is, who grew up in the Community (Harriet Worden, Tirzah Miller). This section is comprised of firsthand, contemporaneous pieces describing the invention of the commune's distinctive feminine costume and how it resulted from necessity. Other writings illuminate how the Perfectionists' highly original system of raising children came about, again from their perspective, simply as a practical measure. Women in these selections express their views of themselves, what they thought of gender relations, and how those relations were lived out in daily routine. The last essay graphically illustrates the influence females wielded when it came to straightening out bad male habits such as the "tobacco principality."

Oneida Community history is most frequently told as the colorful tale of a Rasputin-like leader lording over a religious sex cult. But "the truth is," as they put it and "as all the world will one day see and acknowledge," the Perfectionists saw themselves as "social architects, with high moral and religious aims, whose experiments and discoveries they have sincerely believed would prove of value to mankind."[16] And as the final text shows, they delighted in welcoming visitors into their home. In accordance with the latter sentiment, this book features the writings of individual rank-and-file members. Their texts convey much that is new in the scholarly literature about the Community's early history, its motivating principles, and its distinctive features and practices. In so doing, the selections complement and expand the testimonial legacy of the Community. They convey much that is unavailable from other sources.

And they perform another service. A good reason to read what these articulate folk wrote is to learn something about the contentment in life. "I am sure I was happy," Community member Jessie Kinsley wrote years later. Constance Robertson recorded how her grandmother told her "that there had never been such happiness as they knew in the old Community. I believe this was honest testimony.... They worked, they lived together, they loved one another and above all—or because of this—they were simply happy. They were gay; they played as well as prayed. They saw all of life as good and their own lives as especially fortunate. So—until their last days—they were happy."[17]

Notes

1. John Humphrey Noyes, *History of American Socialisms* (Philadelphia: J. B. Lippincott, 1870).
2. Anthony Wonderley, ed., *Writings from Wallingford: The Connecticut Outpost of the Oneida Community* (Hamilton College Library, Clinton, NY: Richard W. Couper Press, 2020), 59, 62.
3. "music and dancing," "suddenly and totally," and "it made a new society," From "A Community Transplanted. From Putney to Oneida, I," *American Socialist*, August 14, 1879, 261-262. Reprinted in this volume, Chapter 2, Histories.
4. "One of the Four: A Memoir of Charlotte A. Miller, IV" *Oneida Circular*, March 29, 1875, 98. Reprinted in this volume, Chapter 2, Histories.
5. "One of the Four: A Memoir of Charlotte A. Miller, V" *Oneida Circular*, April 5, 1875, 106-107. Reprinted in this volume, Chapter 2, Histories.
6. "One of the Four: A Memoir of Charlotte A. Miller, X" *Oneida Circular*, May 10, 1875, 145-146. Reprinted in this volume, Chapter 2, Histories.
7. "One of the Four: A Memoir of Charlotte A. Miller, X" *Oneida Circular*, May 10, 1875, 145-146. Reprinted in this volume, Chapter 2, Histories.
8. "One of the Four: A Memoir of Charlotte A. Miller, XI" *Oneida Circular*, May 17, 1875, 153-154. Reprinted in this volume, Chapter 2, Histories.
9. "A Community Transplanted. From Putney to Oneida, V" *American Socialist*, September 11, 1879, 293-294. Reprinted in this volume, Chapter 2, Histories.
10. "One of the Four: A Memoir of Charlotte A. Miller, XIV" *Oneida Circular*, June 7, 1875, 178. Reprinted in this volume, Chapter 2, Histories.
11. "One of the Four: "A Memoir of Charlotte A. Miller, XIII, " *Oneida Circular*, May 31, 1875, 170-171. Reprinted in this volume, Chapter 2, Histories.
12. The office of "Community Mother" as regards Charlotte Miller is described in "One of the Four: A Memoir of Charlotte A. Miller, IV" *Oneida Circular*, March 29, 1875, 98 and "One of the Four: A Memoir of Charlotte A. Miller, XVIII", Oneida Circular, July 12, 1875, 222-23.
13. "Bible Argument," Proposition XX, by John Humphrey Noyes; See Wonderley, *John Humphrey Noyes on Sexual Relations*, p. 79.

14. Walter D. Edmonds, *The First Hundred Years, 1848-1948: 1848—Oneida Community, 1880—Oneida Community, Limited, 1935—Oneida Ltd.* (Oneida, NY: Oneida Ltd., 1948); John P. L. Hatcher, *Oneida (Community) Ltd.: A Goodly Heritage Gone Wrong* (Bloomington, IN: iUniverse, 2016); Anthony Wonderley, *Oneida Utopia: A Community Searching for Human Happiness and Prosperity* (Ithaca, NY: Cornell University Press, 2017), 173-79, 191-204.
15. Wonderley, *Oneida Utopia, 11-12.*
16. *American Socialist,* September 4, 1879, 284.
17. Jane K. Rich, ed. *A Lasting Spring: Jessie Catherine Kinsley, Daughter of the Oneida Community* (Syracuse: Syracuse University Press, 1983), 68; Constance Noyes Robertson, ed. *Oneida Community: An Autobiography, 1851-1876* (Syracuse: Syracuse University Press, 1970), xii-xiii.

Bibliography

Certain references given in the text to serial publications of the Oneida Community and the Mansion House are stand-alone citations not repeated in this bibliography. The Oneida Community's periodical, a newspaper-like magazine usually published weekly, went through several changes of name. *Spiritual Magazine* (begun in Putney and published between 1848 and 1850 in Oneida), *Free Church Circular (1850-1851), Circular (1851-1870), Oneida Circular (1871-1876), and American Socialist* (1876-1879). A newsletter printed for internal consumption (*Daily Journal*, 1866-1868) was preceded by the *Community Journal* (1863-1864), which is present in typescript at the Mansion House. *The Quadrangle* was a journal published irregularly out of the Mansion House by Oneida Community descendants between 1908 and 1938. The *Oneida Community Journal* (1987-present) is the periodical of the not-for-profit museum, the Oneida Community Mansion House.

Andrews, Edward Deming. *The People Called Shakers: A Search for the Perfect Society*. New York: Dover, 1963, first published in 1953.

Beecher, Jonathan. *Charles Fourier: The Visionary and His World*. Berkeley: University of California Press, 1986.

Bestor, Arthur. *Backwoods Utopias: The Sectarian Origins and the Owenite Phase of Communitarian Socialism in America, 1663-1829*, 2nd enlarged ed. (Philadelphia: University of Pennsylvania Press, 1970; originally published 1950.

Brisbane, Albert. *Association; or, A Concise Exposition of the Practical Part of Fourier's Social Science*. New York: Greeley and McElrath, 1843.

Carden, Maren Lockwood. *Oneida: Utopian Community to Modern Corporation*. Syracuse, NY: Syracuse University Press, 1998.

Carmer, Carl. *Listen for a Lonesome Drum: A York State Chronicle*. Syracuse, NY: Syracuse University Press, 1995, originally published 1936

Cross, Whitney R. *The Burned-Over District: The Social and Intellectual History of Enthusiastic Religion in Western New York, 1800-1850*. Ithaca, NY: Cornell University Press, 1950.

DeMaria, Richard. *Communal Love at Oneida: A Perfectionist Vision of Authority, Property, and Sexual Order*. New York: Mellen Press, 1978.

Desroche, Henri. *The American Shakers: From Neo-Christianity to Presocialism* (Amherst: University of Massachusetts Press, 1971, first published in 1955).

Dixon, William Hepworth. *New America*, 8th ed., Vol. 2. London: Hurst and Blackett, 1867.

Eastman, Hubbard. *Noyesism Unveiled: A History of the Sect Self-Styled Perfectionists.* Brattleboro, VT: the author, 1849

Edmonds, Walter D. *The First Hundred Years, 1848-1948.* New York: Oneida Ltd., 1948.

Estlake, Allan (pseudonym of Abel Easton), *The Oneida Community: A Record of an Attempt to Carry Out the Principles of Christian Unselfishness and Scientific Improvement* (London: George Redway, 1900.

Fogarty, Robert S. *Desire and Duty at Oneida: Tirzah Miller's Intimate Memoir.* Bloomington: University of Indiana Press, 2000.

----------. *Special Love/Special Sex: An Oneida Community Diary.* Syracuse, NY: Syracuse University Press, 1994.

Foster, Lawrence, Ed. *Free Love in Utopia: John Humphrey Noyes and the Origin of the Oneida Community, Compiled by George Wallingford Noyes.* Urbana: University of Illinois Press, 2001.

----------. *Religion and Sexuality: Three American Communal Experiments of the Nineteenth Century. New York*: Oxford University Press, 1981.

----------. *Women, Family, and Utopia: Communal Experiments of the Shakers, the Oneida Community, and the Mormons.* Syracuse, NY: Syracuse University Press, 1991.

Godwin, Jocelyn. *Upstate Caldron: Eccentric Spiritual Movements in Early New York State.* Albany: SUNY Press, Excelsior Editions, 2015.

Hatcher, P. L. *Oneida (Community) Ltd.: A Goodly Heritage Gone Wrong.* Bloomington, IN: iUniverse, 2016.

Herrick, James B. "In luminatuo lumen videmus," *Quadrangle* 1, no. 2 (May 1908), 11.

Hinds, William Alfred. *American Communities and Co-operative Colonies*, 2nd rev., 3rd ed. (Chicago: Charles H. Kerr, 1908, originally published 1878).

Holloway, Mark. *Heavens on Earth: Utopian Communities in America, 1680-1880*. New York: Turnstile Press, Ltd., 1951.

Horowitz, Helen Lefkowitz. *Rereading Sex: Battles over Sexual Knowledge and Repression in Nineteenth-Century America*. New York: Alfred A. Knopf, 2002.

Huxley, Aldous. *Tomorrow and Tomorrow and Tomorrow, and Other Essays*. New York: Harper and Brothers, 1956.

J. [James Herrick]."Harriet Noyes Skinner." *Quadrangle* 1, no. 8 (December 1908).

Jennings, Chris. P*aradise Now: The Story of American Utopianism*. New York: Random House, 2016.

Kephart, William M. *Extraordinary Groups: The Sociology of Unconventional Life-Styles*, 2nd ed. New York: St. Martin's, 1982.

Kern, Louis J. *An Ordered Love: Sex Roles and Sexuality in Victorian Utopias: The Shakers, the Mormons, and the Oneida Community*. Chapel Hill: University of North Carolina Press, 1981.

----------. "Breaching the 'Wall of Partition between the Male and the Female': John Humphrey Noyes and Free Love," *Syracuse University Library Associates Courier* 28 (Fall 1993),
87-115.

Klaw, Spencer. *Without Sin: the Life and Death of a Utopian Community*. New York: Viking, 1993.

La Moy, William T. "Two Documents Detailing the Oneida Community's Practice of Complex Marriage," *New England Quarterly* 135, no. 1 (March 2012): 119-137.

Leonard, Stephen R. Jr. "Recollections," photocopy of unpublished manuscript. Oneida Community Mansion House Archives, ca. 1951.

Newhouse, Sewell, *The Trappers Guide: A Manual of Instructions*. Wallingford, CN: Oneida Community, 1865.

Nordhoff, Charles, *The Communistic Societies of the United States: Harmony, Oneida, the Shakers, and Others* (New York: Harper and Brothers, 1875).

Noyes, Corinna Ackley, *The Days of My Youth* (Hamilton College Library, Clinton, NY: Richard W. Cooper Press, 2011; originally published 1960.

Noyes, Hilda Herrick, and George Wallingford Noyes. "Oneida Community Experiment in Stirpiculture." *Eugenics, Genetics and the Family* 1 (1923): 377-78.

Noyes, Holton V. "A History of the Oneida Community Limited," unpublished typescript, ca. 1930, Oneida Community Mansion House Archives.

Noyes, John Humphrey. *The Berean: A Manual for the Help of Those Who Seek the Faith of the Primitive Church*. Putney, VT: Office of the Spiritual Magazine, 1847.

----------. *Confessions of John H. Noyes, Part 1: Confession of Religious Experience, including a History of Modern Perfectionism*. Oneida Reserve, NY: Leonard & Co., Printers, 1849.

----------. *History of American Socialisms*. Philadelphia: J.B. Lippincott, 1870.

Noyes, Pierrepoint Burt. *My Father's House: An Oneida Boyhood*. New York: Farrar and Rinehart, 1937.

Olin, Spencer C. Jr. "Bible Communism and the Origins of Orange County, California." *California History* 58 (Fall 1979), 220-32.

----------. "The Oneida Community and the Instability of Charismatic Authority," *Journal of American History* 67, no. 2 (September 1980), 285-300.

Oneida Community. *First Annual Report of the Oneida Association: Exhibiting Its History, Principles, and Transactions to Jan. 1, 1849*. Oneida Reserve, N.Y., Oneida Association, 1849.

----------. *Second Annual Report of the Oneida Association: Exhibiting Its Progress to February 20, 1850* (Oneida Reserve, NY: Oneida Association, 1850).

----------. *Third Annual Report of the Oneida Association, Exhibiting Its Progress to February 20, 1851*. Oneida Reserve, NY: Oneida Association, 1851.

----------. *Bible Communism: A Compilation from the Annual Reports of the Oneida Association and Its Branches.* Brooklyn, NY: Office of the Circular, 1853.

----------. *The Oneida Community: A Familiar Exposition of Its Ideas and Practical Life, in a Conversation with a Visitor.* Wallingford, CN: Office of the Circular, 1865.

----------. *Hand-Book of the Oneida Community: Containing a Brief Sketch of Its Present Condition, Internal Economy, and Leading Principles, No. 2* (Oneida, NY: Oneida Community, 1871).

----------. *Mutual Criticism* (Oneida, NY: Office of the American Socialist, 1876).

Parker, Robert Allerton. *A Yankee Saint; John Humphrey Noyes and The Oneida Community.* New York: G.P. Putnam's Sons, 1935.

Rich, Jane J, ed., *A Lasting Spring: Jessie Catherine Kinsley, Daughter of the Oneida Community.* Syracuse, NY: Syracuse University Press, 1983

Robertson, Constance Noyes. *Oneida Community: An Autobiography, 1851-1876.* Syracuse, NY: Syracuse University Press, 1970.

----------. *Oneida Community: The Breakup, 1876-1881.* Syracuse, NY: Syracuse University Press, 1972.

----------. *Oneida Community Profiles.* Syracuse, NY: Syracuse University Press, 1977.

Sears, Hal D. *The Sex Radicals: Free Love in High Victorian America.* Lawrence: Regents Press of Kansas, 1977.

Spann, Edward K. *Brotherly Tomorrows: Movements for a Cooperative Society in America, 1820-1920.* New York: Columbia University Press, 1989.

Stoehr, Taylor. *Free Love in America: A Documentary History.* New York: AMS, 1979.

Swedenborg, Emanuel. *A Compendium of the Theological and Spiritual Writings of Emanuel Swedenborg: Being a Systematic and Orderly Epitome of All His Religious Works.* Boston: Crosby, Nichols, and Otis Clapp, 1854.

Teeple, John B. *The Oneida Family: Genealogy of a 19th Century Perfectionist Commune, Containing Original Community Photographs and Drawings*. Oneida, New York: Oneida Community Historical Committee, 1985.

Van der Warker, Ely. "A Gynecological Study of the Oneida Community," *American Journal of Obstetrics and Diseases of Women and Children* 17, no. 8 (August 1884), 785-810.

Wagner, Sally Roesch. "The Iroquois Influence on Women's Rights," in *Indian Roots of American Democracy*, edited by José Barreiro, 115-34. Ithaca, NY: Akwe:kon Press, 1992.

----------. "The Untold Story of the Iroquois Influence on Early Feminist," *On the Issues Magazine* (Winter 1996): pagination unknown (Long Island City, NY: Choices Women's Medical Center).

Wayland-Smith, Ellen. *Oneida: From Free Love Utopia to the Well-Set Table*. New York: Picador: 2016.

White, Carol. *A Taste of Heaven on Earth: Harnessing the Energies of Love*. Eugene, OR: Resource Publications, 2020.

Wonderley, Anthony, ed. John Humphrey Noyes on Sexual Relations in the Oneida Community: Four Essential Texts. Clinton, NY: Richard W. Couper Press, 2012.

----------. *Oneida Utopia: A Community Searching for Human Happiness and Prosperity*. Ithaca, NY: Cornell University Press, 2017.

----------. "The Oneida Community's Forgotten Commune," *New Circular* 9 (December 2017a): 1-4.

----------, ed. *Writings from Wallingford: The Connecticut Outpost of the Oneida Community*. Clinton, NY: Richard Couper Press, 2020.

Worden, Harriet M. *Old Mansion House Memories, by One Brought Up in It*. Oneida, NY: Oneida Ltd., 1950.

Index

A

Ackley
    Alice 136, 143, 144, 148, 149
    Corinna 143, 148, 149
    Joseph C. 73
Allen
    Eliza 53
    Emily 13
    Henry 13
    Portia Underhill 177
Amana Community 3
American Socialist 54
American Spiritualism 71
Associationism 4

B

Baker 47
Bassett
    H. W. 123, 124
Beecher
    Lyman 71
Belasco
    Susan XII
Bevan 63
Bible Argument 82
Bible Communism 25
Bottum
    C. L. 120
Bradley 47
    William C. 60
Brisbane
    Albert 5
Brook Farm 4
Brownson
    O. A. 38
Burnham 47
Burt
    Jonathan 6, 54, 64, 69, 73, 81, 109, 110, 162

C

Campbell
    Alexander 38
Circular 98
Civil War 55, 68, 89
Clark
    Maria 45
Clifford
    William Henry 116
Cornelius
    Thomas 71
Cragin 25, 47
    Charles A. 117, 122, 124
    George E. 85, 120, 121, 179
    Mary E. 24, 48, 52, 53, 140, 141
Crawford
    James 38, 46

D

Darwin
    Charles 132
Douglass
    Frederick 155, 164
Downing
    A. J. 14

E

Easton
    Abel 85
Emerson
    Ralph Waldo 4, 98

F

Finney
    Charles Grandison 1, 71
Fogarty
    Robert 134
Fourier 93, 153
    Charles 4, 5
Fourierism 4

Fox
  George 25
Fruitlands 4

G

Graham
  Sylvester 157
Guarneri
  Carl 153
Guiler
  Thomas A. XII

H

Hall
  Harriet A. 48
Hamilton
  Erastus H. 102, 117
Hamilton College 171
Harmonists 131
Hawley
  Martha 144, 151
Hayes
  Rutherford 26, 33
Herrick
  Hilda Hayes 85
Hinds
  William Alfred 127, 128, 179
Hobart
  Ann 144, 150
Howe
  Elias 117
Huxley
  Aldus 10, 132

I

Illustrated Newspaper XI
Inslee
  William R. 118, 119

J

Jones
  J. Winslow 116

K

Kellogg
  Otis 102
Kinsley
  Jessie 22, 74, 102, 134, 180
  Myron H. 124

L

Leavitt 57
Lee
  Ann 3
Leland
  T. C. 72
Leonard 25, 47
  Charlotte 144, 150
  Stephen 150
Leslie
  Frank XI
Lord
  John R. 118
Louis XIV 25
Luther
  Martin 25

M

Madison University 171
Mansion House, 7
Mead
  L. G. 60
Melancthon
  Philipp 25
Miller
  Charlotte Noyes 2, 22, 23, 24, 25, 28, 29, 30, 31, 32, 33, 34, 36, 37, 38, 39, 40, 41, 43, 44, 45, 46, 48, 49, 50, 51, 52, 53, 73, 74, 75, 109, 122, 134, 153, 154, 155, 157, 175, 178
  Elizabeth Smith 137, 141
  John R. 13, 25, 45, 46, 47, 70, 73, 134
  Tirzah C. 127, 132, 134, 135, 136, 141, 180
  William 6
Mills
  William 101

Moravians 3
Mormonism 73
Mormons 3

N

New Harmonists 3
Newhouse
    Sewell O. 13, 69, 109, 110, 111
North American Phalanx 16
Noyes
    Corinna Ackley XI
    Elizabeth 28, 29
    George Washington 2, 23, 25, 28, 29, 30, 40, 42, 44, 122, 136, 162
    Harriet Holton 2, 24, 25, 44, 45, 59, 102
    Horatio 29, 33, 46
    Joanna 29, 33, 41, 46
    John 26, 27, 28, 32, 57
    John Humphrey XI, 1, 2, 3, 5, 6, 10, 11, 12, 17, 21, 23, 25, 29, 34, 36, 37, 38, 39, 41, 43, 44, 46, 47, 50, 58, 61, 73, 81, 82, 84, 85, 95, 97, 102, 109, 111, 117, 122, 128, 132, 135, 141, 147, 159, 161, 163, 175, 176, 178, 179
    Mary 29
    Pierrepont B. XI, 22, 74, 142
    Polly Hayes 26, 27, 28, 32, 41, 45, 48
    Theodore R. 17, 122, 132, 136, 147, 148
    William 28

O

Oneida Circular 23
Owen 93
    Robert Dale 91, 93

P

Parker
    Robert 84
Pawlika
    Lauren XII
Penn
    William 25

Perfectionism 6, 25
Pierce
    L. 39
Prideaux
    Humphrey 43

R

Reeve
    Constance Bradley 177
Richards
    Mark 60
Robertson
    Constance Noyes XII, XIII, 180

S

Sconondoa 70
Scott
    Walter 30, 61
Shaker 3
Shakers 3, 131
Singer
    Isaac 117
Skinner
    Harriet Noyes XI, 2, 21, 22, 24, 25, 27, 29, 31, 32, 39, 40, 42, 44, 45, 46, 48, 54, 73, 75, 132, 137, 140, 143, 144, 153, 155, 157, 175, 177, 178
    John L. 22, 25, 47, 164
Smith
    Gerrit 73, 141
    Peter 137
Spiritualism 73, 94
Stirpiculture 16, 17, 26, 135
Swedenborg
    Emanuel 91

T

Thacker
    Henry 64
Towner
    James W. 89, 90, 91, 93, 102, 103, 104, 113, 115, 179
Transcendentalism 4

V

Vanderwall
　Rhoda 103

W

Wagner
　Sally Roesch 137
Wayland-Smith
　Frank 134
Wayland-Smith Hatch
　Laura XII
Weld
　Charles H. 40
Wesley
　Charles 25
　John 25
White
　Abby 58
Winslow
　Isaac 113, 116
Wonderley
　Anthony XI, XII
Woolworth
　William 102
　William H. 47, 162
Worden
　Harriet M. XI, 13, 127, 131, 132, 134, 137, 139, 142, 144, 151, 159, 180
Wright
　Ellen Nash 177
　Fanny 91, 93

www.ingramcontent.com/pod-product-compliance
Lightning Source LLC
Chambersburg PA
CBHW071843230426
43671CB00012B/2050